An Introduction to Nineteenth Century Germany

Eda Sagarra

Longman

LONGMAN GROUP LIMITED
Longman House
Burnt Mill, Harlow, Essex

First published 1980
ISBN 0 582 35137 5 cased edition
ISBN 0 582 35138 3 paperback edition

Set in 11/12 Baskerville, Monophoto 169
by Keyspools Limited, Golborne, Lancashire.

Printed in Hong Kong by
Sheck Wah Tong Printing Press Ltd

IN THE SAME SERIES:
An Introduction to Nineteenth Century France
by John and Muriel Lough

Contents

Acknowledgements   iv
Illustrations, Maps and Tables   v
Note on currency values   vii

1 Germany and Napoleon   1
2 Authority and the Subject in nineteenth century
     Germany   16
3 The Restoration Era 1815–48   38
4 The Economy   56
     i)   The Restoration Years
     ii)   Industrialisation and the People
     iii) The Industrial Nation
5 The German Revolutions 1848–49   86
6 The National Movement   107
7 The Growth of Prussian Hegemony in Germany
     1850–71   124
8 The State, the Parties and the Army after 1871   143
9 Politics, Government and the Masses (1890–1914)   165
10 The Evolution of German Society 1800–1914   197
11 The Family   231
12 The German Writer and his Public   273

Main historical events: some dates   295
List of Museums in the Federal Republic of Germany
     with a special interest in the nineteenth century   298
Some suggestions for further reading   299
Index   305

Acknowledgements

I would like to thank the German Academic Exchange Service (DAAD) for making it possible for me to visit many museums, galleries and archives while writing this book, and for much incidental help as well. The Dublin Goethe Institute, under its Director, Herr Berthold Dobieß, and its librarian, Fräulein Hesper, have been, as always, wonderfully helpful and efficient in procuring books and periodicals from Germany. Miss Mary Dempsey typed the manuscript with speed and elegance.

Lastly I would like to thank Mrs. Ilse Samuel and the many second-year students in the German departments of Manchester University and Trinity College Dublin, who had to listen to lectures on nineteenth century Germany. For their patience I dedicate this book to them.

E.S.   Dublin April 1978

We are grateful to the following for permission to reproduce photographs;

Amerika-Gedenkbibliothek Berliner-Zentralbibliothek, from *Liederbuch des Deutschen Michel*, 1843: page 42;

Bildarchiv Foto Marburg: pages 20, 134, 251, 265, 270;

Bildarchiv Preussicher Kulturbesitz, Berlin: pages 4, 10, 11, 13, 17, 32, 36, 54, 59, 60, 64, 68, 79, 78, 82, 91 and cover, 93, 119, 130, 135, 141, 147, 159, 187, 200, 219, 222, 223, 239, 249, 252, 257, 258, 263, 277;

Der Deutsche in seiner Karikatur, Friedr. Basserman'sche Verlagsbuchhandlung, Stuttgart: pages 137, 176, 195, 212, 274;

Facsimile Querschnitt durch den Simplicissimus, Scherz Verlag, München, 1963: pages 172, 178, 194, 220;

Mansell Collection: cover (eagle);

Schloss Charlottenburg, Staatliche Schlösser und Gärten Berlin: page 247;

Staatliche Museen zu Berlin National galerie: pages 115, 246;

Staatsgemäldesammlungen, München: pages 114, 254.

Cartoons on pages 172, 176 and 194 by Th. Th. Henie © SPADEM, Paris Sammlungen 1980.

Illustrations, Maps and Tables

Photographs

4 The 'horse thief of Berlin'
10 Kampf: Professor Henrik Steffens calls on his students at Breslau to join the Volunteers
11 Martersteig: Blessing of the Lützow Free Corps 1813
13 'The Rhenish Courier loses everything on his way from the Leipzig Fair' 1813–14
17 The Emperor William I
20 The Park at Schönbrunn, Vienna
32 Roeseler: 'Sums'
36 The Final Exam (Abitur) at a German Grammar School
42 Satiric reference to the 'queue' or pigtail
54 Krüger: detail from 'Parade Unter den Linden'
59 The Lauchhammer works in 1825
60 Maffei's machine-tool factory near Munich, 1843
64 'While the political ambition of the citizen advances at snail's pace, the industrial development rushes by on wheels.'
68 Maffei's machine-tool works near Munich, 1849
70 Thon: an old Thuringian steam hammer
78 Menzel: 'The iron foundry'
82 Thiel: The Berlin Stock Exchange, 1889
91 Death of a student on the barricades in Berlin, 1848
93 Kirchhof: Defending the barricades in Berlin, 1848
114 Overbeck: 'Italia and Germania'
115 Schumacher: Portrait of Heinrich Hoffmann von Fallersleben as a young man
119 The unveiling of the Victory Column in Berlin, 1873
130 Weger: Bismarck in 1871
134 Portrait of an officer
135 Werner: proclamation of the Emperor in Versailles, 1871
137 German Unity. Contemporary caricature
141 The entry of the victorious into Berlin, 1871
147 Hosang: the Emperor reviewing the troops
159 Bismarck at the laying of the foundation stone for the new Reichstag, 1884
172 Heine: 'The English sword'
176 Germans abroad

178 Gulbransson: skit on William II's love of travel
187 On the Charlottenburg Chausée in Berlin
194 Bismarck and Bebel
195 Thiele: 'Tankard types'
200 German society as seen by *Kladderadatsch* 1885 in its railway passengers
212 Oberländer: Mr Commercial Councillor before and after his decoration
219 Gulbransson: strikers at their employer's
220 Cartoon on the rabble from *Simplicissiums*
222 The employment agency for domestic servants, 1889
223 Huisken: servant girls pass the Royal Ulans
235 'Picture of the future' Munich, 1847
239 The German woman lecturer of the future, 1848
246 Begas: Frau Wilhelmine Begas
247 Grassi: Queen Louise of Prussia, 1802
249 'The first woman advocate' as seen in 1897
251 Gärtner: details from 'Panorama from the Werdersche Church'
252 Wunsch: 'Sums'
254 Waldmüller: 'At the window', 1840
257 Father's birthday. Photo 1880
258 Christmas day. Augsburg, early 19th century
264 Knaus: the school yard
265 The Joachimsthal Gymnasium in the late 19th century
270 'The sun-children'
274 Gulbransson: cartoon on culture

Maps

39 The German Confederation 1815
61 The Zollverein and the Tax Union 1834
63 German Railways 1835–65
139 The Evolution of Bismarck's Germany

Tables

144 Germany's population
163 Strength of the German Army 1880–1914
163 Strength of the Navy 1880–1910
190 Membership of the principal Trade Unions in Germany
197 Germany's population in the 19th century
237 Employment of women in the Second Empire

Graph

282 The number of books published in 19th century Germany

Note on currency values

1 taler = 30 groschen = c. 15p or three shillings
1 gulden (Austria) = florin (French name for gulden) = c. 7½p
1 mark (since 1873 official German currency, though taler continued in circulation) = one English shilling
10 marks = 1 gold crown (Krone)
20 marks = 1 Doppel (double) krone = c. one English sovereign

I
Germany and Napoleon

> Should anyone care to inquire about the type of government in
> Germany, the answer must be: Germany is governed in the German
> manner.
>
> (Holberg)

The French revolutionary wars and Germany

When, in the year 1792, the French armies invaded the territory of
the Holy Roman Empire, Germany was a geographical and a
cultural concept, but not a political one. In the years which
followed, neither the French annexations on the left bank of the
Rhine, nor the establishment of the short-lived Jacobin republic of
Mainz, nor further victories by the French armies on German
territory, altered this situation. In 1800 the population of Germany,
between 22 and 23 millions, were subjects of secular and religious
rulers governing more than 300 sovereign political units. Internal
customs barriers on roads and waterways, a variety of coinages
besides the seven 'official' currencies, and a truly bewildering number of weights and measures, provided the commercial counterpart
of the chequered map of the Holy Roman Empire and contiguous
German territories, such as East Prussia, which did not form part of
it. Government in the German manner was indeed a baffling
business as the Danish comic writer Holberg so aptly observed, both
to foreigners and to those few Germans who chose to ponder on such
matters. The vast majority of the population, some 80% or more,
lived and worked on the land, and of the remainder, a sizeable
number, though domiciled in towns or villages, earned their living
mainly by agriculture.

The political divisions were not the only barrier to the creation of
a sense of nationhood in the political sphere. Germany's social

structure on the threshold of the nineteenth century was reminiscent of an earlier age. Essentially, Germany was a *Ständestaat*, a society of corporate estates. The nobility enjoyed exclusive legal, political, social and fiscal privileges, while in the manorial lands of eastern Germany, the peasantry were still largely bound to the soil. In the west the peasant was personally free, but he laboured under many onerous obligations, often the more so because he owed his obligations to a number of different lords, rent to one, labour dues to another, tithes to a third. The lack of a mercantile class in Germany outside Hamburg, Leipzig and one or two more towns, was a salient feature of her society. For the majority of German towns owed their character to the fact that the prince had his residence there, not to its being a commercial or market centre. 'One cannot even buy a pair of gloves here,' lamented a Scottish traveller of early nineteenth century Karlsruhe, a town which was, after all, the seat of the ruler of Baden, a substantial state in the south-west of the country. The educated middle classes, made up of sons of officials, pastors, teachers or master craftsmen, which were growing in numbers in the late eighteenth century, found little outlet for their talents. Aspirants to public office, as the case of Goethe's '*Werther*' earlier exemplified, found themselves automatically passed over in favour of scions of noble houses. In the wake of the Enlightenment, vigorous discussion in periodicals and learned journals was devoted to the future role and function of the middle class citizen, without such concern yielding any tangible benefit for him.

In the towns, trade was still very largely regulated by the guilds, which survived longer in Germany than elsewhere. Although they had long since lost their political role, they continued to exercise a strong social and economic influence in the townships of the Holy Roman Empire. Their firm opposition to technical innovation, their restrictive practices, designed to exclude 'unfair' competition, encouraged the proliferation of the so-called 'illegal craftsmen' who produced inferior goods for lower prices. It was estimated that two thirds of the town dwellers in Württemberg and two-fifths in Brandenburg fell into this category.

The impact of Napoleon on Germany

It was the historic role of Napoleon to have acted as the catalyst both of polity and society in Germany. Not only did he reduce the number of political units through his territorial reorganisation of Germany in the wake of conquest to scarcely more than one-tenth of their former number, but he also wrought changes in her society, both in the lands occupied by the French until Napoleon's defeat in 1814 and also in those which became satellites of the French Empire after 1806. The introduction of the *Code Napoléon* in the Rhineland, the opening of the French market to goods produced there, stimulated the rise of capitalist enterprise in an area which was to become one of Germany's key industrial regions. The continental blockade, which Napoleon directed against England, gave needful protection to young German enterprises from the English competition which was to prove such a disaster for Germany's craftsmen after the Napoleonic era had passed. Napoleon's defeat of Austria and of Prussia, his subjugation of south and central German rulers to the status of French vassals, stimulated programmes of internal reform in the government and administration of those states which served these and their people in good stead.

Political nationalism

Moreover, Napoleonic rule in Germany was responsible for creating a totally new phenomenon in the life of Germany, namely political nationalism. Because of the circumstances of its birth in a time of defeat and occupation, political (as against cultural) nationalism was from the first irrational and chauvinistic. Finally, Napoleon was responsible, if only indirectly, for further alienating public opinion in Germany from the ideas and the ideals of the French Revolution. For both the rulers of Germany and their subjects, the concepts of revolution, emancipation, equality of all citizens, came to be associated irrevocably with the experience of conquest, of exploitation and of national humiliation. In time, the association acquired the received character of a myth, and it retained this character throughout the rest of the nineteenth century and beyond. This prejudiced German attitudes for generations against their own, very limited, revolutionary or radical traditions. As the Socialist, publicist and political theorist, Franz Mehring, put it provocatively in the 1890s: 'The German bourgeois has never himself been a liberator but only a man liberated by others, and at every step he takes, the sound of his broken chains clanks treacherously behind him.' The leaders of the German nationalist opposition to the French were not Kant, Goethe or Schiller; they were Romantic writers, Fichte the philosopher, Arndt, author of the rousing *Geist der Zeit* (1806) and of widely popular patriotic lyrics, and 'Turnvater' Jahn, self-styled apostle of

The 'horse thief' of Berlin (Napoleon steals the horses from the top of the
Brandenburg Gate). Contemporary caricature (c. 181).

Germanic physical culture. They and others, such as the dramatist
Kleist, rejected the political implications of the idea of human
equality, because of its associations with the French Revolution.
They extended their rejection to the rights of ethnic minorities
living within the German borders and a number of them came to
deny the notion of the equality of all citizens before the law. The
ritual book-burning carried out by the chief spokesmen of the
nationalist movement after Napoleon's defeat, the university
students, included a copy of the *Code Napoléon*, with its provisions for
such equality. The very fact that the French had removed
disabilities from the Jews in Germany in the territories occupied by
them (a decision which was revoked in 1815) helped to associate the
movement for Jewish emancipation in nineteenth century Germany
with the stigma of revolution. German Jacobins, to be sure,
distinguished by their belief in the brotherhood of man, made a brief
impact on the public mind in the beginning of the French
revolutionary wars. Their ideas informed the writings of the
intellectual radicals of the 1830s, writers, such as the Young

Hegelians, who applied the ideas of the leading philosopher of the age, Hegel, to inspire political revolution. The German Jacobins also influenced the literary group known as the Young Germans in the mid 1830s and exercised a formative influence on the ideas of the democratic Left in the 1848 Revolution. But numerically, and in spite of the strong support which the Jacobins enjoyed in south and west Germany, they were never more than a small minority and the revolutionary stigma proved a permanent liability.

Territorial changes

In 1801 Napoleon consolidated his victorious campaigns against the Empire in the Treaty of Lunéville, the principal provision of which was the ceding of the left bank of the Rhine to France. Secularisation of ecclesiastical territory in Germany was to provide compensation for German and other princes who had lost their lands, though it was not until 1803 that this took place. Napoleon thus drove a wedge between the secular and ecclesiastical princes of the Empire, and in effect abolished one of the three Estates of that institution. Of eighty-one ecclesiastical princes only three re-mained: the once mighty archbishop of Mainz, now virtually landless, and the Grand Masters of the Teutonic Knights and of the Knights of St. John; moreover the ancient free cities had also been decimated: only Hamburg, Bremen, Lübeck, Frankfurt and Augsburg survived from fifty-one such towns. The imminent demise of the Empire itself was anticipated in 1804 when Napoleon had himself proclaimed emperor of the French and came to Mainz to hold court. In 1805 (on the eve of the war of the Third Coalition), Napoleon wooed and bullied the south German princes; territorial compensations in the form of lands to be taken from Austria and the mediatised princes and the imperial knights gained him the support in men and arms for his campaign against Austria in 1806 and subsequent campaigns. Friendship, a two-edged affair, was cemented between these states and the French Empire in July 1806, when the Confederation of the Rhine was formed. Sixteen German princes, including the rulers of Bavaria and Württemberg, elevated to the rank of kings by Napoleon, and of Baden and Hesse-Darmstadt, now grand-dukes, joined the Confederation of the Rhine under French protection. This was a preliminary to the final dismantling of the Holy Roman Empire scarcely a month later. Few lamented or indeed noticed its passing. The Holy Roman Empire had been in existence for 1006 years, on a parallel with the kingdoms of the

Pharaohs of ancient Egypt and the Ming dynasty in China, but it was no longer a reality for those who had lived so long under its protection, and the identity it had undoubtedly offered Germans even in the last century of its history, had disappeared under the impact of events visiting the nation since the French Revolution of 1789.

Jena and the collapse of Prussia

The year 1806 is not, therefore, a date of crucial importance in German history in so far as it heralded the demise of an ancient institution, although its passing was a milestone on the road to national unification. The significance of that year is that it witnessed the defeat and collapse of the old Fredrician order in Prussia, and as such the beginning of Prussia's association with the national movement, whose leadership she would in due course assume.

For it was at the precise moment of the creation of the Confederation of the Rhine and the abolition of the old Empire, that the king of Prussia, Frederick William III (1797–1840), pedantic in spite of his relative youth, obstinate and of limited capabilities, chose to re-enter the war against Napoleon. Prussia had preserved her neutrality since 1795, when the previous king had negotiated peace with the French. In September 1806 Prussia declared war on France. Scarcely a month later, Napoleon was master of Prussia. The battle of Jena, 14 October 1806, brought not only the military annihilation of Prussia but a moral collapse also. In the peace of Tilsit 1807, Prussia lost all her territories west of the Elbe to Napoleon, who created the puppet kingdom of Westphalia for his brother Jérome, and also those lands she had acquired in eastern Europe during the Second and Third Partitions of Poland. In addition, Prussia was required to pay a war indemnity of some 120 million francs and to contribute to the costs of the French occupation of the territory remaining to her. In subsequent years her people were required to contribute in men and money to the costs of Napoleon's further campaigns, including that against Russia in 1812.

Jena is one of the turning points in nineteenth century Prussian and German history. The response of the Prussian nation to this, its most overwhelming defeat, illustrates the resilience of this remarkable state. The rout of the Prussian army, the panic shown by its officers, the craven surrender of fortresses to Napoleon, was followed by manifestations of craven servility on the part of Prussia's leaders to the conqueror. The whole raison d'être of the Prussian state, its military order, had disintegrated in 1806. Yet within weeks of defeat the Prussian king pledged to dedicate himself to the moral regeneration of the nation, and his people responded with an enthusiasm apparently out of keeping with the cool north German character. He was supported by one of the most attractive personalities of the age, his queen, Louise, born a princess of Mecklenburg-Strelitz, whose warm nature and passionate espousal of the cause of resistance to Napoleon endeared her to contemporaries and to subsequent generations.

The Prussian revival

It was Prussia's good fortune that a remarkable galaxy of talent had assembled in Berlin in these years and that men of ability, character and imagination were given the opportunity to help reorganise government and society in the following years. Their names included Baron Stein, from Nassau, whom Frederick William III summoned to head his ministry in 1807, the diplomat and scholar, Wilhelm von Humboldt, who gave his name to Berlin university, founded as part of the reform programme in 1810, and the charismatic soldier figures, Gneisenau and his Saxon colleague, Scharnhorst, responsible for the humane reforms of army discipline and for the introduction of conscription.

In addition, Prussia had at her disposal a number of able young administrators in central and regional government, who combined something of the visionary quality which distinguished Baron Stein with the practical talents their difficult task demanded. Many of these young men had been schooled at the Hanoverian university of Göttingen, where they had encountered the writings of Adam Smith. They were impressed with the notion that greater liberty given to the individual should be conducive to greater productivity. Stein himself had his personal copy of Smith's '*The Wealth of Nations*' underlined at the point where Smith observes:

> It appears, accordingly, from the experiences of all ages and nations, I believe, that the work done by free men is cheaper in the end than that done by slaves.

Faced with the daunting fiscal problems of Prussia following her defeat and occupation, ministers and civil servants embarked on a course of reform which has been given the name of the Prussian Liberal Era. The reform programme was diverse in its aspirations and by and large, more successful in its economic measures than its social and political provisions. Both in concept and execution, however, it represented a vital contributory factor to establishing Prussia's position of hegemony in Germany in the second half of the century.

Stein's vision was inspired by the ideals of the age of German classical humanism, now drawing to its close. It was a vision which Wilhelm von Humboldt had helped to form and which inspired his reform of the Prussian secondary school system and the idea of founding a new university in Berlin. The reformers were convinced that if the individual were to be freed from the restrictions on his initiative which traditional feudal obligations had imposed upon him, he would cease to regard himself as merely a subject of the prince, and become instead a citizen of the state. The programme of reform included the emancipation of the serfs, municipal self-government, abolition of restrictions on personal mobility, on the sale of land and the prosecution of a trade, and abolition of cruel and degrading punishment for infringement of military discipline, which had made the Prussian army a password for brutal discipline. It was in his famous municipal ordinance of 1808, which gave self-government to the towns of the old Prussian provinces, that Stein came closest to realising his ideals. Before his appointment as chief minister of the king of Prussia in 1807, he had advocated a thorough reform of government. His aim was, as he put it:

> ... to breathe life into the spirit of the community, to make citizens conscious of their powers, to exploit dormant or misapplied skills, to make use of talents now lying idle, and to revive sentiments of patriotism, self-reliance and national honour.

Those who were responsible for finding the massive contributions demanded by the occupying power, believed that the ending of restraints on trade, transfer of property and the facilitating of personal mobility would bring prosperity to the nation and revenue to the state. Freedom of trade was introduced in 1810: this meant that a craftsman could set up a business without regard to the traditional and time-honoured restraints on competition. Furthermore, the prohibition on the sale of manorial estates to non-nobles was lifted. Many of these were in fact already in the possession of bourgeois owners; the legalisation of the process gave encouragement to large-scale investment in land and the development of capitalist enterprise, especially after the agrarian reforms created a surplus of rural labourers. The emancipation of the peasantry, which spanned the years 1807–10, was the most far-reaching of all Stein's measures. It was aimed at providing Prussia with the kind of sturdy patriotic peasantry of which enlightened reformers had dreamed, and which seemed to fit so well into the demands of nascent German nationalism. Prussian bureaucrats remained faithful to their policies of economic liberalism for more than half a century. They did this despite the human problems created by the reform, such as that of the landless peasants unable to subsist on their plot and meet their compensation payments to the nobility, or the countless craftsmen working in over-subscribed trades who failed to make a living, or whose livelihood was destroyed by English competition. The bureaucrats continued to put their trust in a better future for all. As a result of their efforts and their determination to balance the budget in subsequent decades, Prussia was the only German state which found itself with a sound financial basis on the eve of the industrial revolution in mid-century. Moreover, Prussian economic liberalism, although not matched by political emancipation, provided the basis for capitalist enterprise both on the land, where a new entrepreneurial class began to produce grain, sugar and other products for export, and in the towns of the old commercial and new industrial centres.

The wars of liberation

Much of this lay in the future, and for the first years of Napoleon's occupation, from about 1807 to 1811, national morale in Prussia, after initial enthusiasm, was very low. The suicide of the poet Heinrich von Kleist in 1811 was interpreted by many intellectuals as a symbolic act of despair at the continued humiliation of the nation. The decision by Austria in 1809 to challenge Napoleon once again and bring about a rising in Germany proved abortive. Austria was defeated once more, this time at Wagram; and the isolated patriotic manifestations, such as Andreas Hofer's rising in the Tyrol, Schill's effort to overthrow the French puppet kingdom of Westphalia, ended in failure and the death of the leaders. However, changes in the political constellation and the defeat of Napoleon in Russia in 1812, stimulated the growth of a genuine national movement. This was centred on Prussia and had Baron Stein as its chosen leader, although he himself had been exiled from Prussia on Napoleon's orders, since 1808. Stein's famous phrase 'I have only one Fatherland and that is Germany', expressed in a letter dated 1811, inspired students, artisans, poets, lawyers and landowners,

Professor Henrik Steffens calls on his students at Breslau to join the Volunteers. Lithograph of a painting by A. Kampf (1813).

especially, but not only, in Prussia. The university professor in Breslau, the Danish Romantic philospher, Henrik Steffens, joined the volunteer movement and brought his students with him. Women surrendered their jewelry and pastors preached a crusade against the 'godless Napoleon'. Prussia's central role in the nationalist movement was demonstrated when a reluctant Prussian king finally agreed to summon all Germans to arms against Napoleon in March 1813. Though volunteers streamed in from other regions of Germany, the only ruler who gave his support was the duke of Mecklenburg-Schwerin. However, in the course of the summer of 1813, the chancellor of Austria, Metternich, displayed consummate diplomacy and secured the political initiative in Germany for his state.

In August 1813 Austria declared war on Napoleon. The coalition of Austria, Prussia and Russia was led by the Austrian, Karl von Schwarzenberg, whose statue stands opposite that of the great Prince Eugene, dominating the great centre of Vienna, the *Heldenplatz*. Almost seven years to the day after the Prussian defeat at Jena, the allies proved victorious over Napoleon at Leipzig. The Confederation of the Rhine and the Napoleonic states in northern

Blessing of the famous Lützow Free Corps (whose colours were black-red-gold) on 27 March 1813. The poet Körner kneels. Painting by Martersteig.

Germany were dissolved. The south German states hastened to protect themselves by signing treaties with Austria. Metternich, more concerned with containment of Russia in the east than with nationalist concerns at home, would have been content to make peace with France, leaving her the conquests on the west bank of the Rhine. It was Napoleon, not the German patriots, who decided otherwise. He continued the war which came to an end at Fontainebleau in April 1814. The numerous and complex questions facing Europe's statesmen in the aftermath of a quarter of a century of war were to be decided at an international congress which met at Vienna in October 1814, and sat until June of the following year. Napoleon's escape from his exile in Elba and the outbreak of war again provided a dramatic interlude, but ended in his defeat at Waterloo, in June 1815, one week after the massive protocol of the Congress of Vienna had been signed by all the powers.

The Napoleonic wars lasted, with interludes in the fighting, for a whole generation. In that time Germans experienced constant change, changes of territorial allegiance and of political status, and also, in some if not all regions, severe economic dislocation. Many parts of Germany suffered war levies, quartering of troops, high taxation, plundering and requisition by the French troops for years on end, and then, in the last years of the Napoleonic regime, as for example in Hamburg, violent repression and destruction. The loss of the familiar if antiquated framework in which they had lived for centuries, and the extent and the duration of the wars, conferred on Germans a totally novel sense of their own national identity. Napoleon is therefore rightly regarded as the father of German nationalism, and this is obviously one of the most significant consequences of his intervention in German affairs.

Germany and the Revolution

But equally important is the way in which the Napoleonic wars in Germany, with all the attendant political and social disturbances and the suffering these caused the population, came to be seen both by the authorities and the people as a direct consequence of the French Revolution. Preoccupation, indeed obsession, with re-volution characterised German statesmen and political thinkers throughout the nineteenth century, from Metternich to Bismarck, from Karl Marx to Jakob Burckhardt, though the conclusions which they drew from their reflexions were very different.

As late as 1871, when the Swiss historian and political philosopher Jakob Burckhardt resumed his lectures on the French Revolution which had been interrupted by the Franco-Prussia war of 1870–71, followed by the unification of Germany under the Second Empire, he introduced them with the following remarks:

> As for the title of this course of lectures, I should like to add that the whole period up to our own day, has in fact been one of revolution, and it may be that we have only reached the beginnings of the second act. For those three apparently tranquil decades from 1815 to 1848 have revealed themselves to be merely an interlude in the great drama, and this drama appears to be merging into one single action, contrasting with the whole known past history of our world.

Not only were the authorities and the intellectuals in nineteenth century Germany obsessed with the fear of revolution. The experiences of the Napoleonic era, the disorientation and insecurity of those twenty years had led Germans to see political and social change as the work of 'foreign' intervention and to react against it instinctively.

Both the French Revolution and Napoleon influenced the course of German history in the nineteenth century very profoundly. They did not, however, influence it in general in the direction of western Europe, i.e. towards the goals of liberalism, the creation of representative institutions and a free press and the emergence of a powerful bourgeois class. These ideals were undoubtedly in vogue in the 1830s and 1840s, but they gained no lasting hold on the imagination of the German nation. The reasons for this lay mainly with Germany's political tradition and inherited social structure, rather than with Napoleon, but it was of very considerable importance for the future that change in general during the period

The Rhenish Courier loses everything on his way from the Leipzig Fair (1813–14). Contemporary satire on Napoleon's defeat at Leipzig in 1813 and its consequences.

DER RHEINISCHE COURIER
verliehrt auf der Heimreise von der Leipziger Messe alles

of the French revolutionary wars was seen by the inhabitants of Germany to originate *from outside*.

Throughout the nineteenth century, and indeed up to the collapse of the Third Reich in 1945, revolution seemed to the German public mind something abhorrent, the negation of 'freedom', as the Germans had been educated by tradition and experience to understand it. The brief experience of revolution in Germany itself, in 1830, 1848 and 1918 only served to reinforce this instinctive response. Freedom, to simplify a complex phenomenon, was interpreted by most Germans as security from disturbance rather than the protection of the individual from the power of the state and other institutions.

Napoleon and the Germans

Napoleon and the Napoleonic occupation of Germany were responsible for the creation of a German national identity in the political sense. But the response to Napoleon's person was not without ambiguity. Both during and after the war he exercised a powerful spell on the imagination of Germans generally. Those who became aware of their country's anomalous position, by experience of the war or reflection on it, could not but be fascinated by the notion of a single human being altering the destiny of his own nation – and that of countless others besides. The person and the myth of Napoleon exercised a particular fascination on Germany's writers, both during and after his lifetime. Kleist, in his notorious *Catechism of the Germans* (1809), written during the French occupation of Prussia, made the Emperor the focus of a new aggressive German patriotism. Others, such as Heine, were moved by the notion of a man overturning the habits of mind, the prejudices of a society, by his act of emancipation of the Jews. His highly stylised account of Napoleon's entry into Düsseldorf in 1811, which he had witnessed as a boy of fourteen, was made to seem like the witness of a sacramental act. He wrote it many years after the event, in 1822, against the background of mounting discrimination against Jews in Germany, and published it as part of '*Ideen: Das Buch le Grand*'. The Austrian playwright, Grillparzer, a contemporary of Heine, set a monument to Napoleon's endeavours and to the transience of human achievement in his play '*König Ottokars Glück und Ende*' (1825), although he strenuously denied the parallel. His young contemporary, the tortured genius Grabbe, wrote his '*Napoleon oder die Hundert Tage*' (1831) in order to demonstrate the power of the mob, whose only concern is their own appetites, to destroy the work of individual genius. The response of governments to Napoleon was equally varied and ambiguous. Many attempted to separate the person of the Emperor from the revolution which had brought him forth, and the majority accepted Napoleon's legitimacy, both as ruler of France, and erstwhile ruler of much of Germany. Even the public censor felt called upon to intervene in many regions of Germany after 1815 to forbid public criticism of Napoleon 'in the interests of upholding the monarchic principle'.

German governments were inspired by Metternich thus to postulate an essential continuity of German history between 1789 and 1815. Their motives in doing this were aimed to prevent the ideas of the French Revolution from affecting Germans, and to preserve the position of the traditional ruling elites. Over the nineteenth century as a whole, the pervasive influence of Napoleon and the Napoleonic era was evident in the stimulus, both direct and indirect, which it administered to the German economy by way of political change – what Marx was to call Napoleon's 'cleansing of the German Augean stables', his salutary abolition of innumerable petty princedoms.

Engels declared that Napoleon was the creator of the German bourgeoisie, and certainly in the Rhineland, which benefitted in many ways from the period of French administration, this is true. But the most pervasive influence of all, perhaps, was the fascination that Germans felt for the association between personal power and national aggression typified in Napoleon. It was this peculiar blend which Bismarck seemed to his contemporaries to embody, and which in their eyes gave him authority to determine the form of national unification in 1871.

2

Authority and the Subject in nineteenth century Germany

> Traditional habits of obedience in Germany are associated with our princely houses, and these cannot be simply transferred to any other object or institution.
>
> (the historian Dahlmann, *Foreword to the draft Constitution of 26 April 1848*)

The Monarchy

> Fleiß, Gehorsam sind die Pflichten,
> Welche redlich zu entrichten
> Gute Bürger sich bestreben:
> Aber so nach Pflicht zu leben,
> Prägen Schulen nur allein
> In das Herz der Jugend ein.*

sang the children of Ravensburg in the kingdom of Württemberg on the annual school feastday in the year 1811. In acknowledgement of the author of such a felicitous state of affairs, the chorus answered:

> Heil dem König, heil dem Staat,
> Wo man gute Schulen hat!
> Da jauchzet Jeder wonniglich:
> Es lebe König Friederich!†

Few people would take a school song as a gauge of contemporary values, and yet the sentiments expressed in this ditty have a certain representative character for Germany, even beyond the time in which they were recorded. The idea that the school is a main agent for conditioning the populace in their political and social attitudes

---

* 'Hard work and obedience are the duties which good citizens strive honestly to discharge. But only schools can imprint on the heart of youth the habit of a dutiful life.'
† 'Hail the king, hail the state, providers of good schools! Let everyone join in joyous song: Long live King Frederick!'

The Emperor William I (1876)

and that the state authorities should provide for their needs in this respect was widely accepted throughout the century. Characteristic of the early decades, by contrast with the later years, was the special mention of the monarch or local ruler as the provider for his subjects.

Germans in this revolutionary age felt a close bond with their princes, something which was no doubt a result of the familiarity of most sovereigns to their people. Indeed, the most effective rulers in eighteenth century Germany had rightly enjoyed the reputation of being accessible to their subjects: the case of Frederick II of Prussia (1740–86) and the miller Arnold enjoyed considerable publicity in Germany in the nineteenth century and was quoted in defence of the German paternalist system.*

---

* A miller named Arnold took his sovereign, King Frederick II of Prussia ('the Great') to court over an alleged injustice on the part of the latter. The miller was found to have no case but the king expressed his pleasure at the confidence expressed by so humble a subject in the rule of law in Prussia.

A Tyrolean pedlar called Peter Prosch told in his memoirs how he had come on foot to Vienna to lodge a complaint against the local authorities in his native village with the Empress Maria Theresa (1740–80); she listened to his grievance and even ordered a couple of dozen pairs of gloves from him. The accessibility of the prince continued to be a characteristic of political life in nineteenth century Germany also. The monarch was no abstract concept but a person who had immediate influence on one's life. Thus when the professor of philosophy at Breslau university, Danish-born Henrik Steffens, aspired to join the volunteers to fight Napoleon in 1811, he requested the king of Prussia to give him permission. He received a letter signed by the king giving him leave of absence and appointing the forty-year-old academic a sub-lieutenant. The term *Landesvater*, father of his country, was commonly used as a synonym for the prince in the Restoration period (1815–48) by ordinary people as well as the authorities. In his pioneering and influential biography of Frederick II of Prussia, published 1818–37, J. D. E. Preuß, a Prussian schoolmaster and archivist, devoted almost one quarter of his four-volume opus to *Friedrich als Landesvater*, outlining his achievements for the material well-being of his people. The loyalty felt by the subject to his ruler was part of his own identity, his roots. At this stage in Germany's history it was by no means synonymous with a sense of national identity. This is well illustrated by the attitudes of people in northern Frisia, in the duchy of Schleswig which until 1866 was subject to the king of Denmark. These attitudes are described with insight and vividness by Friedrich Paulsen, later professor of education in Berlin university and author of the standard history of educational institutions in Germany. He came from a village near Husum, birthplace of the writer Theodor Storm. Paulsen recalled the feelings of the local inhabitants in mid-nineteenth century Schleswig: the local population was

> ... German in their political sympathies; they had been involved in the war against Denmark (in 1848) but without great enthusiasm, because they were unaware of any kind of repression on the part of the Danes. For people simply felt ... that Schleswig's history, character and contacts made it part of Denmark.

His own father identified himself with such sentiments. Frederick VI of Denmark, he told his son, was the king he had grown up under, and he had often seen him in his youth; his successor, Christian VIII, was also to him the local ruler.

For the generations who grew to manhood before the 1830

Revolution, the monarch *was* the state. Paulsen's father (born 1806) was a small independent farmer in an outlying but not unprosperous province which was largely German-speaking, though not a member of the Confederation. Paulsen himself, born in 1846, owed his more overtly German loyalties in part to the fact that he had been sent to grammar school at Altona near Hamburg, which was in Holstein and therefore in the German Confederation. Here his fellow countrymen, the Mommsen brothers, Theodor and Tycho, were also educated.

While the ordinary individual remained faithful to the old ways throughout the first half of the century and continued to identify the prince with the state, even during the upheavals of the Napoleonic days, many, not least those responsible for government and administration, knew that things were changing. At the opposite end of the social scale to the Frisian peasant Paulsen, the Austrian emperor, Francis I (1804–35), complained when told of the mounting national debt, 'Yes indeed, the state is going to make beggars of us all'. To him, as to the king of Prussia and to the latter's son, later Frederick William IV, ministers and state officials were increasingly intruding on the royal prerogative. The abstract notion of the 'state' was thus gradually supplanting traditional dynastic loyalty. During the Napoleonic wars the civil servants, especially, but not only, in Prussia, had gained a considerable reputation for efficient and imaginative administration and for patriotism. In Prussia ministerial and official power was invariably greater under weak kings, such as Frederick William III, and here in the years 1807–13, civil servants had pioneered far-reaching reform programmes. Their reforms had included emancipation of the peasantry, a measure of self-government for the towns, important educational measures at school and university level; their initiative was largely responsible for the Customs Union of 1834 and they made other notable contributions to the revolution in communications in mid-century Germany. State officials in Hanover and Saxony, who here as elsewhere in north Germany were of mixed noble and bourgeois origin, put through peasant emancipation, electoral reform, and in the former state the so-called Basic Law of 1833. It was the abrogation of this last-named measure by Queen Victoria's uncle, the new Elector Ernst August, in 1837 which brought the protest and dismissal of seven civil servants, professors at the university of Göttingen. In south Germany government ministers and their civil servants played an important part in absorbing into the administration of Bavaria, Württemberg,

Hesse-Darmstadt and Baden those territories which had been acquired after the abolition of the Holy Roman Empire in 1806. For the inhabitants of many of such territories, especially of the small former Imperial Free Cities, the officials represented all that was new and contrary to well-tried ways. Their administration, based on the capital of the state, seemed impersonal and remote to the conservative small townsman. Furthermore, it robbed him of the feeling of having a say in the regulation of his affairs. Hence, when severe economic hardship afflicted tradesmen and rural folk in the 1840s, it was to the king, not to the officials, that men of initiative turned, believing that if he knew of their troubles, he would help. The same attitude was true of Prussia too, although it had a much longer tradition of centralist government than the southern states. In Bavaria over five hundred prominent citizens submitted essays in the mid-1840s, in answer to a request by King Ludwig I, on the subject of the causes of distress in his kingdom.

The monarchic order seemed a guarantee of stability to a generation which had experienced the French revolutionary wars and Napoleon. While the incident of the Grimm brothers helping to draw the carriage of the returning grand duke of Hesse-Kassel into his capital in 1815 is often referred to by modern historians as a

The Park at Schönbrunn, Vienna. German rulers – in this case the Austrian Emperor – generally allowed their subjects to walk in the gardens of their residences.

typical example of the sycophancy of Germans towards their rulers, the same or similar such incidents can be seen in the context of the time as illustrating people's pleasure in heralding the restoration of solid and 'caring' government after the arbitrary and ineffective administration of King Jérome in Westphalia during the Napoleonic occupation.

The dynasties as a whole proved dexterous in putting the impression across that it was they rather than 'the people' who had liberated Germany from Napoleon. As 1813 receded into the past, the volunteer movement which participants had seen as the seed of a citizen militia, was represented by the authorities as a breach of the law, and as such morally ambiguous, even wrong. Particularly in south Germany, which did not modernise as rapidly as the north, and where society was felt to be more socially homogeneous, loyalty to the dynasties remained strong. Such loyalty was thought of in terms of personal affection and even a degree of familiarity – thus the kings of Bavaria and the emperors of Austria, with few exceptions, spoke with a pronounced local accent, and this habit was contrasted by south Germans and members of the small central German states with the abstract state patriotism felt to be typical of Prussia. And yet paradoxically it was in the four south German states, which, unlike Prussia in the first half of the century, had constitutions, that the person of the monarch was expressly declared 'sacred and inviolable'.

The revolution of 1830, despite its relative lack of violence, administered a severe shock to rulers and their governments. The policy of the Austrian chancellor, Prince Metternich, the 'strong man' of the German Confederation, had been to isolate Germany politically and if possible intellectually from western Europe. 1830 seemed proof that this policy had faltered, if not failed. Accordingly, the authorities grew less self-assured, more arbitrary in their repressiveness; this was felt acutely by writers, victims of a censorship whose mindlessness earned Heine's witty character-isation in chapter twelve of his '*Ideen: Das Buch le Grand*' (1827). The entire chapter consisted of the following:

The German censors . . .
. . . . . .
Idiots . . .
. . . . . .

(It was customary for the censor to substitute a blank for an offending word.) Trenchant and lively criticisms of the monarchy began to appear in the 1830s and increasingly in the 1840s, fastening on the weak point of the institution, the personal silliness or inadequacy of individual rulers. Certainly Ludwig I of Bavaria (1825–48) and Frederick William IV of Prussia (1840–61) offered ample scope to satirists, and most students of German are familiar with Heine's entertaining strictures. Even more damning was the publication of the sexagenarian Ludwig's amorous poems to the dancer Lola Montez, including one effort entitled '*Lolas Busen*' which was circulated surreptitiously in the 1840s. Somewhat earlier, and in a more serious vein, the writer Paul Pfizer observed in his '*Briefwechsel zweier Deutschen*' (Stuttgart, 1832), that nobody believed any longer in the divine right of kings, but that those in authority had arbitrarily decided to cite such a claim in defence of the status quo. Republican sentiments were expressed by young academics, the Young Germans and Young Hegelians, towards the end of the 1830s. Though few in number they were to win considerable public influence in the Rhineland in the 1840s. The majority of the educated public, now becoming conscious of political matters, eagerly speculating over their beer or their coffee on the rights and liberties of the subject, were desirous only of constitutional reform within a traditional framework. The same attitude is largely true of the revolution of 1848, taken as a whole, although in making this point one must not underestimate the extent of genuine revolutionary activity, especially in Baden in the south-west, in many urban centres throughout the Confederation and in the Rhineland, where August Bebel, later leader of the Socialist party in Germany, recalled being beaten up by his classmates for expressing loyalty for the monarchy in 1848 (Bebel's father was a Prussian NCO). A. de Tocqueville's claim, which became widely disseminated through the work of the sociologist, Wilhelm Riehl's '*Die bürgerliche Gesellschaft*' (1850), that the revolution stopped before the thrones of the princes, is, if not absolutely true, generally accurate.

The churches

The Protestant Churches

In any discussion of authority and its agents in nineteenth century Germany, most Germans would invariably have made reference to the individual Christian churches. Yet the very real decline in the influence and in the authority of the churches over people's lives between 1800 and 1914 makes the twentieth century historian reluctant to concede very much importance to institutional religion in that period. At the time, however, and especially in the first sixty or seventy years of the century, the Christian churches as an institution seemed a permanent feature of the social landscape, and religious practice continued for most people to be a necessary part of their everyday lives. It was natural, given the close association between throne and altar in the Lutheran areas of Germany since the Reformation, that the Protestant church was a firm ally of the monarchy. Most German monarchs and their nobility were personally pious throughout the nineteenth century. Thus, in strong contrast with his great uncle, Frederick II of Prussia, Frederick William III and his sons Frederick William IV and William I, who ruled from 1797 to 1888, were deeply devout and at the same time thoroughly dogmatic in their views on the church's role in society. King Frederick William III regarded religion as the source of moral regeneration in Prussia after the catastrophic defeat of the old order in Jena in 1806. He planned as part of his programme of moral reforms to heal the split between the Lutheran and the Reformed (Calvinist) churches in his territory. In 1817, on the three-hundredth anniversary of the Lutheran Reformation, he brought about the formal union of the two: henceforth the Protestant church in Prussia and in a number of other German states came to be known as the Evangelical Church (as it still is today).

More controversial was the Prussian king's determination to eradicate the rationalism which had come to be characteristic of Protestant theological thinking in the eighteenth century. State governments in the eighteenth century, under the influence of the Enlightenment, had stressed above all the utilitarian role of the clergyman in society – Herder had once complained that he and his colleagues were but *Beamte im Talar* (civil servants in vestments). The moral and pedagogical role of religion predominated over matters of faith and doctrine, but when Frederick William III came to the throne, he was determined to realise his vision of a pious and contented nation through the restoration of the religious and social function of the church. He would brook no opposition to his ideas. His clergy and his people must, he determined, misapplying a famous phrase of Frederick II, '*nach seiner (Seiner) Fasson selig werden*' be saved according to a royal recipe. The churches were to use the liturgy that he, as head of the church, had designed and none other. Religious affairs excited an extraordinary degree of interest in the 1820s and 1830s, even outside Prussia. Contemporary literature and the press are full of references to it. In consequence of the king's authoritarian attitudes, dissenting clergymen were dismissed and the judicious award of titles and decorations, notably the so-called Order of the Red Eagle, won support for the royal policy. As Heine put it in his second '*Brief aus Berlin*', 'the liturgy . . . will fly from one church spire to the next on the wings of the Red Eagle'. In this context the remarkable movement known as the Friends of Light, centred on Prussia and Saxony and which counted among its leaders many of the king's most dedicated clerical opponents, drew crowds of several thousand to what were ostensibly religious meetings in the 1830s and early 1840s. The political character of royal ecclesiastical policy, as also of public protest organised by the Friends of Light, was clear to contemporaries, though it would be wrong to deny a deep religious impulse to those involved. The attitude of those members of the clergy who supported the king, and they were the majority, smacked of opportunism. This was to prove very damaging to the public image of the church in Prussia in subsequent decades. Moreover, the permanent association in the public mind between 'throne and altar' (always in this order), a phrase much bandied about by those with a vested interest in the status quo, alienated those people from the church who had most need of it. This was particularly true during the upheavals attendant on industrialisation, particularly in the second half of the century. In general, up to about 1870 custom continued to exercise a strong influence on contemporaries, as Fr. Paulsen observed:

> Custom determined the response of those indifferent and even of those hostile (to religion). It was not until after 1870 that this changed.

The same remained true of rural areas until several decades later, but in the industrialised cities the decline was very rapid after 1870. By 1874, for example, only 20% of Protestant couples in Prussia were married in church, though 62% of babies were baptised.

The Catholic church

The position of the Catholic Church in Germany is rather different from that of the Protestant churches, although it was perhaps still more authoritarian in its attitude towards its members. Religious practice among German Catholics remained strong even after the onset of the industrial revolution and in urban areas such as the Rhineland. Traditional piety continued to be characteristic of both the educated classes and the masses in Catholic areas of Germany well into the modern age, though not without a price being paid for it. This price was an increasing tendency to withdraw from confrontation with modern living and the separation of Catholics from those of a different or no creed. Many of the Church's leaders, most notably the redoubtable Bishop von Ketteler of Mainz (1811–77), adapted their pastoral practice to the needs of their time, though their social consciousness remained with a traditionally paternalistic framework. Care of the sick and aged, and of the socially deprived, both in and out of institutions, was actually extended by the religious orders in the nineteenth century long before the state began to legislate for their needs. Although the need to protect the ignorant against the danger of mobility inherent in modern society was the prime mover, the Catholic Church understood the needs of those affected by the upheaval in their lives characteristic of the industrial age and tried to make provision for the physical needs of its members. This included such enterprises as the hostels for artisans, founded by Adolf Kolping, and orphanages and hospitals. That the church cared for those in need was something that its members were aware of and showed their approval of by their support. Catholic lay organisations proliferated too, especially in the late nineteenth century, and helped to centre people's lives on their membership of the Catholic Church. However, as in other European countries, the church authorities did not see fit to prepare people to meet the challenges of modern living, but rather to shield them from contact as far as possible. To do otherwise, in their view, would encourage a critical spirit which might be dangerous. The papal Syllabus of Errors of 1864, which listed some eighty 'errors' of modern society, including liberalism, socialism and modern science, remained binding on the faithful in Germany and elsewhere well into the twentieth century; this affected both the Catholics' own attitude and also the view with which it was regarded by the rest of society. One of the very few Catholic thinkers to show an early awareness of the long-term dangers of such attitudes was the political philosopher, Franz von Baader (1765–1841). In a now famous article on the proletariat, which was written as early as 1835, he made the assertion:

> The intellectual poverty or ignorance and hence the vulnerability of this class of the population is no less dangerous to the church than their physical poverty and need to the secular government.

Catholic devotional manuals, instructions in the schools and from the pulpits continued to be authoritarian and simplistic, earning for Catholics from their fellow Germans the not-unfounded charge that they were anti-intellectual. The relationship of the Catholic Church and Catholics generally in Germany to the state was one of acceptance of its authority, except where it diverged in matters of faith and conscience from the position of the Catholic Church.

An instance of the latter was the so-called *Kulturkampf*, or conflict between the state and the Catholic Church in Germany, which occurred in the second half of the nineteenth century. The *Kulturkampf* was engineered, at least in part, by Bismarck's determination to isolate the racial minorities in the new Reich, who were mainly Catholic, and to undermine the power of the Catholic political party, the so-called Centre Party. But it was also a challenge to the Catholic Church by the German liberals. They wished to reserve to the state such matters as education and marriage in which the Catholic Church claimed responsibility over their members. The *Kulturkampf* dominated the middle years of the 1870s, but by the early 1880s peace was made between church and state in Germany. Catholics proved themselves thoroughly conservative in their outlook and in their readiness to side with what were known as the *staatserhaltende Kräfte* or 'loyal classes', against liberalism, social democracy and revolutionary excess. One of the results of the *Kulturkampf* was to make Catholics in the Second Empire very sensitive to the charge, used also with considerable effectiveness against Jews and Socialists, that they were not 'as good Germans' as the next, on account of their international connections. The dexterous association by apologists of Prussia of Protestantism, liberalism and the Prussian nation as the forces which had created and unified Germany, put Catholics on the defensive. Frequently, especially in the decades immediately preceding the First World War, Catholics tended to associate themselves somewhat osten-tatiously with nationalistic posturings. The most apt summary of the problematic position of the Catholic Church in nineteenth century Germany was probably that voiced by von Baader when, with considerable perceptiveness, he noted as early as 1833:

> Since the (catholic) clergy, who hold the reins of power, ... were attacked by the Protestants, they never tried to show their superiority over them, but rather remained in negative and defensive opposition. ... Catholicism, far from being in a state of revolution or even dissolution, has sunk into a state of stagnation.

The nobility

Throne and altar represented clear institutions of authority for the individual in Germany. Another such repository of authority was, oddly enough in the so-called bourgeois century, the nobility. It was in fact one of the most remarkable features of nineteenth century Germany, that her nobility, especially that of Prussia, showed itself able to resist the apparent force of European history in this period and to consolidate its position as a ruling elite. This was achieved mainly by the support and favour of the princes in the early decades and in later years by state governments. This enabled the German nobility to uphold traditional claims to senior positions in the army and civil service. A further source of their success derived from their ability to adapt themselves to changing economic conditions. Thus, at the beginning of the century, after initial difficulties and a period of severe crisis for agriculture following the end of the Napoleonic wars, in which many of the great landed estates changed hands, the landed nobility in the eastern provinces of Germany entered a period of unprecedented prosperity. This lasted from the mid 1830s to the late 1870s. The price of land increased threefold between 1825 and 1875; between 1816 and 1866 the amount of land producing crops doubled in size. The export trade brought unheard-of wealth to the landowners, and the manorial estates of east Germany paid no tax until 1861. Even after that date corrupt practices often ensured that the tax burden was placed on other sections of society. The legendary exclusiveness of the nobility in Germany proved to be capable, on closer examination, of fairly loose application. A Prussian edict of 1739, which was adopted by the Prussian Civil Code in 1794, declared that the marriage between a nobleman and a commoner of peasant or lower middle class stock was invalid and the children illegitimate. However, the same edict stated, should an impoverished nobleman marry such a person who had money with the purpose of seeing his home and line survive, this was in order and the children could succeed. Similarly, the prohibition on the sale of manorial land to commoners was overruled when economic necessity demanded. In the agrarian crisis already referred to, particularly between 1816 and 1825, a large number of commoners came to own such land. These, or their children, became, as the nineteenth century commentator R. Meyer put it, 'bourgeois Junkers', but Junkers nonetheless. In theory the Junkers might not engage in trade. In practice, from the mid 1820s onwards, the landowners of lands east of the Elbe made a great deal of money from capitalistic farming. They learnt modern business methods from their new bourgeois neighbours, they continued to export grain and now produced substantial amounts of spirits from potatoes, sugar from sugar-beet for export and internal markets. When overseas competition threatened the livelihood of these east Elbian landowners, the state in 1879 introduced protective tariffs and in subsequent years had these tariffs raised fivefold. In the course of the nineteenth century as a whole, the Prussian nobility increased their landholdings from two million hectares to two and a half million. Above all, as the sociologist, Ferdinand Tönnies, pointed out in the course of a brilliant analysis entitled '*Deutscher Adel im 19. Jahrhundert*' and published in the '*Neue Rundschau*' in 1912, the German nobility showed their talent for self-preservation through alliance with 'other powers'. These 'other powers' included the state, banking and industrial circles, and, towards the end of the century, the various pressure groups, such as the Farmers League (*Bund der Landwirte*), which came to exercise very considerable influence on government decision making. The nineteenth century in Germany saw the end of the hostility between what the mid-nineteenth century conservative philosopher, Fr. Julius Stahl, had called '*die Feudalen und die Gouvernementalen*' (the landed gentry and government authority), not least because of the preponderance of the former or members of their interest group, in cabinets, senior official positions and the army.

In the remaining two-fifths of Germany, that is, in the non-Prussian part, the preponderance of the nobility was generally very much less, with the exception, perhaps, of Mecklenburg or Hanover. In Bavaria, although more and more members of the nobility came to depend on a civil service career or the army for a living and, after 1848, on industry, they did not claim the kind of prescriptive right to senior posts which the Prussian nobility considered they should enjoy. In Bavaria, too, the crown's interest in preserving and promoting a wealthy aristocracy prevented them from becoming an exclusive caste. Thus, of the marriages which took place between members of the Nuremberg patriciate between 1806 and 1900, 309 were with members of the bourgeoisie and only 237 with fellow nobles. Many of the former mediatised princes (that is, princes who had lost lands and sovereignty on the collapse of the Holy Roman Empire) gravitated to the state service. Many, indeed, went to Prussia to enter the bureaucracy or embark on diplomatic careers, but those who went to the Bavarian service, such as the erstwhile Bavarian prime minister, Chlodwig von Hohenlohe, later governor of Alsace-Lorraine and from 1894–1900 imperial chancellor, retained something of the common touch which generally characterised the south German nobility.

For Germany as a whole the political and legal privileges enjoyed by the nobility in former times were gradually eroded in the nineteenth century, a movement which began with the legislation of the Napoleonic period, and received further impulses during the revolutionary year 1848–49 and in the 1860s. However, the landed nobility, its ranks now swelled, particularly in Prussia, by wealthy bourgeois, came close to recognising that property was more important in a capitalist era as a basis of power than social status and traditional privilege. On the land, despite the so-called emancipation of the peasantry, they retained their authority over the rural populace, particularly since surplus population drove the more energetic and potentially critical members of the labour force to emigration overseas or migration to the German industrial centres. In the last years of the century landowners in eastern Germany took to engaging many hundreds of thousands of seasonal workers from Russia, Poland and Austria who were, in effect if not in name, serfs.

The Prussian upper house became virtually an exclusive social club of the first estate after the 1848 revolution; the lower house was increasingly dominated after the so-called Constitutional Conflict of the 1860s either by the nobility or those favourable to the conservative interest. The same became increasingly true of the civil service, including even the judiciary, which up to the founding of the Empire had been staffed mainly by bourgeois or members of the lower nobility who shared common liberal attitudes. Though the manorial estates lost their tax immunity in 1861, the financial policies of the Prussian minister of finance, Johann von Miquel, in the nineties effectually restored the status quo. The special concessions given to the agrarian interest in the form of protective tariffs, export credits, special freight rates, exemplifies what the economic historian Hans Rosenberg has referred to as their highly developed sense of position both in terms of political power and social rank. They well understood Bismarck's dictum, 'whoever has his hand on the lever of the legislature will not hesitate to use it'; they exploited the legislature to bolster their economic position on which their privileged status depended. Even the reform of local administration, the *Kreisordnung* of 1872, which substituted the authority of the state for that of the local landowner, resulted in the approximate identity of the two. The vast majority of *Landräte* in Prussia, that is the chief local authority, were in fact noblemen, even at the end of the century. As has been said, the nobility retained their special position in the army and the diplomatic career.

This situation was in part brought about by the attitude of other elements in society towards the German and particularly the Prussian aristocracy. The bourgeois plutocrats, for example, who were in general far more wealthy – in the year 1900, out of 3,142 millionaires only 856 were noble – did not develop an independent class consciousness based on their economic position, but rather aped the values of the feudal elite. In their own person, or in that of their children, they aspired to membership by intermarriage or by acquisition of landed estates, and were widely successful. The academic elite also accepted the continued privileged status of pre-industrial elites, and even the consolidation of their power. Prior to 1848, the members of the academic world had been the spokesmen for the emancipation of the middle classes, but by the end of the nineteenth century they had come to believe that their own special status within the world of university, school and the profession of letters depended on the preservation or rather petrification of the status quo in a rapidly changing industrial society.

The state

During the nineteenth century the source of authority in Germany, if not its exercise, passed gradually away from persons and corporative estates to the state as such. Ruling elites of former times aimed to retain their power by identifying their interests with those of the state. In the case of the churches this largely failed, in the case of the nobility it was successful to a remarkable degree. The concept of authority retained and even enhanced the association it had long possessed with protection and security (*Geborgenheit*) for the vast majority of the population, even when, as in the late nineteenth century, it was exercised by an increasingly centralised state government and not by the persons to whom Germans had traditionally and on the whole willingly given their loyalty. The main reasons for this was the demonstrable success of the Prussian, and, after 1871, of the Prussian-German state in increasing the power and the status of the nation in Europe; additionally the state was seen to be responsible for the impressive rise in living standards in the population as a whole, however unevenly this increase might be distributed. Moreover, respect for authority was instilled in a variety of ways in the day-to-day life of the individual. The most obvious source of this was the family, particularly for paternal authority. However, it would be difficult to prove that the family in Germany was more authoritarian than it was in Victorian England.

Certainly, with the present state of research on the German side, it could not be done conclusively. Although memoirs, literature and letters can provide countless instances of paternal rigour and even severity, there are also innumerable testimonies in the same sources of affectionate interest shown by both father and mother in their children. Moreover, memoirs of cruelty towards children, as for example in the memoirs of Carl Fischer or Adelheid Popp, cited in a later chapter, were generally occasioned by dire physical need in the family and frustration in the parent at his continued inability to provide for his family. The lovelessness of many an English childhood spent in institutions away from the family or deprived by fate of family life is far less frequently attested for Germany, while the beneficial influence of family life as evoked in memory is constantly referred to in autobiographies, especially, but by no means only, among the middle and upper classes.

School as an agent of authority

Although family life was regulated and disciplined, it would seem that a more systematic agent of promoting obedience in the subject and respect for the authority was the school. German rulers, especially Saxon, Prussian and Thuringian princes, had long been personally concerned in education, primary, secondary and tertiary. Primary school education was generally made compulsory (in theory, if not always in practice) in the course of the eighteenth century, and in the early decades of the nineteenth century examination requirements were introduced for entry into a number of the professions, including the civil service. This was more effective in northern and central Germany than in the south. In fact, as evidence shows, the high reputation enjoyed by the German school system was often rather relative, i.e. a good deal less bad than the British, French or Spanish. Thus, in 1818, one-third of Berlin's school-children could not even write their names. School premises in Prussia, including even the second half of the nineteenth century, were often extremely primitive, the teachers poorly paid and poorly housed. The primitive teaching methods employed are frequently recalled in memoirs, of which the following extract is typical:

> In those days being able to read was an extraordinarily difficult art, and its acquisition at school according to the old methods often took years, and those who did not come regularly might never learn to read with ease. The exercise was as follows: diagrams were fixed to apparatus on the tables; every two or three pupils had one to themselves, aided by an

'The arithmetic class' by A. Roeseler. A traditional primary school (1898).

'assistant' complete with stick and pointer. First the diagram with the letters; then one with syllables a-b:ab, b-a:ba etc.; finally diagrams with words a-p:ap, f-e-l:fel, *apfel* (apple). If a pupil in one year or two, though it could be three, four or more years had worked through the tables, he was put on to catechism, first the short then the full length catechism, only then could he enjoy the fruits of reading: learning by rote.

Certainly, even when at the end of the century the percentage of literates in the population was almost 100%, compared with some 82% for France, 20% for Spain, literacy did not imply the ability to think for oneself. To the minority of the population who enjoyed post-primary education, which in any pre-industrial community was invariably a small section, the support given by the authorities to the educational system, grammar schools, universities, and technical schools, could only enhance very greatly the reputation of the state in their eyes. However, the numbers of German primary schoolchildren who went on to higher schools were few indeed: in 1865 they represented 5.7%, 6% in 1896 and 7.2% in 1906 of the total population. And even after the industrial revolution was well in train, the additional money spent on state education tended to benefit more or less the same section of the community.

However, in noting this fact one should still remind oneself that Germany was still considerably more progressive in this area than Britain or France, for, although the percentage of working class children who got to grammar school or university in the nineteenth century was negligible, the 20% of lower middle class children who did so compares very favourably with any European country in the same period. Nor was entry to higher education restricted on religious or ideological grounds: there was no equivalent in Germany to the Test Acts in Britain, which discriminated against Nonconformists and Catholics up to 1871. In Germany the highly authoritarian organisation of teaching and lecturing and the hierarchical structure within the teaching profession were acceptable to the majority of the middle classes because of the clear professional and social advantages the system enabled the successful among them to enjoy. It was made abundantly clear in Wilhelmine Germany, as in the kingdom of Württemberg in 1811 (see above) that the principal aim of educational institutions was to provide good, industrious and obedient citizens.

The Army

A further institution which had a similar function was 'the school of the nation', the army. The post-1945 accounts of army life in imperial Germany have dwelt on the brutalisation of the citizen on the parade ground. Franz Rehbein's account is often quoted, an unusual document coming from the pen of a former rural labourer:

> We were lucky on that occasion that we only got shouted at. Though indeed in the army any excuse is enough to let them beat you. On such occasions I, like the rest of my comrades, got not just beatings, kicks, boxes on the ear, but once I got such a wallop from my corporal on the back of the neck that the blood gushed forth from mouth and nose.
>
> That to ill-treat someone who cannot hit back is nothing but an act of cowardice, scarcely occurred to those thugs. Quite the contrary, they

were proud of the way they behaved and with typical Prussian
corporal's arrogance, they felt they had done something to satisfy their
superiors. And what of the superior officers? They 'hear nothing, see
nothing and their Heavenly Father feeds them all the same'. As long as
they can get away with it they close, not just one eye but two, all so as not
to undermine discipline, which is sacred.

Let no one come to me with talk of the German soldier's sense of
honour. As far as I'm concerned no greater lie exists. Indeed what
happens is that the natural sense of honour in a man is systematically
destroyed by such degrading treatment.

The cartoons from *Simplicissimus*, from 1896 onwards, underlined
the less attractive aspects of army life which Remarque's horrific
portrait of NCO Himmelpfennig in *All quiet on the Western Front* in
the 1914–18 War was later to make world-famous. But probably the
majority had agreeable memories of the three-year military service
or the one-year volunteer service for those who had spent six years in
a grammar school and had passed their leaving exam. They had
seen a bit of the world, made friends, had their photographs taken in
smart uniforms to hang framed on their walls for posterity, and for
those who finished their voluntary service satisfactorily the
institution of reserve officer brought members of the middle class
within a stone's throw of the ruling elite, and gave them a pre-
eminent social status within their circle.

The consequences: subject or citizen?

While such institutions reinforced among Germans in the Empire a
natural sympathy for the forces of law and order which was the
product of their history over the previous two centuries, they also
offered serious resistance to the gradual evolution of a liberal society
in Germany. The external manifestations of authority and the
responses of the large majority of the populace perpetuated the
Untertanengeist ('subject mentality'), which Heinrich Mann was one
of the few contemporary writers to pillory in a systematic fashion.
(His famous novel, '*Der Untertan*' ('Man of straw') was withdrawn
from serialisation after war broke out in 1914 and was only
published in 1916.) There was, too, despite the achievements of the
1860s and 1870s in the field of legislation, considerable legal
discrimination in the Empire on the grounds of creed, race and sex.
There was also much tacit social discrimination against real or
potential critics which became much more marked in the decades
immediately preceding the war than had been true of the early

years of the Empire. The national minorities, Poles, Alsatians, Lothringians and Danes were the principal victims of this, but so too were other minorities in different ways and in varying degrees, the Catholics, Jews, Socialists, and, towards the end of the century, members of liberal parties and organisations also. But, on the other hand, as has been noted, Catholics and Jews were not excluded from university on religious grounds as they were in England, though they might find themselves discriminated against if they applied for university chairs. However, the attitudes of authority towards the Socialist movement resembled at times the character of a witch hunt. The paternalist and hierarchical organisations of both state and society saw in the republican Socialist Party, which counted Marx and Engels as its spokesmen, as neither more or less than the state's most intractable enemy. Between 1878 and 1890, Socialist organisations were prohibited in Germany. Even the liberal parties in parliament, with the exception of the Left Liberals, voted for this measure, which was introduced by Bismarck in 1878. Both the pre-industrial elites and new interest groups, such as the industrialists, felt that universal suffrage, as instituted by Bismarck for the Reichstag elections in 1867, had given their enemy a weapon which must eventually undermine the state. Towards the end of the century, these groups favoured abolition of universal suffrage. The best method to bring this about, a number of their spokesmen believed, including Emperor William II himself, was a government-provoked coup d'état followed by restrictions on constitutional rights of the citizens. Although notice of such a 'preventive act of hostility' by the authorities and their agents against the alleged enemies of the State lost its actuality about 1900, the military retained very considerable emergency powers over the civilian population, without however this fact arousing much hostility in the public. After 1890 the anti-Socialist law was repealed and the ruling classes saw the Socialist Party go from strength to strength in general elections. In 1912 it was the largest party in parliament. It did not matter that they knew, and that the Socialist leaders knew, that the Socialist Party would never be tolerated in office, despite the allegedly constitutional character of the state. The idea that a party professing republican sentiments could ever be a government party, or even a loyal opposition, representing as it did the interests of more than a third of the German population, was something the ruling classes in Germany were not prepared to contemplate. In Prussia they and their supporters opposed with great determination any amendment to the three-class franchise

The Final Exam (Abitur) at a German Grammar School. Late 19th century engraving.

which continued to regulate elections to the Prussian parliament until 1918, and which was introduced into industrialised Saxony in a form even more advantageous to the upper class in 1896. This was of very considerable importance because the limited competence of the *Reichstag* over legislation gave the state parliaments major powers over those living within the boundaries of the state, as for example in education. Even the experience of the nation at war, in which the Socialists supported war credits and members and supporters of the Socialist Party proved themselves loyal and disciplined soldiers, failed to modify the monolithic attitude of the ruling elite of the Empire. A by no means untypical expression of prevailing views as regards the liberalisation of institutions in Germany was voiced by an army officer, one Colonel Bauer, towards the end of the 1914 war:

> It must be emphasised over and over again, equal franchise for Prussia means the end of Prussia, as it does for any state. What is the point of all

these sacrifices if at the end we are to be suffocated in Jewry and the proletariat?

The maintenance of such a franchise condemned the masses to minimal representation in matters of legislation. The limitations imposed by Bismarck on the power and effectiveness of parliament and the political parties, especially the failure to win budgetary control of the army or ministerial responsibility, questioned the very fact of Germany's claim to call itself a genuine constitutional state.

The course of the nineteenth century in Germany saw a diminution in the arbitrary exercise of power by princes and their agents, but a considerable extension of the range of state activities in the lives of its citizens. Respect for the authority of the state and its representatives in public life, at work, in the army and at school, was probably greater and more freely given by the majority at the end of the century than at the beginning or in the middle, and there was, on the whole, a strong sense of commitment on the part of public servants to the state and the people they served. But by an often facile tendency among supporters of the regime to equate obedience and orderliness with public virtue and by rejecting criticism as invariably destructive, imperial Germany robbed itself, as it were, of the mirror in which it could gain perspective on its society and institutions, and enjoy an invaluable and indeed necessary source of evolutionary change.

3
The Restoration Era 1815–48

The German Confederation

The settlement which was devised for Germany after the expulsion of Napoleon was the work of European statesmen at the Congress of Vienna. On 10 June 1815 a German Confederation (*Deutscher Bund*) of thirty-eight states was set up under its aegis (a further state, Hesse-Homburg was created in 1818). The Austrian Emperor, Francis I, formerly Holy Roman Emperor Francis II, became president of the German Confederation. The Holy Roman Empire was not restored in the 'Restoration' but simply the monarchic order in German lands. The Austrian ruler retained the title of Austrian Emperor, which he had assumed in 1804, and in his capacity as president of the Confederation, was empowered to declare war and sign peace in its name. The very loose federal structure of the German Confederation was reminiscent more of Napoleon's own creation, the Confederation of the Rhine (1806–13), than of the old Empire. In theory at least, the Confederation had the right to accredit its representatives abroad, but in practice little use of this right was made. On the other hand, the sovereign princes of the larger German states sent ministers to other German courts, as well as abroad. There was only one federal institution, the *Bundestag*, or Federal Diet, which sat at Frankfurt. It was not in any sense an electoral assembly but a conference of ambassadors from the various states. It exercised executive authority, most notably with regard to maintaining public order. Measures dealing with the control of public opinion, censorship of books and periodicals, banning of writings, and imprisonment of 'dangerous' authors, fell within its members' jurisdiction and earned it a bad reputation among contemporary liberals and later nationalists. The cumbersome character of the Confederation, the imbalance between the power of the individual sovereign states and

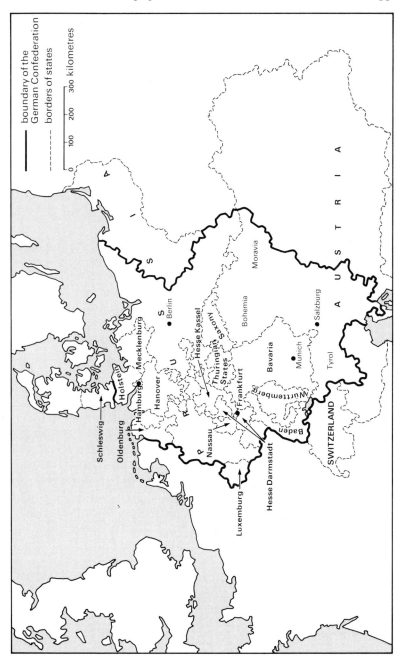

The German Confederation 1815

the Confederation as such, stunted its development into a genuine federal state. The Frankfurt Diet remained the only organ of government, although the provision was later made for the defence of the *Bund* by the Federal Law of 1821; a federal army was composed of three contingents from Austria, three from Prussia, one from Bavaria and three from the remaining thirty-six states. It was in fact not a federal state, a *Bundesstaat*, but rather a federation of states or *Staatenbund*, to which England, Denmark and the Netherlands also belonged, by reason of their sovereignty over Hanover, Holstein and Luxemburg respectively. This proved to be an insuperable obstacle to the advance of national unification, and earned the Confederation an undeservedly bad reputation among nationalist historians, which has continued to influence people's views to the present day.

The chief raison d'être of the Confederation in the eyes of its principal architect, Metternich, the Austrian chancellor, was to fill the power vacuum in central Europe with a stable regime, and thus to serve the wider ideal of a European balance of power. A complicated series of territorial exchanges and annexations accompanied the introduction of the new order into Germany in 1815. Of these, the most important was the expansion of Prussia into western Germany by her acquisition of the Rhineland and Westphalia. The real significance of these territories for the future of Prussia and Germany lay in their mineral riches and commercial traditions. At the time of the Congress of Vienna, Prussian aggrandisement was supported both by the Austrian chancellor and the British foreign minister, Castlereagh, because they believed it would benefit European security. The subsequent history of Europe, at least until the 1860s, suggests that they were correct in their assumptions. The strengthening of Prussia was specifically designed to provide an effective counter-balance to the potential aggressor states, France and Russia, in the interests of European peace. The Confederation in fact made little impact on the European public mind, though it was regarded, and no doubt rightly so, as an agent of peace. Its main effectiveness lay in the way it buttressed the restoration of the traditional monarchical states in Germany and perpetuated territorial divisions. The energies of its most important statesman, the Austrian chancellor Metternich, who directed its affairs for thirty-three years, were successfully aimed at stifling the national and liberal aspirations of the people who lived within its borders.

Many abortive plans for a new Germany had been mooted in the last months of 1814 and the spring of 1815, which had tried to take into account the very divergent interests concerned. These included those of the great powers of Austria and Prussia, the medium-sized states, such as Bavaria, Hanover and Saxony, all of whom were bitterly hostile to Prussia and jealous of her success, and also of the so-called mediatised princes, that is, those princes who had lost their sovereignty during Napoleon's dismemberment of the Holy Roman Empire. Finally there were the interests of the patriots, who aspired to a united, constitutional Germany, but whose lack of influence was amply demonstrated in the course of 1815, and whose lack of genuine popular support was made evident in the years which followed. In the event, the formation of the German Confederation was a rushed job, largely because the question of Germany seemed unimportant to the great powers, and the decisions as regards its form were taken under the stress of Napoleon's escape from Elba. In the light of this renewed threat to European security, the sovereign princes of Germany and representatives of the four city states of Frankfurt, Hamburg, Bremen and Lübeck agreed to form 'an indissoluble Confederation' dedicated, as the protocol termed it, to 'the preservation of the internal and external security of Germany and to the independence and inviolability of the constituent German states'. In fact the problems of Germany had never occupied a central position in the deliberations of the European powers. To them Germany was what contemporary functionaries might call a 'non-problem'. The statesmen were far more occupied with conciliating Tsar Alexander of Russia, at the same time as they were determined to contain his ambitions of westward expansion. The problems of Saxony and of Poland, which were related to the Russian question, and which were also intimately bound up with the present ambitions and future strength of Prussia, preoccupied the delegates to the Congress of Vienna to the exclusion of discussion on Germany as such. The Federal Act (*Bundesakte*) constituting the new state was not drawn up until 10 June 1815, a whole day after the long protocol of the Congress had been duly signed by the European statesmen. It was then belatedly added to the solemn *acte finale*, but by that time many of the delegates had left Vienna and could not append their signatures.

In the several states of the German Confederation from 1815 to 1867 (when it was dissolved), rulers and their ministers promoted the idea of monarchic, or, as in the case of the city states, oligarchic paternalism as the best form of government for the people. In the early years, the old-fashioned pigtail or *queue*, associated with eighteenth-century absolutism, came back into use, especially among civil servants or aspirants to the state service, for the authorities looked on it as a sign of loyalty and general reliability. In the stories of the Romantic writer, E. T. A. Hoffmann, these pig-tailed bureaucrats appear as quaint philistines, the butt of ironic and even demonic wit for their underlings. But there is no doubt who is master, and Hoffmann's grotesque fantasies on the subject of Germany's new ruling class, the bureaucrats, contain a mordant twist: although himself a writer of genius and an accomplished composer and conductor, he was forced by circumstances to return to his former profession as lawyer in the Prussian state service at the end of the Napoleonic wars, and – most bitter irony of all – he became a member of the commission responsible for drafting the reviled Karlsbad Decrees (1819), directed against Germany's intellectuals. He did not live long enough to witness the first effective protest against the new order, namely the revolution of 1830, for he died in 1822. The revolution did not mitigate the repression of liberal and democratic opposition in the Confederation, but it gave immense stimulus to criticism and to political speculation. Overnight the pigtail became the symbol of an antiquated political system and as such was widely pilloried in satiric verse and broadsheets. Though the content of these was usually mild in tone and crude in execution, they represented an important step in the growth of political awareness in Germany as a whole, which is a striking feature of the 1830s by contrast with the decade preceding it.

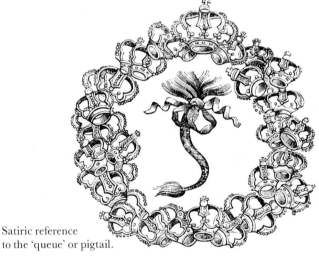

Satiric reference
to the 'queue' or pigtail.

Constitutions

The autocratic attitudes of individual German rulers and their governments, as well as that of the Federal Diet which was their collective voice, were the more bitterly resented by the liberal-minded citizenry of post-1830 Germany, because the Confederation had at first seemed to promise an era of constitutional government for the nation. Article 13 of the *Bundesakte* had given specific pledges of constitutional government under the new regime. In southern Germany and some of the central states, this pledge was redeemed in the years after Vienna. The state of Nassau, most fittingly, since it was the home of the great reformer Baron Stein, had anticipated these developments by bringing in a constitution even before Napoleon's fall, in 1814. After the formation of the Confederation, Weimar, Goethe's home, was the first state to do so, in 1816; Bavaria and Baden followed suit in 1818, Württemberg in 1819 and Hesse-Darmstadt in 1820. In the case of the southern states, which had made considerable territorial gains in the Napoleonic wars, constitutions were primarily aimed at creating a sense of common identity for the state as a whole. This was particularly desirable for Bavaria, for she had acquired Franconia, parts of Swabia and the Palatinate, territories having very different political traditions and, for the most part, a Protestant population.* Baden, in the south-west, possessed the most liberal constitution of all, which included a lower house of parliament, elected on a property qualification. The debates in the Baden chamber were the object of very considerable interest to Germans in the years between 1815 and 1848, known as the pre-March era (*Vormärz*)†, and many even travelled to Karlsruhe to witness them. However, although south German liberals liked to draw attention to their superiority over their northern countrymen, especially in Prussia, by virtue of their being members of modern constitutional states, the limits of constitutional sovereignty in practice were constantly demonstrated. Liberal spokesmen, including highly respected professors, such as Karl Rotteck of Freiburg, Robert Mohl of Tübingen, shared the lot of north German colleagues in that they lost their university chairs for

---

* An example of how slow people are to break loose from historical ties – an important lesson of history which many Germans and others fail to appreciate – is the fact that people in Bavaria still distinguish in common parlance between 'Old Bavaria', pre-Napoleonic Bavaria, and 'New Bavaria', the territories acquired by the kingdom Bavaria under Napoleon.

† 'pre-March' refers to the fact that the 1848 Revolution broke out in March of that year.

their public criticism of the system. The university of Freiburg was actually closed by the Baden authorities for some time, in order to remind intellectuals who was master. Particularly in his attitude towards universities and the press, Metternich demonstrated the limitations of sovereignty enjoyed by individual states in the Confederation. In 1819, taking as an excuse the murder of the playwright Kotzebue by a radical student called Sand, the Austrian chancellor put pressure on the principal German states to accept stringent surveillance of the universities, and a censorship of books, pamphlets and journals. This constituted a very serious obstacle to the development of political education and the free exchange of ideas in Germany. These measures, known as the Karlsbad Decrees, won the active support of the Prussian king, who in the same year dismissed the last of his liberal ministers, Wilhelm von Humboldt and Boyen, the latter of whom was one of the authors of the humane military reforms of the Napoleonic era. Württemberg's representative at Frankfurt offered vigorous and at first successful resistance to the decrees but was eventually relieved of his post under pressure from Vienna. Bavaria showed her independence in a way which was to be characteristic of her relations with powerful German states throughout the nineteenth century – *fortiter in modo, suaviter in re,* that is, she accepted them only in so far 'as they were not in contradiction to the sovereignty of the constitution and of the law', but she accepted them. Just a month prior to the promulgation of the decrees, Metternich met the Prussian chancellor, Hardenberg, in Teplitz. The fruit of their talks was that Prussia pledged herself not to introduce a representative assembly for her very disparate territories, but to perpetuate the individual identity of each province by granting *landständische Verfassungen,* that is, constitutions based on the traditional provincial assemblies. Repeatedly during the Restoration and again in the revolutionary year of 1848–49, Prussia publicly showed her deference to Austria's wishes in constitutional and other matters. Throughout the years 1815–48, Prussia's rulers demonstrated that they were much more concerned with the preservation of monarchical prerogative and the power of the privileged estates, the nobility and the bureaucracy, than with the conciliation of their subjects and the gaining of popularity in Germany. On five occasions King Frederick William III promised his people a constitution, but he did not implement his promise and it is doubtful whether he ever intended to. However, there is some considerable evidence from contemporaries that the conviction expressed in 1815 by the

Prussian historian Niebuhr carried much weight in Restoration Germany, namely that 'freedom rests far more on administration than in constitutions'.

The system and its critics

It is perhaps surprising to later generations that contemporaries should have offered little tangible resistance to the Restoration, given the talents and energies evinced by the patriots in the years 1806–15. But one must remember that the heady experience of a united Prussian nation offering successful resistance to Napoleon during the Wars of Liberation had concealed the fact that the real executive force had been the landed nobility and the higher civil servants. These acquired or retained positions of influence in the state during the Restoration era, and, although a number of individuals expressed critical views about the system, particularly in Prussia, these were invariably in the form of criticism from within. On the other hand, artists, intellectuals and university students who had identified themselves so totally with the *Erhebung*, the rising against Napoleon, found themselves faced after 1815 with the mundane task of earning a living, of getting into or back into government service in an increasingly competitive society. This was, for example, the case with the poet and lawyer, Eichendorff (and Hoffmann, already mentioned), the writer and lawyer, Karl Immermann, the university professors, Schleiermacher and Steffens, and many more.

There were, however, some notable exceptions to the general political apathy of the post-war years. One such was the students' political organisation known as the *Burschenschaften*, which originated at the Weimar university of Jena at the end of the Napoleonic era, and which suffered persecution at the hands of the Federal authorities under the Karlsbad Decrees. But in general Germans took little part in the European-wide conspiratorial movements of the 1820s and subsequent years, which were dedicated to the realisation of national and liberal goals. Even the 1830 revolution, which swept across Europe and brought fundamental changes in a number of states, had little obvious impact on Germany. Bloodshed was rare and the main gains of protest, the expulsion of the elector of Hesse-Kassel and of the duke of Brunswick, the latter of which had reigned, in the historian Treitschke's words, '*voll fürstlicher Unverantwortlichkeit*' (with due princely irresponsibility), over his territories, were achieved with minimal violence. The importance of 1830 in Germany lay not in political or institutional change but in the way in which the revolution shaped the consciousness of a new generation of university graduates, who entered the civil service or attempted to support themselves in the profession of letters. In general, it remains true that the Restoration settlement continued to be accepted by Germans from all regions and classes with greater acquiescence than the circumstances attending its birth might have seemed to warrant.

Lack of mobility, especially in the first twenty years of the Restoration period, the small and self-contained units in which most people lived, were important factors in accounting for the political mood of these years. Although the Holy Roman Empire had disappeared over a generation ago, an observant German traveller in 1832 (the writer Fanny Lewald) noticed how people in the south and west of the Confederation spoke of the village three miles away as 'abroad': they had probably never been as far away from home themselves, or if they had, they continued to regard it, as indeed had been the case in their fathers' time, as being a different state from their own. There was also in the country at large a general sense that the political system under which they lived was a rational one, designed to accommodate as far as possible a variety of conflicting interests. Not least of these were the counter-claims of privilege and tradition on the one hand, and modernisation of society and state on the other. Many people believed that the holders of the highest offices in the land, were themselves bound by obligations which all but the most irresponsible, as for example the expelled elector of Hesse-Kassel, discharged. In March 1948, on the centenary of the outbreak of the 1848 revolution, which marks the end of the Restoration era, the then president of the Austrian Republic, Karl Renner, characterised the climate of the Restoration period critically but acutely: 'In the Vormärz state, all the members were fixed in a rigid hierarchical system, and every single member was subject to one above him, even the monarch himself, who was bound by the obligations imposed on him by the traditions of his house.' The system was undoubtedly an authoritarian one, and very occasionally, as in the case of Georg Büchner's home state of Hesse-Darmstadt, a vicious one, but in general those who endured its intolerance of liberal or other criticism, such as the historian, publicist and author of the first history of German literature, Georg Gervinus, bore witness to its underlying humanity. He, along with six colleagues, including the Grimm brothers and the distinguished constitutional historian, Dahlmann (later president of the Frankfurt

Assembly in 1848) had lost his university chair at Göttingen in 1837, when the seven professors protested against the unconstitutional ways of the new sovereign, the elector Ernst August of Hanover. Yet, a constitutionalist through and through, Gervinus could write dispassionately about the German governmental system in 1847, a year before the revolution: 'When the present regime is overthrown we will have no crimes against habeas corpus to redress, no servitude to abolish, no ridiculous privileges to topple.'

Several factors helped to explain the widespread acceptance of the Restoration of the German Confederation of thirty-nine states, despite the failure of the Congress of Vienna to create that unified nation state, to which patriots had aspired. On the one hand there was the people's awareness of the critical economic and social problems of post-war Germany, and on the other a widespread feeling, both in Prussia, which comprised some three-fifths of the Confederation, and in the constitutional states of southern Germany, that Germany was reasonably well governed. Belief in the essential integrity of the system was substantial for over a generation after 1815. Commentators, both academics and publicists, frequently brought home to their readers the contrast of present times with the kind of government Germany had known in the eighteenth century. The natural conservatism of the middle classes was thus re-enforced by a characteristically nineteenth century optimism and belief in progress. Characteristic also of their traditional political quietism was the tacit assumption that political progress was not the result of bourgeois effort, but was the gift of well-disposed rulers to diligent and loyal subjects.

The social order

The most effective force in assuring the acceptance of the system as a whole – and in all this we are speaking of the average rather than the individual citizen – was the social structure of the middle class. By contrast with her western neighbours, Germany possessed no bourgeoisie in the *Vormärz* with cosmopolitan connections and outlook. The nearest thing to such an institution, though numerically too small to merit the name, was the group of Jewish bankers and businessmen, whose commercial enterprises in Berlin, Hamburg, Breslau and Königsberg etc. enjoyed the support of related firms in Paris, London, Amsterdam or Rome. Members of the well-to-do commercial and professional families, scattered across the country in centres such as Hamburg or Berlin, Frankfurt,

Mannheim or Leipzig were local notables, so-called *Honoratioren* –
not bourgeoisie in current nineteenth century sense. The typical
middle-class German was in fact a *Kleinbürger*, whose salient feature
was his local egoism; he was a frequent butt of satire, epitomized in
what became in this period the national stereotype '*der deutsche
Michel*', but unruffled in his self-assurance. The petit bourgeois
complacency, satirized over and over again by Heine, as in '*bei uns
geht's hübsch ordentlich zu*' ('we're alright Jack') from '*Schwäbische
Schule*', was a product of the German's ignorance of other ways.
Perhaps not surprisingly, the most vivid insights we possess of social
and political injustice in the Restoration era, were written by those
few members of burgher society who were mobile, namely the
journeymen, who played a prominent role in the 1848 revolution,
or the students and intellectuals, whose protest became vocal after
the 1830 revolution. The predominance of the *Kleinbürger* and the
greater importance given to the local over the national issues in the
years from 1815 to the early 1840s, go far to explain the success of the
Restoration not simply in terms of political control but also of public
attitudes. As Marx put it provocatively: 'The basis of German
morality and honesty, not just of individuals, but of the classes too, is
... that self-effacing egoism, which makes a virtue of provinciality
and narrowness and accepts it as such in others.' And he added
tartly, 'Even the moral awareness of the German middle class
derives solely from their consciousness of being the general
representative of the philistine mediocrity of all other classes.'

Despite the widespread social problems of Germany in the
Restoration era, whose principal causes were massive regional
population increase and a backward economy, despite the fact that
industrialisation was beginning to acquire momentum in certain
areas in the 1830s and early 1840s, the social order remained
generally static and showed only limited signs of any tendency
towards mobility.

The reform movements

However, it would be incorrect to attribute the political stability of
Germany in this period wholly to social causes or to the defective
political awareness of her people. Of vital importance in creating
confidence in the state were the reform movements of the early
nineteenth century, particularly in Prussia, and the fact that these
had been introduced by the governments and their civil servants,
most of whom were of middle-class origin. The reform legislation

was designed to set aside the traditional absolutist order in which 'human beings were not regarded as such, but as chattels of other men in the state'. The original aim of the Prussian legislation was thus avowedly liberal and humanistic. It appealed to men of liberal sentiment, and confirmed their belief in the fundamental goodwill of the administration; it retained their loyalty in subsequent decades until about 1840, even though benefits promised did not always materialise. The individual however enjoyed, as a direct result of government intervention on his behalf, in the early years of the nineteenth century a far greater degree of economic liberty and, though to a more limited extent, more political rights than he had in the eighteenth century. In Prussia, for example, permission to marry was freed from restrictions and remained so henceforth. Most other states followed suit, though in the south German constitutional states of Bavaria, Baden and Württemberg, and in Hanover, restrictive legislation was introduced at various times, between 1818–52: couples intending to marry had to give evidence of possessing sufficient substance to support themselves. Furthermore, the emancipation of the peasantry, notably, but not only, in Prussia, represented a major political concession, however harmful the economic consequences for the individual might be.

Emancipation changed the status of a large proportion of the population from that of 'subject' to, in theory at least, 'citizen'. State governments gave direct encouragement to greater regional mobility in their territory, by introducing freedom of movement and freedom of trade. In 1810–11 full freedom of trade was introduced in Prussia. In 1816, the taxes payable by the individual on leaving his place of domicile, were abolished. However, those trades still organised on guild lines continued to exist, though they largely lost their powers of compulsion. The trade tax levied on anyone who opened a workshop or began to ply a trade, was designed as a useful source of state revenue and occasionally used to protect trades which were over-supplied, such as inn-keeping. By and large, the kind of freedom of trade which Prussia introduced and maintained was not acceptable to the Free Cities and to the states of central and southern Germany. Bavaria and Hanover brought in full freedom of trade, but then imposed restrictions in order to counteract the social problems, which seemed to those affected to be a direct result of the reforms. For the middle classes, perhaps the most significant reforms concerned education. The reforms initiated by Wilhelm von Humboldt, during his time as head of the department of Cults and Instruction in 1809–10, and implemented by Prussian civil servants in subsequent years, gave the middle classes access to status and allowed them a degree of upward social mobility, through academic and technical qualifications. Other states, notably Saxony, Baden and Württemberg, followed the Prussian model. Civil servants, teachers, engineers and skilled workers alike saw state education as the means of personal advancement, and if necessary, of overcoming disadvantageous family or economic circumstances. Another, less obvious, factor in conditioning young Germans, especially university graduates, in their attitudes towards their political environment, was their dependence on the state for employment.

Voices of protest

The role of the state, then, both as a source of order and security, and also as a major provider of employment, had an important bearing on political behaviour and conservative outlook. In the 1830s a dedicated attempt was made by a number of university graduates to create an alternative source of employment in journalism, and at the same time to foster critical awareness among their fellow countrymen of the repressive character of the political system. These were the Young Germans, the Young Hegelians and their associates whose mentors in this respect were Heine, and, less readily acknowledged by them, the Frankfurt journalist Ludwig Börne. Severe repressive measures were imposed by the *Bundestag* in the mid 1830s. In 1835, a number of writers were disciplined and imprisoned, and their works proscribed, notably those of the Young Germans. But it was perhaps less the actual repression than the political and social structure which prevented radicalism from being more successful. As Börne said, in the fulsome tones characteristic of early nineteenth century German liberalism, the main problem was the lack of a cultural centre:

> We lack both a capital city which could provide the focus for all rays of light, a market for the products of the spirit, and we lack popular representation, whereby the best of the masses are chosen to represent them as deputies and take counsel and make decisions. The critical newspapers can indeed perform the function of such chambers of deputies, but the majority are no more than mere dwelling places, in which comfortable paterfamilias who pass themselves off as editors act just as they will. There is no way to create a public opinion in our nation.

Although the impact of the younger generation, either on the system or the political outlook of the majority, was not very incisive, the variety of critical enquiry into political and social structures and Germany's position in the world was very considerable in the 1830s and particularly in the 1840s. The relevance of such enquiry was made manifest in the revolutionary disturbances of 1848 and 1849, but the lack of numbers and of cohesion of the intellectuals, and their lack of political experience, which became obvious in 1848, consigned the extraordinarily interesting and pertinent ideas of such men, to a mere episode in nineteenth century German history. However, their relevance to the post-1945 situation in Germany, where both the Federal Republic and the Democratic Republic have sought to legitimise their existence through reference to Germany's past, has been amply demonstrated in the work of contemporary historians, literary critics, political philosophers and sociologists.

With the establishment of the German Confederation, Metternich achieved his principal aims – to preserve peace for Germany in Europe and ensure internal stability by isolating the Confederation from the mainstream of European political ideas. His regime as chancellor of Austria and as the major policymaker in Germany lasted as long as the Restoration era itself, until he fled before the Viennese revolutionaries in March 1848. 'It is no little achievement to have controlled Germany for a generation and a half', Bismarck commented aptly later. Yet although Germans as a whole showed themselves remarkably quiescent in an age which has often been called 'the age of revolutions', and in middle and old age many looked back on these years as a halcyon time, the mood of the time, as expressed in contemporary literature was often very different below the surface from what an observer of the public life of the country might assume. In the literary and philosophical writing of the time, and in satirical poetry and local doggerel, we encounter a profound sense of unease, which was directed less perhaps at the present crises than the future of civilised society in Germany. The poetry of Lenau, the romantic Hungarian nobleman, or that of Platen, whose classical forms never mask the underlying tension, is a particularly apt expression of the earlier part of the epoch, the 1820s and early 1830s. The formal mastery of their medium, lyric poetry, is an attempt to overcome an anguish of spirit, an existential *Angst* indeed, which was expressed in terms of the contemporary situation. The popular literary figure of these years, *der Zerrissene* (from *zerreissen*, to tear asunder), a disillusioned observer of the human scene, is another expression which was firmly anchored in contemporary problems. *Der Zerrissene* appears in the work of the two great innovators in German drama in this period, Grabbe and Büchner, the latter in his black comedy, '*Leonce und Lena*' and was satirised by Nestroy in his magnificent comedy of the same name; he appears also in the popular novels of Immermann and others. The fear of pauperisation among German burghers as the population increased without an accompanying increase in business or food to support it*, the lack of employment prospects for the educated, the anxiety for the future, such emotions informed the works of philosophers and poets alike. Some believed in an imminent holocaust. Metternich's vocabulary, according to the historian Treitschke in his '*History of Germany in the nineteenth century*' knew only five metaphors, all of them concerned with natural catastrophe. These were: volcano, conflagration, deluge, plague, cancerous growth. Shortly before his death, which took place two years after the inconclusive 1830 revolution, Goethe observed that a war 'like the Thirty Years War' appeared imminent. The sage historian of ancient Rome, Barthold Niebuhr, who chose his words carefully, wrote in the preface to the second edition of his '*Roman History*' (1830):

> Unless God comes to our aid in some miraculous manner, we are faced with a catastrophe on the scale experienced by the Roman world in the middle of the third century: destruction of prosperity, freedom, education and knowledge.

Prophetic utterances by widely read authors, such as Heine, Börne and the English poet Byron, conjured up visions of imminent class war more than a decade before the appearance of the Communist Manifesto in 1848. Börne warned his contemporaries:

> When the middle classes have won equality for themselves, the lower classes suddenly become aware of the inequality in which they live; they learn to recognise their own wretched state, and that must inevitably bring about a war between rich and poor.

Heine asked rhetorically in chapter 29 of his '*Reisebilder*',

> 'What is the great task of our times?' His answer – emancipation.
> Not just emancipation of the Irish, the Greeks and the Frankfurt Jews, the West Indians and other oppressed peoples, but the emancipation of the whole world, and especially that of Europe, which has come of age and is wrenching itself free of the iron leading-strings, in which it has been so long held by the privileged, the aristocracy.

---

* Büchner prefaced '*Leonce und Lena*' with a quotation from Alfieri:
  E la fama? ('And what of fame?') *E la fame?* ('And what of hunger?')

At the same time, the popularity of chiliastic visions spread among indigent craftsmen, who constituted the new proletariat. By the late 1830s the works of early French socialist thinkers were beginning to circulate in Germany, and were being widely read by travelling journeymen and students.

Towards the end of the 1830s, a change in the temper of the nation gradually made itself manifest. Unease gave place to protest, specific grievances were aired, and political poetry became immensely popular. The Young German poets, Freiligrath, Herwegh and the author of what was to become the twentieth century German national anthem, Hoffmann von Fallersleben, found themselves household names. Indeed Freiligrath made a substantial sum of money from the sale of his poetry and was even able to support his family on the proceeds in the first months of his expulsion from Germany as a political radical in the mid-1840s. It was in the provinces rather than in the big cities that this change of temper was first noted. In the early 1840s a traveller to Berlin from Königsberg (Fanny Lewald) was amazed at the sleepy paternalism of the Prussian capital. 'Politics for people in Berlin are the doings of the royal family,' she wrote, 'while for us in East Prussia it is what the government does or does not do.' However, this changed overnight in the course of the next years, and Berlin, Vienna, Frankfurt and other big cities had become the focal point of political agitation by the middle of the 1840s.

The new political fluidity found expression in all sorts of ways. Although public meetings were banned, the religious revivalist movement known as the 'Friends of Light', with its centres in Prussia, Saxony and the central German states, drew crowds of several thousands of people of widely varying social origins. Farmers, apprentices, pastors and teachers met with craftsmen and intellectuals and even Berlin seamstresses to hear popular speakers. An interesting aspect of the movement, which was essentially political rather than religious in character – its leader, Pastor Uhlig, was dubbed the Saxon O'Connell after the popular Irish agitator, Daniel O'Connell – was the use of the new railway stations for the meetings. The novelty of travelling by train naturally increased the attractiveness of protest, although travel was only possible for the better-off. Thus the Thuringian town of Köthen, which was already an important railway junction in the early 1840s, became a popular venue and developed its buffet facilities at the station to accommodate the large numbers. Another sign of renewed political awareness was the widespread popularity of the illustrated satirical

'Parade Unter den Linden'. Detail of painting by Franz Krüger (1837). Many famous contemporaries, including the actress Stich-Crelinger and her daughters, and the opera singer Mantius, are portrayed.

papers, which the new king of Prussia, Frederick William IV, who came to the throne in 1840, freed from the censorship. The satire was often savage, as was that of the political chansons and broadsheets, which proliferated in Germany during the revolution of 1848.

By the mid-1840s, before the full effects of the European agricultural crisis had become visible, it was already apparent to those responsible for the preservation of order at every level in the German Confederation, from the local official in the provinces to the ministers in Vienna, Dresden, Berlin and Munich, that society as a whole was becoming increasingly alienated from the state. Governments showed their awareness of what was happening by trying to be seen to conciliate the populace. However, the dimensions of the social problems affecting Germany, which resulted from increase in population among farmworkers and craftsmen, followed by a series of bad harvests and a downswing in the economy in the mid-1840s, proved to be far too great for any administrative measures to solve. Across a wide section of society the feeling was rife, which a decade earlier had only been held by disaffected intellectuals, that the state was becoming a machine which 'is only aware of things, but pays no heed to human beings'.

The end of an era

In the event, the Restoration settlement was not overthrown by the ferment of political and social ideas of the 1840s. Despite the extent of social distress and political grievances in the nation was a whole, despite the influence of figures such as the utopian journeyman, Wilhelm Weitling, on radical artisans in the 1840s, or the agitation of the democrats Moses Hess, Marx and Engels in the Rhineland, the revolution of 1848 did not achieve the overthrow of the social order nor the destruction of the political settlement of 1815. The Confederation was reconstituted at the end of the revolution and lasted for almost another generation till 1867. But 1848 marks the end of the Restoration era, because the revolution abolished the last vestiges of the traditional corporate state (*Ständestaat*) and brought constitutional regimes to the two major states which hitherto had none – Austria and Prussia. More important, though as yet imperfectly understood by participants and observers alike, 1848 brought a change in the political balance between Austria and Prussia in the Confederation, which predetermined its end.

The Restoration era was thus brought to an end, not by the energies of the German people, but by the economic power and political will of Prussia. The vital role of economic initiative, as exercised by Prussia in the years 1815–34, in determining the character of political change in Germany, was not apparent to contemporaries. However, despite the seemingly stagnant character of the Restoration epoch, Prussian enterprise constituted a dynamic force, which the industrial revolution developed to the full.

4
The Economy

i) The Restoration Years

Germany on the eve of the industrial revolution

One of the most effective sources of the state's authority in Germany at the end of the nineteenth century was its economic strength. The manner in which the state had participated in the industrial revolution, and had thereby generated very great wealth, and the fact that it had been seen by the governed to do so, were important aspects of the politics of persuasion in that country. At the same time the relatively short time-span in which industrialisation occurred in Germany, the coincidence of the take-off into sustained industrial growth with national unification and major movements of the population, created problems for the German nation of a different kind and on a greater scale, than those experienced in neighbouring European countries.

That the industrial revolution constituted, in Carlo Cipolla's apt phrase, a break in the continuity of history, that it changed fundamentally a way of life which had not altered in its essentials since Roman times, is especially evident in nineteenth century Germany. In the year 1800 there was only one city in Germany of over 200,000 inhabitants, three of more than 100,000; in 1900 there were seventy-three German and three Austrian cities of 50,000 or more inhabitants; Vienna had increased her population by 490%, Berlin by 872%. In 1800 Berlin had an estimated 20% of her population of 170,000 and Cologne one in four inhabitants on some form of public relief; three-quarters of a century later, Berlin was the most expensive and one of the most ostentatiously prosperous cities in the world, while Cologne was a thriving metropolis. In 1800 some 90% of Germany lived in rural areas; by 1891 the urban population had outstripped the rural populace for the first time in her history (in England and Wales the date was 1851). In 1800 some 90% of Germany's people earned their living in agriculture, in 1907 less than 30% did so; at the latter date 42% were employed in industry, and 22% in the tertiary sector (service industries). In 1800 and for many years to come, Germany had notoriously bad roads; innumerable toll barriers inhibited mobility of people and goods. Lack of mobility was a general feature of German life at the time and one which was reinforced in innumerable ways by the restrictive legislation of local rulers and corporations, and by the traditional habits of people. 'Very many people, especially women, never saw a town', wrote the historian of education, Fr. Paulsen, of his north Frisian home in the 1850s, where his parents were small farmers. In contrast, by 1900 Germany had a network of rail, road and waterways on which her commerce and industry depended, and which enabled her to exploit her geographical position in Europe in a positive way totally unknown in her previous history. The development of Berlin in the nineteenth century into being the commercial and industrial centre of Germany, and finally the populous capital of the German Empire, is indeed remarkable, and, like the industrial revolution itself, is a socio-cultural fact of the first order of importance. But perhaps it is the history of the small and medium-sized towns which really brings home to us the re-volutionary nature of the changes wrought in Germany by her economic development. The Ruhr town of Essen, where the Krupp family erected their steelworks and Alfred Krupp, in the 1870s, built his two-hundred room Villa Hügel, had only 9,000 inhabitants in 1850; in 1870 it had 57,000, in 1910 295,000. Similarly Dortmund and Duisburg, mere hamlets in 1850, had in 1910 214,000 and 331,000 inhabitants respectively.

In areas which were not industrial centres, such as the south and north-east of Germany (except Upper Silesia), growth was much less spectacular, and the quality of life changed at a more leisurely pace. This was something which struck north Germans with some force in their contacts with the south, as Th. Mann remarked when he came to Munich from Lübeck in the 1890s, an impression which he recorded in a way not especially flattering to the Bavarians in his character of Herr Permaneder ('*Buddenbrooks*'). Some regions were scarcely touched by the industrial revolution, even as late as 1900, and though the population growth was rapid and sustained, population density in Germany as a whole in 1914 was in fact much less than in England or Belgium (120 inhabitants per square kilometre as against 239 and 259). However, by the end of the nineteenth century, most Germans, wherever they lived, had become anxiously aware of the pace of change, and while nationalist feeling inspired a sense of pride in the country's economic and military strength, the arts, especially the pictorial arts and literature, reflected the sense of unease and even disorientation felt by many Germans as citizens of a great industrial power.

The beginnings of industrialisation

The transformation of Germany from a rural to a predominantly industrial economy did not in fact span the century, but was concentrated on the years after 1850. The many factors inhibiting industrial development in eighteenth century Germany continued to be operative for some years after 1800, even in those areas where industrialisation occurred first: Berlin and the Rhineland, the Ruhr valley, Silesia, Saxony and the Saarland. The most important of these factors was the political division of Germany, which still remained a problem after the 314 independent territories and some 1400 semi-autonomous territories of the late eighteenth century had been replaced by thirty-eight sovereign states when the German Confederation was set up in 1815. The disparity in size between these states was a further inhibiting factor – Austria had 115,533 sq. miles in 1815 (excluding her Italian possessions), Saxony 5,787, Schwarzburg-Sonderhausen a mere 333. Furthermore, many regions were linked economically with adjoining non-German regions rather than with each other. Most states had a traditionally disproportionate military budget, which directed resources away from trade and commerce, and a long-established and long lasting tradition of domestic self-sufficiency, which high taxation and lack of mobility reinforced. In 1648 Germany had lost control of the mouths of the Oder and the Vistula; the effect of her political divisions in the following century and a half had been to cut her off from profitable overseas trade enjoyed by west European powers. Denmark's control of the Sound, high tariff walls with her neighbours, France, Russia and Austro-Hungary, were further disadvantageous features of Germany's position in the early nineteenth century. At this time her few commercial and industrial centres were sited inland, with the exception of Hamburg and the less important Bremen and Danzig. The provincialism so characteristic of her people at the beginning of the nineteenth century, which was a product of her history in the early modern period, acted as a deterrent to effective industrial and government

The Lauchhammer works in 1800. Contemporary lithograph.

enterprise. Adventurous spirits, concerned to change the provincial character of Germany, encountered the physical obstacles of toll barriers and a multiplicity of currencies and weights and measures, laws restricting movement of labour, freedom of trade and indeed even the traveller's passage from one town or village to the next. When the Prussian civil servant responsible for the department of trade in the Ministry of Finance, von Maaßen, prepared to introduce a modified tariff in 1818, Prussia had sixty-seven distinct customs areas, and a traveller from Hamburg to Berlin crossed some sixty-three custom frontiers. Fr. List, the great economist, clearly foresaw economic interdependence among the German states as the forerunner of national unification and power. In 1819 he petitioned the Diet of the Confederation to help remove these barriers, declaring that 'thirty-eight custom boundaries cripple inland commerce and produce much the same effect as ligatures, which prevent the free circulation of the blood'. In subsequent years he argued forcefully for the creation of a centralised railway system, editing the vigorous '*Eisen-Journal*' to foster public awareness of its potential for economic and military power. Though he died by his own hand in 1846, disillusioned with the apparent failure of his mission, his ideas were much discussed in his lifetime and influenced Prussian and German state policies after his death.

Maffei's machine-tool factory near Munich (1843).

A revolution in communications, the necessary first step to industrial progress in Germany, took place in the years between the 1830 revolution and the expulsion of Austria from the Confederation in 1866. This took the form of the reduction of tolls on rivers, highways and canals, the gradual improvement of roads and waterways, and then the building of new ones, and of course the railways. A necessary part of this process was the gradual development of the regional press, both newspapers and journals, to reach a readership beyond their immediate locality and to help forge something approaching a national public opinion. An early instance was Fr. List's '*Eisen-Journal*', already mentioned, but one must not discount the influence of periodicals edited by literary men and historians who played a formative role in the process, such as Heine (in his '*Briefe aus Berlin*'), Gutzkow, the most prominent of the so-called Young Germans, and Gervinus, author of the first history of German literature, the political historian Dahlmann, and many others.

The Customs Union 1834
The two innovations which most readily captured the imagination of the public in the 1830s were in fact the Customs Union and the

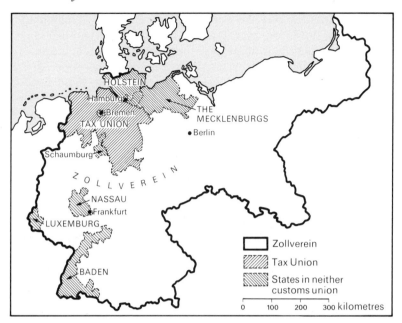

The Zollverein and the Tax Union 1834

first railway, which occurred almost simultaneously, in 1834 and 1835. Economists disagree on how far the Customs Union directly stimulated productivity in the way the railways did. Undoubtedly it greatly stimulated the appetite of businessmen and the public for mobility, and therefore, from an economic point of view, is important as a factor attacking the characteristic inertia of Germany before the industrial revolution. At midnight on 31 December 1833 customs barriers were raised, internal tariffs abolished in nearly three-quarters of Germany and a liberal external tariff introduced. The Prussian initiative in persuading several German states to join, despite strenuous opposition from Austria and the states of the north-west, was to prove important both economically and psychologically. The driving force behind the scheme had been the desire of the Prussian government to have goods transported without tolls through the enclaves and larger territories, which separated Prussia's scattered possessions in the west and the east. The dexterity with which she pursued this goal, and the experience gained in negotiations over the next thirty years, her readiness to sacrifice financial to political gain, won her the grudging acknowledgment of both participant states and those outside the Union. Initially, neither Austria, Baden, Nassau and

Frankfurt, nor the Hanseatic cities and Hanover and Mecklenburg, would join, but most, apart from Austria, Hamburg and Bremen, became members in subsequent decades. Austria, which, in contrast with Prussia, favoured protectionism, sedulously opposed the Customs Union. The Austrian delegate to the Federal Diet (*Bundestag*) at Frankfurt declared in December 1833 that the whole affair was 'one of the chief nails in the coffin of the Confederation', a prophetic phrase indeed. Although in the 1850s Austria secured a privileged relationship with member states, this was lost in the 1860s. Shortly afterwards the correlation between economic and political leadership in German affairs was amply demonstrated as Prussia unexpectedly defeated Austria, and expelled her from the Confederation. The south German states, Austria's allies in the 1866 war, proceeded to sign military agreements with their recent foe, Prussia, not least in order to retain their profitable economic links with that state.

The Customs Union tariff was one of the most liberal in the world, despite the infant state of German industry, and the volume of goods increased rapidly from 1834 onwards: by 1845 revenues to the member states had risen by 90%, the population only by 21%. This increase in revenue – each member kept a share of the total based on population – was irresistible even in times of strain. In a paradoxical manner, the revenue continued to be distributed between member states, even when those states were at war with Prussia in 1866.

The railways
The stimulus offered by the railways to industrialisation is much more evident. The building of railways linked peripheral areas of German territory which were vital to the development of her economy – the Ruhr, Rhineland, Silesia, the Saar, which possessed important mineral deposits. It began to transform business and to place it on the basis of a market economy. The first railway lines were used mainly for passengers, the first of all being the seven kilometre track between Fürth and Nuremberg in 1835 – where today the magnificent German transport museum is aptly sited – followed by Berlin to Potsdam in 1837, which carried 2,000 passengers daily in the early 1840s, and then Brunswick to Wolfenbüttel, one of the few early railways which was state-owned. Something of the contemporary enthusiasm for this technological wonder is captured for us today in the work of a local craftsman in Wolfenbüttel. On a delicate Biedermeier coffee set, housed in the

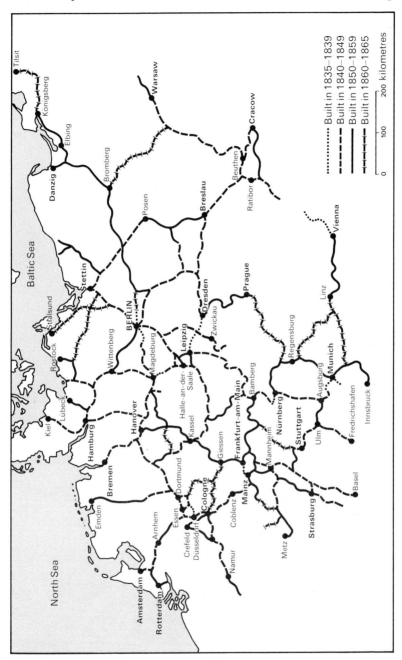

German Railways 1835–65

ducal palace at Wolfenbüttel, he painted the town's first station, its first locomotive and various contemporary scenes connected with the great event.

More significant from the point of view of the economy was Germany's first long line, covering the 115 km from Leipzig to Dresden in Saxony (1837), followed by important lines in the Ruhr and Rhine, Cologne to Minden, Cologne to Aachen etc. By 1840 Germany had 549 km of line, and the next decades (apart from 1848) saw rapid progress. There were nearly 6,000 km in 1850, and over 11,000 in 1860. With the opening of the great bridge over the Rhine at Cologne-Deutz, a few hundred metres from Cologne Cathedral, in 1859, northern Germany was spanned by railways running from Aachen, near the Belgian border, to Memel not far from the Russian frontier. On the eve of the Great War (1912) there were over 60,000 km of railways in Germany.

Initially it was private enterprise rather than the state which supplied the impetus and the capital for the railways. The shareholders of what proved to be the extremely lucrative Dresden–Leipzig railway, linking the royal with the commercial capital of Saxony, raised sufficient funds in a single day for the whole enterprise. Dividends to shareholders in some of the boom periods of railway construction were very high indeed, at times as much as 40% p.a. Accordingly, in the so-called Promoters' Boom of 1871–73, based mainly on a railway expansion programme, many small investors risked their life savings in hopes of emulating those whose connections had apparently earned them legendary fortunes. After the crash of 1873 had claimed numerous victims, victims of their own greed and gullibility and of the corrupt practice of some

'While the political ambition of the citizen advances at snail's pace, the industrial development rushes by on wheels.' Caricature (1848).

dealers, the railway programme slowed down. In the last decades of the century progressive nationalisation took place; south German governments generally owned their own railways and in central and northern Germany too, the railways began to be used by the government as part of its policy of social engineering. Preferential tariffs were granted by Bismarck in 1884 to exporters, to the East Elbian landowners transporting their grain, and to the directors of heavy industry. It was the consumer, already carrying the burden of Bismarck's protective tariffs, introduced in favour of the same groups in 1879, who in effect subsidised the costs.

The fact that the industrial revolution in Germany was not indigenous but was derived largely from Britain and France, and that it occurred relatively late, meant that in general labour was not tied up in declining industries – the linen industry, especially in Silesia, was an exception – and the accumulation of a massive labour force was possible in the peak periods of railway building. Furthermore, German entrepreneurs were able to benefit from the advanced technology of their more progressive neighbours. Initially the German railways were equipped with British rolling stock, but Germans were soon in competition. Thus in 1837 August Borsig, a carpenter's son from Breslau, and a pupil of the Berlin Technical School, set up a locomotive business in Berlin with some thirty employees. In the year of his death (1855) Borsig, now the employer of 1,000 men, sold his 500th locomotive to the Prussian railways.

ii) Industrialisation and the People

The labouring classes

On the eve of the nineteenth century the German labourer and his family still lived their frugal lives in a patriarchal world. Not many working men could be aware of modes of existence different from their own. As a north German periodical noted in 1791, the ordinary worker was at all times patient 'once he has the hope that things aren't going to get any worse'. The Prussian minister Wollner observed smugly in 1784 that 'the working man is an obedient creature. He does not complain, does not criticise the decrees of his territorial sovereign, but obeys with alacrity'. However, as a number of artists, philosophers, civil servants and journeymen were aware, fundamental changes were already taking place in the social condition of the labouring classes. Those most immediately affected were the men whose skills and traditions had always entitled them to an 'honourable estate' in the eyes of society: the artisans. The introduction of machines, over-population in certain areas of Germany, excess of supply over demand, and the poor quality of much workmanship, affected their economic situation in the late eighteenth century, and eventually their social position.

A vital factor of social change was the Enlightenment. The ideas of the Enlightenment had a profound, if delayed influence on the craftsman class, and in the long run a socially divisive effect. By stimulating interest in education as a means of social betterment, such ideas caused the more intelligent and adventurous artisans to look elsewhere for opportunity. The traditional craftsman showed no interest in innovation or improved tools or techniques – where might he learn them? – and his standard of living fell inexorably. It was indeed a formidable task in late eighteenth century Germany to improve oneself by one's own efforts. Apart from the obvious difficulties of restraints on movement and trade, poor communications, an undeveloped economy, there was no focal point, no capital city to which the talented provincial might look. Yet some individuals brought off extraordinary feats of endurance in pursuit of education and social betterment. A goldsmith's apprentice, K. F. Klöden (1782–1858), from the province of Posen, whose memoirs recall sordid poverty with photographic precision, was one such individual. Son of a non-commissioned officer in the Prussian army, who had wrecked his family's happiness by drunkenness, Klöden grew up in bitter need. Without money, resources or patronage, he had but one book, the widely popular German adaptation of Defoe, Campe's '*Robinson der Jüngere*', which inspired his childish ambition. He eventually learned the goldsmith's trade, saved to have lessons as an engraver, to become an accomplished performer on flute and guitar, denying himself sleep in a fourteen-hour working day, to learn foreign languages. When trade was bad during the French occupation, he supported himself by giving lessons, and eventually entered Berlin university as a mature student, to end his life as founder and director of a well-known vocational school in Berlin, the *Gewerbeschule*, which the novelist Theodor Fontane attended in the 1830s. J. C. Fischer, son of a metal-worker in Schaffhausen, is another example: from modest beginnings he travelled abroad, managed to gain admission to Faraday's lectures at the Royal Institute, worked at the Woolwich arsenal, and returned home to found the machine tool factory in Switzerland which still bears his name.

Not everyone had the will or the constitution for such feats. As the Napoleonic wars and inflation followed the bad years, and these in turn were succeeded by famine and plague in many parts of Germany in 1816, increasing numbers of people in the lower levels of society found themselves threatened with starvation. Manufacturers and factory owners in the Rhineland, Silesia and Bohemia appeared to offer an alternative means of livelihood. But in the years after the Congress of Vienna internal markets were limited and German goods could not compete abroad with English goods; accordingly the supply of labour exceeded demand and wages remained low. However, in bad times skilled workers seemed to have been kept on by employers, and the unskilled dismissed. They regarded themselves as an elite army of workers with their background in the craftsman class.

Unskilled workers came from a wider variety of social backgrounds: they could be retired soldiers, poverty-stricken land labourers, or even members of the bourgeoisie who had failed in commercial enterprises. For all these the factory offered an alternative to beggary. Indeed, although the conditions of work and the standard of living enjoyed by factory workers or those employed at home by the manufacturer could seem grim, the factory system as such preserved a considerable proportion of the population of Germany and Austria from beggary at best and at worst starvation. Within the factory itself the work-force was anything but homogenous, at least until well into the second half of the century. Differences in social background, in skills, legal status of the worker, and job performed brought with them corresponding differences in status and wages. Wage differentials could be very considerable in this transition period between the older manufacturing and the new factory systems; 11:1 was not uncommon, 14:1 was recorded in a spinning factory in Chemnitz, Saxony.

Industrialisation in Germany was at first slow and piecemeal. The take-off into sustained industrial growth in Germany did not occur until after 1850, though many areas in the Rhineland were becoming industrialised in the 1830s. Some regions, such as central and southern Bavaria, remained untouched by it until the twentieth century: Munich only had its first large works when the Krupp concern opened a munitions factory there in 1917. Between the late eighteenth and the mid nineteenth century factories were opened in the old manufacturing areas of Germany such as Saxony; smaller

Maffei's machine-tool works near Munich (1849). Engraving.

existing enterprises such as coalmining, textiles and metalworking expanded, and old traditional crafts such as cigar-making (as in Hamburg-Altona) were organised on a capitalist basis. The main industrial centres were the Rhineland, with the Ruhr and Wupper valleys, Saxony, Silesia, Bohemia and Berlin. Here there was a tradition of skilled work, technical know-how, and large sources of labour. Railway lines were opened linking Cologne and Aachen, in the late 1830s: gradually, over the next forty years, a nationwide network centred in Berlin was established. Major road building projects had been begun in the early nineteenth century, were shelved after 1815, but taken up again in the 1830s; prior to this Germany had been notorious for its poor, indeed lamentable roads. Another significant change which contributed to the growth of the economy in Germany in the first half of the nineteenth century was population increase. The population of Germany increased between 1800 and 1870 from under 23,000,000 to almost 40,000,000. The increase was predominant in rural areas; it was influenced by several factors, among them the emancipation of the serfs in Prussia (1770–1810) and the abolition of dues elsewhere, which encouraged early marriage. After 1815 a series of bad harvests and cattle plagues drove ever-growing numbers into the towns. Thus Vienna increased its population between 1827 and

1847 by 42.5%, the textile town of Barmen in Wuppertal between 1800 and 1900 by 1,000%. The rise in population in early nineteenth century Germany, unlike in Britain, was more the result of a remarkably high birth rate than of advances in medicine and social hygiene. Child mortality did not decline significantly until the 1880s, infant mortality not until 1900.

Labour relations

In the early decades of industrial expansion, a paternalist relationship often existed between employer and worker, particularly in those areas with an established manufacturing tradition. In the Wupper valley, for example, many of the new factory owners, such as Friedrich Engel's family, were Calvinists. They might make heavy demands on their employees, expecting them to work twelve and fourteen hours daily, but they felt responsible for their physical and moral welfare. They and their wives knew each individual worker, and in bad times, such as the years after 1815, they subscribed large sums to feed the destitute population of their town. Time and the continued expansion of the factory system changed this. As the number of the employed grew, personal contact became difficult. While the sons of the factory founders no longer attended church, they retained an ethically based sense of responsibility for those under them, but a different generation grew up alongside them, self-made men, many of whom had worked their way up from the factory floor. These men had the relentless materialist outlook of doctrinaire capitalism. Profit or loss determined policy. The German worker, whether factory hand or pieceworker at home had great powers of physical endurance; he only resisted when he felt that those who were in authority over him had ceased to care; this is the situation which the Silesian dramatist Gerhart Hauptmann (1862–1946), whose grandfather had been a weaver, portrayed so movingly in his play, '*Die Weber*' (1892), half a century after the celebrated revolt of the Silesian weavers in 1844; this was the underlying cause of the emergence of a proletarian self-consciousness between 1848 and 1870 and of working class support for the Socialist movement from the 1860s onwards.

Working hours and conditions

The working day in the nineteenth century, as in previous times, was extremely long. The concept of annual holidays was non-

existent, though the artisans had a traditional *Blauer Montag*, or
holiday on Monday, which was abolished for factory workers in the
1840s. The average working day before 1870 was anything from ten
or twelve to fourteen or even sixteen hours, and in good times men
would work far into Saturday night. In the mid 1850s it was still
unchanged from the late eighteenth century, on average fourteen
hours, ten years later thirteen, and in 1870 twelve. It depended –
and this fact was becoming increasingly clear to those concerned –
on the degree of organisation in a particular area of production.
Only in 1900–5 was there a ten hour working day introduced by
law, and even then employers felt sincere moral scruples at thus
exposing men to the dangers of drink. Robert Bosch, founder of the
Bosch electrical firm, was much criticised by fellow industrialists for
his radical innovation: the eight hour day, which he introduced into
his Stuttgart works in the late 1890s. They called him 'Red Bosch'.

Ventilation and sanitation in factories and workshops were either
non-existent or extremely primitive. Dust from cotton and glass,
lead from paint, unprotected dangerous machinery, restricted
space, all these took a terrible toll of life and health. Writing of the
Bohemian glass industry in the early 1860s, where he worked as a

An old Thuringian steam hammer. Engraving (1870).

six-year-old child, the Austrian anarchist Josef Pankert recalled the
ravages of 'the proletarian's disease', tuberculosis, and commented
'the products which are used all over the world for trimmings,
buttons, brooches, ear-rings and other ornaments for women, men
and children give no idea of the massive amount of suffering,
wretchedness and human lives which lie crystallised within them'.
An observer in a textile factory in the late nineteenth century
described how men on a fourteen hour shift had tin receptacles
around their necks from which they snatched food at second-long
intervals while operating machines. Such conditions made
absenteeism on grounds of illness extremely common, and
encouraged workers to move frequently. Thus in 1900 a textile
factory owner offered a large bonus to anyone who would stay more
than three months. An annual turnover of 50% of the labour force
was not uncommon even at this late date. If a factory worker had
survived thirty or forty years of employment, he was not necessarily
entitled to a pension either from his employer or from the state until
Bismarck's social legislation of the 1880s; even then the sums paid
were derisory. However, there were many responsible employers
such as the Krupps, who set up an insurance scheme for their
workers as far back as 1836, though the paternalism which inspired
such forethought could have its negative side as well. Mining
communities all over Germany had a centuries-old tradition of
caring for their own, as did the state owners of the salt and coal
mines in the Salzkammergut in Austria. Workers often took the
initiative in founding so-called *Liebesvereine* or charitable associations to look after their sick colleagues or their dependents. One
of the earliest of such examples is the Kettenhof cotton factory in
late eighteenth century Austria: such efforts were but a modern
expression of the guild tradition of caring for one's fellow members.
The traditional ethos of the guilds survived in other ways too:
provision of facilities for women workers in industry was usually
minimal and this could lead to prostitution. Yet the men often put
pressure on one of their number who had made a girl pregnant to
marry her; if he resisted they could force him to leave the district.
But for the vast majority of workers in industry throughout these
early years of expansion, life was hard, often wretchedly so and the
rewards of effort non-existent. For most, 'their path ended in the
poorhouse, where it had often begun'.

The wages of industrial workers in Germany and Austria
remained low until about the 1860s, when things began to improve
slowly but permanently, although the improvement was at best only

relative. Before that time a man was often forced to have wife and children work to support the family. The very size of the supply of female and child labour was a constant factor in keeping wages depressed, and prevented a rise in living standards until after mid-century. The exploitation of child labour may not have been on quite the same scale as in England, but it was scandalous nonetheless. It may seem surprising that the paternalist Prussian and Austrian governments were slow to introduce legislation to protect young children. It was not until the years between 1850 and 1869 that such legislation began to be effective. Nor, with some few exceptions, was it the practice of German governments to set up commissions of enquiry into abuses on the part of employers, as was the case in Britain. Conditions of life for poor children in industrial areas are starkly represented in dialect poetry, and in the very considerable body of surviving letters and memoirs of workers, many of which are now available in paperback. The situation in the cottage industry was at least as bad as in the early factories, and lasted much longer, since it was not exposed to public opinion and was remote from the authority of the state. Later in the century in 1882 a sociologist, G. Schnapper-Arndt, spent many months in villages in the Taunus near Frankfurt and published his findings in a detailed study. He described children as young as three and four at work for long hours with their mothers, while the schoolteacher estimated that the children spent up to six and seven hours a day at work over and above their schooltime. Julius Bruhns (1860–1927), later a journalist in the Social Democratic Party, contrasted the ideal of the family wage-earners with reality in recalling his early years in Hamburg-Altona, where his father was a cigar-maker:

> Some people enthuse at the sight of a family where young and old are busily employed in a narrow room, seeing the fruits of their combined labour growing in front of them. It all looks rather different when one forms part of the charming family circle oneself.

Some parents ill-treated their children, forcing them to work against their will, but the majority found it natural, and the younger children tried to outdo the achievements of their elders. Such children never really learned to play.

Housing

There were no very large cities in Germany before the nineteenth century – even Vienna and Berlin were less than a quarter of a million inhabitants in 1800 – and one of the most immediate problems facing immigrants from the countryside seeking factory work was housing. In Vienna in the 1830s the population increased four times as fast as living accommodation; many were forced to share their room or even their bed with shift workers. The poor musician, Jakob, in Grillparzer's short story '*Der arme Spielmann*' (1847) was one such example. It was a common practice in Berlin in the 1840s to rent a *Schlafstelle* (sleeping space) in an already overcrowded habitation. Inmates of such houses were constantly and sharply controlled by the police, asking for their papers and enquiring about their means of livelihood. If one was out of work in Berlin and unable to pay for a bed, one could be classed as a beggar and sent to the dreaded *Ochsenkopf*, a punitive institution with a treadmill which the Great Elector (1640–88) had opened in the city to discourage the work-shy. The authorities seemed to believe that coercion was the best way to deal with the growing problem of pauperism in the 1840s, when conditions grew rapidly worse both on the land and in the towns. Despite the tradition of benevolent despotism in Prussia and in Austria they rarely felt called upon to make some material provision for the casualties of the machine age, apart from a reluctantly administered poor relief. It was speculators who provided the first barracks to house the labourers in the north of Berlin; the most notorious area was the Voigtland, near the Hamburg gate, which Ernst Dronke, a colleague of Marx on the '*Neue Rheinische Zeitung*', described in his book, '*Berlin*' (1846) as composed of seven great blocks, where some 2,500 men, women and children lived in 400 rooms. Karl Gutzkow describes similar conditions in a chapter of his novel, '*Die Ritter vom Geiste*' (1850–52), '*Die Brandgasse*', which he knew from experience.

Diet was in keeping with the grim surroundings. In northern and eastern Germany it was, to quote a phrase from the 1830s, 'Irish', that is, mainly potatoes. A treat, recalled the Social Democratic functionary Wilhelm Bock (1846–1931) of his Thuringian childhood, was a herring for the family of three 'which would never be eaten up at the one meal'. The Aachen factory inspector described the diet of millhands in his area in 1857 as consisting of bread, potatoes, coffee water and a little oil. In the same decade the Prussian authorities appointed county commissioners to investigate the conditions of both factory and domestic workers in Silesia. Their reports (1858–66) made clear how precarious was the existence of the industrial worker even in good times; 'in times of economic depression it could become calamitous' (Th. Hamerow).

Workers and the social question

It is not too much to say that physical survival was a major problem for the urban working class and for workers in cottage industries until the 1870s and beyond. It is scarcely surprising that relatively few recorded their reminiscences before that date, and that the slender body of imaginative literature on the subject was generally written by middle-class sympathisers. The first major writer to concern himself with the social conditions of his contemporaries in a literary work was Georg Büchner, whose interest in the subject was first aroused by the depressed rural workers in his native Hesse and whom he tried to rouse to revolutionary action by his pamphlet entitled '*Der hessische Landbote*' (1834). Büchner was in fact primarily concerned with the human condition and only secondarily with the oppression of the proletariat, but in the figure of the soldier, Woyzeck, in the drama of the same name, he created the most sensitive and powerful portrait of proletarian man in German nineteenth century literature. He had, however, no experience of urban workers and died at the early age of twenty-four in 1837. A group of writers with whom he was briefly associated, the Young Germans, interested themselves in a rather abstract way with the condition of working men and women. The poets Freiligrath and Herwegh had close, if transient, links with early communist thinkers, and Freiligrath's poetry certainly influenced the social thinking of the young Engels. Only Karl Gutzkow, the self-styled leader of the movement, wrote about the working classes in a major novel. He showed insight and imagination in portraying the everyday realities of their lives, but literary convention did not yet admit the lower orders to be heroes of epic works and, although the factory hands, Dankward and Karl Eisold, and the seamstress Luise Eisold in '*Die Ritter vom Geiste*' (1850–52) are much more keenly observed than the central figures, Gutzkow was not a literary innovator nor indeed a social reformer. Ernst Willkomm's novel '*Die Sklaven*' (1845) about the exploitation of factory workers was much more forthright, while Robert Prutz's '*Das Engelchen*' (1851), which also treats the problem of the Silesian weavers, was a moving exposé of what people suffered and would continue to suffer as long as industrial capitalism was allowed to continue without control. By far the most trenchant comment on conditions of life in early industrial Germany and indeed the most acute understanding of the message of communism came from the pen of Heine. His deadpan summary of Karl Marx theory of the two class society is expressed in '*Die Wanderratten*':

Es gibt zwei *Arten von Ratten*,
Die Hungrigen und die Satten . . .

('There are two types of rat, the hungry and the fat'); in '*Das Sklavenschiff*' he likens the lot of modern workers to the barbarous conditions of bygone galleyships; his '*Die schlesischen Weber*' (1844) helped to bring pressure to bear on the authorities to do something to succour the starving and desperate domestic workers in Silesia. The rhythm of the verse echoes the rattle of the loom, and the monotonous repetition of the chorus '*Wir weben*' ('we weave') seems to presage the inevitable day of reckoning for the oppressors of the poor who weave feudal Germany's shroud. Heine was much attracted to a younger contemporary, Georg Weerth, who died at the age of thirty-four in 1856. Weerth worked briefly with Marx on the '*Neue Rheinische Zeitung*', and used his considerable talents as a social satirist and humorist in the cause of reform. It was in that journal that he published his most famous work, '*Leben und Taten des berühmten Ritters Schnapphanski*'*, an attack on the establishment which the censor duly suppressed. He tried to use his talents to draw attention to the plight of the poor all over Germany, the farmers in the Eifel, Ravensburg, and Senne, near Bielefeld, the industrial workers in Berlin, Westphalia and Silesia. After the failure of the revolution Weerth's works, like those of many other political writers, were forgotten; it is only in recent years, especially through East German scholars, that attention has been focussed on his work.

A much more comprehensive picture of life at the lower levels of society in these early years of industrialisation than that seen in the works of middle class writers is to be found in the memoirs of artisans and journeymen, factory hands and day labourers. The importance of these reminiscences as social documents is being recognised by historians, and one of the things they bring home to us is how very localised the changes in German society were until the last decade of the century. In the industrial areas the towns were overcrowded, and the sanitation lamentable, people lived, worked and died without knowledge of each other. Yet only a few miles away, where roads were still unmade or unmended and the railways had not yet been built, life went on as it had for centuries before. Or, more often,

---

* The figure of Schnapphannski appears twice in Heine's most famous satirical poem, '*Atta Troll*' (1847).

industrial enterprise and rural life went on side by side. Thus, in Brunswick in 1869 an iron foundry was in production, and a steel works was being built, yet every evening the herdsman brought the cows back to the town gate, and every cow found her own way home to her byre. The craftsmen continued to exist in large numbers until after the middle of the century, but the number of masters exceeded that of apprentices, and their output was small and constantly threatened by the new methods of production. Yet they continued to think in terms of former times. For them the plutocrats who were taking their livelihood from them were not a new economic force but fellow masters who 'had got above themselves', *geldstolze Krämer* ('puffed-up money grubbers'). Paul Ernst (1866–1933) recalls in his evocative memoirs based largely on his father's reminiscences the case of a cabinet-maker in his native Harz who was forced to work for a local furniture factory. Asked to price his work in terms of so much per article, he committed suicide in despair at these new and incomprehensible ways. Ernst recounts another telling anecdote about the former miners at Andreasberg, also in the Harz, who worked in a factory opened by the Hanoverian government when the mines had ceased to pay. In 1848 news of the revolution came to the village. The men working at the factory immediately assembled, donned their old mining dress, took their lamps in their hands, and went down to their old shafts. Instead of wild revolutionary songs they sang their 250-year-old miners' anthem, greeting the chance to work once more in the mines:

> Frisch auf, ihr Barkleit, jung un alt,
> Sad frisch und wohlgemuth,
> Erhebet Eure Stimmen bald,
> Es wird noch warden gut.
> Gott hot uns ollen die Gnad gegabn,
> Dass mir von edlen Bergwark labn,
> Drumm rufft mit uns der ganze Hauf:
> Gluck auf, Gluck auf, Gluck auf!*

---

* ('Come all ye miners, young and old,
  Be glad and of good cheer,
  Raise up your voices now,
  All will be well again.
  God has given us all the grace
  To live from the noble craft of mining,
  And so let us all join in the call,
  Hurrah, hurrah, hurrah!')

A sense of superior social status, even if this was not borne out in the nature of their employment, their wages or standard of living, remained with the artisans until 1848, and in the less industrialised regions for many years longer. They believed in the value of education, for its own sake as the mark of a self-respecting man, and as a means of acquiring standing in the community. Even in hard times and a mean environment, artisans and their wives made strenuous sacrifices for their children's education, and if many failed and were depressed to the level of the unskilled labourer, others succeeded. A tradition of cultural awareness also survived in these circles. Thus, the Solingen metal workers on low wages in the 1850s had pianos and other musical instruments in their homes as a matter of course. Paul Ernst's father, a miner, bought Schiller's collected works in 1859 for six talers. This represented four weeks wages.

Pauperism

Contemporaries, both the authorities and the middle classes, had been much exercised by the problem of pauperism in the 1830s and 1840s, and by the emergence of political champions of the oppressed in the 1840s. Many believed then that pauperism would undermine the whole structure of society. Appeals for action by governments came from a variety of individuals, from the philosopher Franz von Baader, who taught at Munich university, from Friedrich Harkort, a leading Rhenish industrialist and philanthropist, and from Bishop Wilhelm von Ketteler of Mainz, a pioneer of social involvement by the Catholic Church. Public opinion became alarmed in the early forties when famine threatened some areas of the country, but people liked to comfort themselves that it was so much worse in England. Heinrich Bettziech, a democratic journalist, wrote his '*Physiologie Berlins*' (1846) to disabuse them. Those at the bottom of the social scale lived far worse than animals. They had nothing:

> Not a bed nor a table, without firewood, clothes, shoes or stockings, no work, no money, no potatoes, no prospects, no consolation, no charity, hope only of the workhouse or a miserable death in the Charité (poor house) – only rags and straw and dirt and vermin and hunger, hunger howling in their entrails.

It must seem surprising that Prussian governments in the Restoration era should have shown such little initiative in what contemporaries called 'the social question'. The Prussian reform movement was partly responsible for their attitude. Despite the

dismissal of his more liberally minded ministers by the king in 1819, the authorities remained convinced by many of the arguments of economic liberalism, particularly that industry ought to be left to benefit the country in its own way. It was not until the 1840s that gradual disillusionment set in; the benefits of such a policy were not forthcoming. The actual impulse to do something about the situation came not from the central government but from the provinces. A factory owner, one Johann Schuhard, had been moved to address the Rhenish provincial assembly in 1837 after a wretched child labourer had attempted suicide. The depth of feeling in his speech comes over even in the dry style of the protocol: such a child

> was forced even as a child to work like a slave, and just as his childhood
> was grim and joyless, so his whole life was one of need ... and how glad
> he must be now to be in his grave, and to be rid of his wretched life?

With the help of the new governor of the Rhineland, von Bodelschwingh-Velmede, Schuhard brought pressure to bear on the Berlin government: the result was the first Prussian law for the protection of children in factories (1839). It was but a modest beginning, and it was not implemented for more than a decade, but a beginning nonetheless. The same spirit of disappointment with the effect of uncontrolled industrialisation is apparent in the Prussian Trade Ordinance of 1845 and its supplement in 1849. The minister of finance, Thile, roundly told delegates from factories in 1846 that industry was 'the cancer of the land'; the new law had favoured partial restoring of the guilds in Prussia and the abolition of the truck system of payment. The experience of 1848 convinced the authorities in several German states that the new ways were pernicious, and the Prussian king in particular made strenuous efforts to encourage the traditional crafts at the expense of the manufacturing industries. But already by the late 1850s political considerations brought a return to a less paternalistic economic policy. By the late 1860s the unprecedented expansion of the economy and the ever growing demand for labour had led to some slight amelioration of working conditions; though the problem of living conditions only grew worse and the problems of hard times, illness and over-large families seemed hardly touched upon.

Opposite: Adolf von Menzel's famous painting. 'The Iron Foundary' '1875).

iii) The Industrial Nation 1850–1913

From the point of view of the economy, the second half of the nineteenth century, or rather the years 1850–1913, falls into three periods. The first, which was the time when take-off into sustained industrial growth occurred, runs from 1850–73. It is possible to speak of sustained industrial growth in the second half of the century despite the character of the next period, 1873–95, known as the Great Depression, which followed on the stock exchange crash in 1873. Although widespread unemployment, recession and stagnation, and a fall in real wages, were features of this time, especially between 1874 and 1880, not all branches of production were affected equally during this time. Some escaped almost unscathed: heavy industry for instance, adversely affected in 1873–80, made very great strides in the decade 1880–90. The third period, 1896–1913, saw what is often called the second wave of industrialisation, and one in which the revolutionary change in Germany's economy, and therefore in her political and military potential, became clearly evident. The first period is characterised by a change in technology, as for instance, the changeover from water and charcoal to coal as the main source of power in industry, and by the organisation of production in terms of a market economy.

The state and the industrial revolution

In contrast with the history of industrialisation in Britain, the state in Germany, especially in Prussia, played a significant role in this process. The state contributed above all to improving the 'non economic environment' (Supple), as, for example, in the early decades of the century, by abolishing feudal land tenures and removing intermediary local authorities, whose taxation and other powers restricted enterprise. If German governments did not systematically promote industry, apart from Silesia and the Saar, they helped industry indirectly in a host of ways: they invested in the infra-structure, made vital provision for technical education, facilitated credit, guaranteed interest on shares, taxed business profits relatively lightly. The 1850s and 1860s saw the reform of the currency, though only after 1870 was there a unified currency, the mark, based on the gold standard. These decades also witnessed the removal of restrictive legislation on mining, and, especially relevant in the south German states, the abolition of forced laws of settlement, with the introduction of freedom of trade and movement of labour. Yet, despite the traditionally large military budget in German states, despite the fact that the German army after 1871 grew in proportion to the rise in population (40,000,000 in 1871 and 67,000,000 in 1913), and despite Bismarck's social welfare policies of the 1880s, the government's share of expenditure per head of the population remained relatively low in the nineteenth century. At no time did it rise beyond 6% of total consumption, and it was always in percentual terms less than that of Britain.

Distribution of labour

In the years 1850–73 very rapid progress in the modernisation of German industry took place, in spite of a sharp downturn of the economy in 1857. However, the changes did not yet affect people's way of life as it was to do in the next two generations. Thus, the main mass internal migration did not really begin until after 1871; the percentage of the population who lived in communities of 2,000 or less in 1871 was still almost constant at 71.5% (1830 73.5%); some 50% still earned their living in agriculture. In the forty-three years between the founding of the Empire and the outbreak of war, however, Germany changed from an agrarian to an industrial state. The proportion of those earning their living in agriculture declined both relatively and absolutely, the numbers of domestic servants stagnated and declined. The value of the products of industry and trade rose above that of agriculture in the late 1880s. The size of enterprises rose, the number of independent businessmen, traders etc. declined steadily – from 32% of all those earning in 1882 to 22.3% in 1907: this tendency was particularly marked in industry and crafts, 41.7% to 17.6% (1875–1907). A further feature of the same period is the growth of white-collar workers in industry and trade, in commerce and banking, insurance and transport; this employment sector grew in relative terms very much faster than the labour force (1·9% of the total employed in 1882 to 5·2% in 1907). The actual numbers of women at work increased very considerably according to the official statistics, from 2,941,000 in 1882 to 6,422,000 in 1907*. With the expansion of office work, middle class

---

* W. Hoffmann has pointed out that the 1882 census, unlike that of 1907, largely ignored the work of female family members on the farm, and that the figures are more properly 3,935,000 for 1882.

women found it possible to find the kind of work that was considered more or less suitable to their station in life.

Industrial growth

A clear feature in the development of the German economy under the Empire was that the production of capital goods grew much more rapidly than that of consumer goods. Although textiles were her largest industry in the 1850s and 1860s, in the following decades this was overtaken by heavy industry where extraordinary growth rates occurred. Coal output, some 30 million tons in 1871, grew from 60 million tons in 1887 to 190 million tons in 1913; the production of lignite and iron ore more than quadrupled in the latter period (1887–1913); steel output increased tenfold from 1880 to 1900, its cost now a mere tenth of what it had been in the 1860s. Germany's most spectacular achievements in this context were gained in the new chemical and electrical industries, and in optics and precision instruments, where, by the end of the century, she easily led the world. By 1914 she was the second trading nation of the world, 75% of her exports being in manufactured and semi-manufactured goods to Europe, the Americas and Africa, and she

The Berlin Stock Exchange. Drawing by E.Thiel (1889).

had significant invisible overseas earnings. However, in contrast with a few decades previously, she was no longer a major exporter of food and although she was self-sufficient in root crops, and continued to be a major sugar exporter, she had a shortfall of some 40% in her grain requirements. This deficiency was to prove serious in the latter years of the Great War.

Finance and industry

The financing of industrial development was only placed on a systematic basis after the middle of the century. Prior to this, the merchant bankers of Frankfurt, Berlin and Hamburg had catered in a general way for the needs of government and the aristocracy. Return on investment was low in the 1830s and 1840s, and although the railways attracted finance, both public and private, fairly easily, people were slow to risk money in industrial ventures which brought uncertain returns. It was foreigners, British, French or Belgian businessmen or traders, who were prepared to do so. In Prussia as late as 1846 only 1,100 persons were employed in financial and credit institutions. This changed after 1850. The French *Crédit mobilier* of the Pereire brothers provided the model for the numerous credit banks set up to promote manufacturing enterprises in the period 1850–73. The *Crédit mobilier* used the savings of small investors for this purpose and was prodigiously successful up till the mid-1860s. Heinrich Heine's uncle Solomon, from Hamburg, was one of the shareholders, as was the Cologne banker Abraham Oppenheim. Oppenheim and his French associates, the Pereires, gave backing to the Darmstadt Bank of Commerce and Industry, opened in 1853. In 1856 the Rhinelander David Hansemann, with the aid of Gerson Bleichröder (Bismarck's extremely able banker), reorganised the Discount Co. of Berlin as a credit bank; in the same year one of the first non-local banks, the Berlin Commercial Co., was set up, a joint venture between Bleichröder and Mendelssohn of Berlin, and Mevissen and Oppenheim from the Rhineland. All three developed into great German banks in the Empire, along with the so-called great D-Banks, the Disconto, Dresden and the Deutsche Bank, the largest of them all. All these maintained very close links with industry, and, through the presence of their representatives on the boards of industry, exercised influence on investment and longterm business policies.

The development of the giant German banks from the 1870s was a major factor in promoting the tendency towards concentration in industry which was a salient feature of the industrial scene in late nineteenth century Germany. In the 1880s cartels and vertical combines began to develop in heavy industry and in the chemical and electrical industries. Of the 250 such combines existing in 1900, 200 had been founded in the decade following Bismarck's change-over from free trade to protection (1879). Rationalisation of this sort not only enabled producers to keep up prices on the home market, but also to sustain a greater network of agents at home and abroad, with lucrative effect on exports, and to finance industrial research. The close association between industry and banking led to banks investing in the German export drive (both of goods and capital) and in overseas enterprise such as the Berlin–Baghdad railway in the early twentieth century. There was relatively little public criticism of the tendency, nor was there any attempt by the governments to arrest it, since they believed it promoted industrial efficiency. Neither the authorities nor the public, apart from a handful of politicians, were sensitive to the political implications of the emergence of these great power blocks, though this is one of the aspects which has preoccupied historians in post-1945 Germany.

The consequences of the industrial revolution

The extraordinary changes in the German economy in the nineteenth century are indeed revolutionary, and, in common with all revolutions, this one took its toll. While Germans were quite alive to the military and political implications of their new industrial power, the rapidity of the change, and the sharp fluctuations to which growth was subjected, especially in the years from 1873 onwards, left a profound impression on the public mind. The 1873 crash had a particularly pervasive effect. It was essentially the result of structural weaknesses, over-capacity, excessive speculation and too rapid injection of the 5 milliard francs of French war indemnity into the economy. People, however, saw it as a failure of the system, as a conspiracy of the 'new men' – not, however, 'faceless conspirators', since the pictures of those who had made off with creditors' money, usually to America, gazed down from 'Wanted' notices on street corners and public posting places. The fact that a number of these were Jewish had the incidental effect of imprinting a visual image of the 'exploiter' in the minds of the gullible. This tendency was sedulously fostered by the purveyors of anti-Semitism, which became a prominent political issue in Germany in this decade. The cyclical disturbances of the early years of the German

Empire coincided with a natural period of disillusionment after the excitement of successful wars and unification, and this made people reject the spirit of free enterprise, while continuing to enjoy the benefits it produced. A call for protection was answered by the government under Bismarck, who introduced legislation to shield interest groups (landowners, heavy industrialists) whose political and social dominance the authorities were concerned to preserve.

A striking feature of life in late nineteenth-century Germany was the increasing role played by the state and the authorities in people's lives. This was prompted by the changes in the patterns of living as a result of the industrial revolution, such as the influx of rural workers to the towns, especially from the feudal society of the east, urbanisation in general, with consequent need for water, sewage disposal, housing, urban transport etc. State welfare legislation, which Bismarck introduced in the 1880s and which made some provision for old age, sickness and accidents at work, whatever the political motives behind it, was another aspect of this; by the end of the century, all industrial workers outside cottage industries and handcrafts were insured. In the body of critical analyses of life in Imperial Germany it is not perhaps appreciated what a very great legislative effort went into providing for the citizen. Although later commentators have tended to interpret the authorities' concern to legislate for an ever-increasing number of aspects of the citizen's life as a prime example of the excessive regimentation in the Wilhelmine Empire, contemporaries on the whole did not see it in that light. On the contrary most believed that the measure of good government could be taken in the way in which transport, communications, cleansing and other public services were run, and public order assured. It is certainly the case that the amount of the annual budget spent in the provision of public services generally, including social welfare in the widest sense, rose steadily in the years between 1871 and 1914. The distribution of state expenditure changed also, the percentage which was spent on the armed forces declining relatively from some 52% of all state expenditure in 1871–74 to some 27% in 1910–13: the beneficiaries were education, health, social insurance and public welfare. State and society grew thus ever more inter-dependent in the last decades of the century. This was a general feature of European societies at this time, in the case of Germany the fact that state intervention was much more deeply rooted in the country's historical traditions meant that this development served to increase people's sense of obligation to the state. It also, however, increased their expectations.

5
The German Revolutions 1848–49

Perhaps no period in Germany's history exemplifies more vividly the dictum of the historian Leopold von Ranke that 'jede Epoche ist unmittelbar zu Gott' (literally: 'every age stands in direct relationship to God'), namely that any attempt at an objective portrait of an epoch is inevitably coloured by the hopes and fears of the age in which such an attempt is made. Not only the judgement on the achievements and failures of the revolution of 1848 but even the emphasis on the salient issues differs widely according to the perspective of the writer's own time. While the historians of Bismarck's age and those of the Third Reich saw 1848 largely in terms of betrayal and failure of the national movement, while ignoring almost entirely its social revolutionary character, those writing under the Weimar Republic, or in our own time in East and West Germany, sought to legitimise the authority of their regimes by establishing direct links with the ideologies and institutions of 1848–49. The stimulus given by historians of the German Democratic Republic to study of the social and economic history of the revolution has been most fruitful. Although their very proper emphasis on this aspect of *das tolle Jahr* ('the crazy year') has in time led to exaggerations, particularly by attributing a greater influence on events to Communist groups than they actually possessed at the time, their work has assisted historians in the west in their efforts to see the period of the revolution more precisely in the context of the time. Western historians have generally refrained from reiterating moralistic notions such as betrayal, pusillanimity etc., which in East European accounts still occasionally prejudice our understanding of events.

Origins of the Revolution

The immediate domestic causes of the revolution were however political rather than social. The archaic character of German governments in the context of nineteenth century Europe had been arousing increasing disquiet among Germans throughout the Confederation since the revolution of 1830. The German governments were not, on the whole, guilty of flagrant abuse of power. The Confederation represented a very considerable advance on the irresponsible government of many eighteenth century German rulers. Moreover the paternalism of state governments in the Restoration era had certain material advantages for the population which they appreciated. Governments were often more aware of the problems of industrialisation, for example, than any other agency, though they were not very effective in dealing with them. However, among both the propertied and the educated classes, and more particularly in the craftsman class, the feeling that government administration had lost touch with the governed became prevalent about 1840 and was an important cause of popular disturbance in 1848. The proportion of state budgets spent on the military and the court contrasted with that directed towards ameliorating the marked and widespread misery. From about 1840 onwards governments' own demonstrable loss of confidence in their ability to deal with the problems of German society became an important cause of the revolution. The desire for political unity was a further important contributory cause. It was fed by a variety of streams, romantic-nostalgic, liberal-rationalist, practical-commercial. A large proportion of civil servants in German states, who later played an active part in the parliaments and assemblies during the revolutionary year, were drawn from the intelligentsia and the propertied classes. Many of these civil servants had been in prison in youth for political activities, some had been disciplined, some had been forced to resign from office. They were far more immediately aware of the social and economic problems of their society than princes and ministers, but their lack of a regular channel of protest, or indeed their lack of ability to rectify injustice and to deal with the problems was a further immediate cause of the revolution. The social and economic grievances of the German populace had a major influence on revolutionary disturbances in 1848 but were not in themselves a direct cause of the revolution. Thus the agrarian uprisings of February 1848, which recurred at different times throughout the subsequent thirteen months from March 1848 to May 1849, took place alongside rather than within the general revolutionary movement. They were part of the age-long popular revolt against oppression and feudal dues. In general,

once their grievances had been aired, and particularly after the
legislation in the Frankfurt national parliament and the assemblies
at Vienna and Berlin had rectified their grievances, they and their
spokesmen lost interest in the revolution. Nor was 'proletarianisation' as such a direct cause. However, the influence of the social
question on the broad spectrum of the middle classes was extremely
important, predisposing them towards political radicalism.
Ideology was in fact a direct and powerful influence on events,
particularly French Socialist ideology, which helped to channel a
widespread sense of grievance into specific demands to the ruler.
The fear of proletarianisation in the *Mittelstand* was a further
important contributory cause of revolution throughout Germany,
particularly in the south. No worker, in fact, attended the secret
Communist meetings organised by Friedrich Engels in Elberfeld;
supporters came from the *Mittelstand*. In general, revolution was the
work not of those who were forced to endure social deprivation, by
famine and pauperisation, but by those who observed this and
strove to put an end to it.

The European Context

Both the outbreak and the course of the revolution in Germany
were dependent on factors operating in other parts of Europe.
The overthrow of the bourgeois king, Louis-Philippe of France,
on 24 February 1848, provided the impetus for the outbreak of
widespread popular disturbance in Germany. Moreover, the fact
that most European countries were preoccupied with revolt at home
prevented their rulers, notably the Tsar of Russia, Nicholas I, from
coming to the aid of the German princes. The German rulers were
very aware of this. The revolutionary leaders in Germany in 1848
retained a real or apparent freedom of movement as long as the
great powers most nearly concerned with events in Germany were
prevented by their own domestic problems from intervening. This
period ran from March to the late autumn of 1848. Furthermore,
events in France stimulated a genuine fear of a French invasion
among many German rulers and made them more ready to
conciliate popular opinion. The princes, even more than their
subjects, were always influenced by historical analogies, and the
events of the spring of 1848 aroused memories of the French
revolution of 1789 and its consequences. Alexis de Tocqueville's
often-quoted dictum, that the German rulers yielded at the sight of,
rather than under the onslaught of, the revolutionaries must be

understood in this context: the princes had a clear understanding that they could preserve their position only as long as the European powers were able to support the status quo. However, it is also true that many rulers of the smaller German states, as for example the Duke of Saxe-Coburg-Gotha, were not at all hostile to the idea of greater liberalisation of their administration, but up to this time had not been inclined to stand out against Metternich's authority in the Confederation; they therefore readily yielded to the demands of their subjects.

The Course of Revolution

i) *Germany*

The 'glorious revolution weather', as one commentator described it (Theodor Fontane), brought demonstrators out into the streets during the first weeks of March 1848. These and the following weeks saw the granting and implementation of constitutional government in almost all the German states. Elections to a national assembly in Frankfurt, charged with the task of drafting a national constitution for a new, united Germany, elections also to constituent assemblies in the two largest states in the Confederation, Austria and Prussia, were the work of April and early May. The initiative to summon a national assembly of Germans to Frankfurt came mainly from the south and west, where for nearly a generation prominent citizens in the state service, lawyers, teachers, clergymen and others, had been closely identified with the movement for constitutional reform. On 31 March prominent liberals met in Heidelberg, at the so-called Pre-Parliament (*Vorparlament*), to make arrangements for the national elections, and at the end of their deliberations formed a committee of fifty to manage the details. Neither the Heidelberg meeting nor the elections themselves represented an overthrow of state power. By the time the Pre-Parliament met, most German states, including Prussia, had appointed liberal ministers and approved the extension of the franchise. The elections to the Frankfurt Parliament, it was decided, would proceed according to the electoral laws of each state, which of course varied considerably. The rapidity and the ease with which most German princes seemed to capitulate to the demands of demonstrators and petitioners was remarkable, especially to the revolutionaries themselves. Vienna and Berlin apart, remarkably little violence occurred on either side, and even in Berlin, where over-precipitate action by the military led to the deaths of some 230 civilians who had assembled to petition

the king, subsequent events gave a paternalist air to the initial stages
of the revolution there. The king, over-anxious to conciliate, rode
on the streets wearing the black and red and gold of the revolution;
he bared his head at the funeral of the fallen. Much comment was
aroused by the public's being given permission to smoke on the
streets. Fontane remarked on the fact that collection boxes had
actually been put out on the street in front of the Arsenal (*Zeughaus*)
and on the bridge nearby to collect alms for those who had been
wounded on the barricades. His father, who had hastened to the
capital on the morning of Tuesday 21 March from his home in the
provinces on receipt of his son's account of the outbreak of the
revolution on the previous Saturday, hesitated to enter the royal
palace which now stood unguarded. '*So eigentlich gehört man doch da
nicht hinein*' ('The likes of us don't really belong there') he observed,
reflecting the feelings of many burghers, however positively they
might feel towards the new order.

   Although it is easy to exaggerate the clarity of political alignment
throughout the revolutionary years, the fateful difference between
moderate and radical liberals (the latter termed 'democrats' in the
contemporary parlance) already made its appearance during the
first weeks. This division, which was at once ideological,
psychological, political and a matter of tactics, was the single most
important cause of the revolution's eventual failure. It robbed the
institutions of the revolution of their impact by delaying their
constitution until the favourable moment was past, and frightened
passive supporters into transferring their allegiance back to the old
authorities. Prior to 1848 those opposing the regime included a wide
variety of elements, from civil servants and professional men to
anarchist students, and they had possessed a cohesion merely by
the fact of being in opposition. The speed of the revolutionaries'
success in March split this opposition. At the Heidelberg Pre-
Parliament, which sat from 31 March until 3 April, this became
apparent in the tactics of two committed social revolutionaries, von
Struve, son of a councillor of state in the Russian service (and owner
of the Berlin apothecary in which Fontane was employed during
1848) and the energetic young lawyer from Mannheim, Friedrich
Hecker. These two men were determined to turn the Pre-
Parliament into a type of French revolutionary convention, but,
having failed to do so, or to even win seats in the interim Committee
of Fifty, had recourse to direct action. On 12 April 1848, they
declared Germany a republic and led an uprising in Baden, which
was crushed scarcely a week later by federal troops. Struve and

Death of a young student on the barricades in Berlin on 18 March 1848.
Engraving of a drawing by J. Kirchhof.

Hecker were joined by a legion of German revolutionaries led by the popular poet Herwegh, from Paris, accompanied by his energetic wife, Emma, and a host of Polish exiles. This somewhat motley band had spent many hours exercising on the Champ de Mars outside Paris in previous weeks. Their disastrous performance at such an early stage of the German revolution did much to alienate public opinion from violence, not least because Herwegh's contribution exposed him and his ideals to ridicule. One of the victims of the engagement on the federal side was General Friedrich von Gagern, whose brother, Heinrich, was to preside with genial statesmanship over the deliberations of the national assembly at Frankfurt as its president. The sight of a member of a distinguished German liberal family being killed in defence of the now liberalised Confederation, by what could easily be represented as a power hungry splinter group, filled most supporters of national revolution in Germany with foreboding.

ii) *The Frankfurt Assembly*
Elections to the Frankfurt Parliament took place on 1 May and 8 May. Theoretically based on universal manhood suffrage, in fact there existed several electoral laws with varying property and age qualifications which excluded voters in many states. Moreover the use of the 1816 federal population census as a basis for calculating electoral districts led to serious under-representation in those states such as Prussia and Saxony, whose population had risen since 1816 by over 50%. In the absence of any party political structure, electors tended to return men for their personal qualities and, as might be expected from Germany's provincial character, for their local associations. Thus Heinrich Laube, Young German poet and later director of the Viennese Burgtheater, who lived in Leipzig, was elected to represent the Karlsbad spa, where he had frequently taken the waters. The Frankfurt Parliament was no gathering of 'the men of the people'. Of those who sat there over the thirteen months of its session, 764 or 95.5%, had been to grammar school (*Gymnasium*); 657 (81.6%) had enjoyed a university education. The fact that the lower orders were scarcely represented directly (four craftsmen, but no workers, were elected) is more anomalous to twentieth century commentators that it seemed to contemporaries. However, somewhere in the region of 20% of the representatives from commerce and the professions were men of humble social origins who had risen to rank and wealth. The high proportion of civil servants among delegates derived in part from these men's opposition to the pre-1848 regimes. The vast majority were men in the prime of life, aged between thirty-five and fifty-five, and they included an unusual number of poets and scholars. The best known were the Swabian lyric poet, Uhland, (whose ugliness surprised his lady admirers), the philosophers, Arnold Ruge and Fr. Th. Vischer, who was also a poet and university professor, the brothers Grimm, the historians, Dahlmann, Droysen and Gervinus.

The German National Assembly sat at Frankfurt from May 1848 to June 1849, when its radical rump was forcibly disbanded by Prussian troops. It opened in an atmosphere of intense awareness of the historical moment, whose memory, evoked in autobiographies of participants and observers decades later, can still manage to

Students and youths defend the barricades at the Kronen – and Friedrichstraße
on 18 March 1848 in Berlin.

communicate the atmosphere of that marvellous day, when the bells
rang throughout the city of Frankfurt, and the black, red and gold
flags of liberal Germany bedecked all public buildings. The
members processed to the great *Paulskirche* for the first session, where
the gallery was filled with an excited crowd of observers, including a
large number of women. 'A fine and imposing circular building, the
choir supported by pillars, opposite which stands a dais' enthused
the novelist Fanny Lewald on her first visit, 'where pulpit and altar
once stood, the presidential tribunal now stands. The scene
immediately conjured up Herwegh's much vilified lines, "Tear the
crosses from the earth!" Here this has been done for the sake of the
people, and the German flags now flutter where once the image of
the Crucified hung.'

The Frankfurt Parliament was immediately faced with the task
of creating its own procedure. It had many major and minor

difficulties to contend with, notably the lack of parliamentary experience (only the Baden members had genuine experience of parliamentary sessions), the 'north German passion for long speeches' (Vischer) and the determination of the radicals to turn every item into a question of principle. In the view of the Swabian professor, Friedrich Theodor Vischer, it all made the work of the parliament as slow as the judgements of the notorious Imperial Chamber of Wetzlar long ago. The discussion of the basic rights of the German people, the first item on the programme, would, according to one commentator, take at least until April 1850, if things were not speeded up. However, under Gagern's efficient presidency, special committees were appointed, charged with a variety of tasks, and the work of the assembly proceeded systematically, if indeed with excessive deliberation. By the end of June, a Regent *(Reichsverweser)* had been elected – the Archduke Johann of Austria – and he arrived to take up his duties. By the beginning of August, a provisional central government was in office, composed of men from all parts of the country.

The status of the members, the responsible attitude of parliamentary procedure, the lack of violence in Frankfurt and in general during the summer months of 1848 in Germany, gave the Frankfurt assembly nationwide authority. Subsequent events, starting with the September riots of 1848, proved how little real power the Frankfurt Parliament actually possessed. It had no army of its own, it had no treasury. But if one can put aside historical hindsight – an extraordinarily difficult feat in the case of the German revolutions – and assess the situation from the point of view of contemporary German princes and their governments, and in terms of the opinions and expectations of the people at large, one sees events in a different light. It seems clear that the Frankfurt National Assembly, and, to a lesser extent, the two assemblies which met at Berlin from May to December 1848, and at Vienna from June to December, possessed for a period of months sufficient influence at least to institutionalise the reforms won in the spring of 1848.

However, the purpose for which the Frankfurt Parliament had been summoned was a dual one: the creation of a constitution and the unification of Germany. In the view of contemporaries these tasks were not separate ones, but aspects of the same problem, and it is therefore not appropriate to argue, as some have done, that the liberals of 1848 should have concentrated either on the one or the other. Those who had suffered for their political beliefs and activities under Metternich's regime and those who had merely theorised, were equally aware that the different historical traditions of the German states, ranging from the arch-conservative duchies of Mecklenburg to the relatively liberal Baden, would make nonsense of a constitution unless a unified form of state was set up at the same time to implement it. Moreover, liberals were painfully aware that the system of the German Confederation had made it relatively easy for foreign powers, notably Russia, but also Austria, to influence the minor German princes in favour of autocratic rule. The creation of a centralised state would, they believed, prevent this happening in the future, or at least it might limit the power of foreign powers to intervene in German affairs. The deputies did not in fact give sufficient consideration to the relationship between the assembly and the existing institutions of the German Confederation, such as the Federal Diet in Frankfurt or indeed the states themselves. The Federal Diet was formerly, and again from 1850 to 1866, an assembly composed of princely ambassadors. It had been greatly modified in the light of the events of March and included many prominent liberals, such as Mathy, appointed by the new governments. The Diet welcomed the deputies to the Frankfurt assembly in an address in May, but the tactless refusal on their part to read out this message, and the decision to abolish the institution of the Diet in June, were tactical as well as psychological errors. Such conduct brusqued state governments and robbed the assembly of what would have been a most useful liaison office and source of topical information in the critical late summer and autumn months of 1848. In their determination to institute some form of centralised government, the politicians at Frankfurt tended to lose sight of how much they needed the support of the existing state governments in their work. This is particularly true as regards Prussia, which remained much more directly involved in the German situation during 1848 than did Austria.

iii) *Austria*

The history of Austria during the revolution is extraordinarily complex, but in all its permutations exercised a constant influence on the course and outcome of the German revolutions. Austria, that is, the western part of the Habsburg monarchy, exercised presidial powers in the Confederation. For centuries the Austrian ruler had been Holy Roman Emperor and from 1815 he was president of the German Confederation. In this capacity he had to be party to the decisions taken at Frankfurt. The choice of an Austrian archduke as imperial regent and the inclusion of an able Austrian, von Schmerling, later Austrian prime minister, in the provisional central government with the portfolio of the interior, was an acknowledgement of this fact. These appointments also constituted an attempt to influence opinion in the Danube monarchy in favour of the National Assembly as the legitimate government of Germany. But the Austrian authorities had, from the outset, given far less support to the Frankfurt Parliament than had other German state governments. Large areas, notably Bohemia, had boycotted the elections. Only 133 of a total of 193 electoral districts actually sent representatives. Events of May and June within their own state borders occupied Austrian state authorities to the exclusion of all else. The first Vienna rising on 13 March, which had led to Metternich's flight, and the appointment of a liberal government, was followed on 25 April by an imposed constitution, which satisfied few parties, least of all the left-wing. On 15 May, three days before the opening of the Frankfurt Parliament, a further Viennese rising occurred, prompting the flight of the Habsburgs to Innsbruck, and yet another rising on 26 May. The opening of the Pan-Slav Congress in Prague under the sage direction of the Czech historian, who was so incomparably knowledgeable about Austria, Franz Palacky, the Czech rising in June and its suppression by General Windischgrätz, had much more immediate relevance to Austrians than the debates in far-away Frankfurt. In general, Germans in Austria were themselves far more preoccupied with their own relations towards other ethnic groups than with German national unity, and supported the German cause mainly in order to ensure the continued hegemony of their own national group in Austria. The leaders of the revolution in Vienna were more able than those in Berlin, but their success aroused the resentment of rural areas, where the emperor's intervention to abolish the robot (or statutory labour services) and other onerous feudal services, ensured the loyalty of the peasantry to the monarchy. Moreover, the absence of the court from Vienna until the beginning of August 1848 brought with it a loss of trade in the city and consequently serious unemployment and a loss of sympathy for the revolutionaries among the population. It became clear to a wide variety of groups that Austria, in fact, stood to lose far more by granting a liberal constitution and national liberties, than would Prussia, or states with purely German inhabitants, such as Hanover, Saxony or Bavaria. The essential dilemma of German nationalists and liberals in 1848–49, with regard to Austria, was well characterised by a

Prussian diplomat, named Gustav von Usedom, who wrote in his *'Politische Briefe'* in 1849, 'Austria can do nothing for the organic development of the state or for the freedom of peoples without disintegrating; so she decrees that nowhere else in the world should anything be done for these things.'

iv) *Prussia*

The alternative to Austria as leading power in Germany, was seen by liberal politicians from many different areas of Germany, including Mathy and Bassermann from Baden, Droysen who represented Schleswig-Holstein, or Gagern from Hesse-Darmstadt, to be Prussia. Admittedly, Prussia's unpredictable king, Frederick William IV, had disappointed the hopes placed in him during the early days of the revolution. However, the fact that the Prussian army under General Wrangel continued to bear the burden of the war being waged by German federal troops against Denmark over Schleswig-Holstein, won Prussia sympathy among the supporters of the German cause. It was during the revolutionary years that a number of able and energetic men gained a clear appreciation of the Prussian leadership in German economic affairs and that the term *kleindeutsche Lösung** was coined.

The decision by the Frankfurt Parliament to offer the elective imperial crown to the Prussian king was made on 28 March 1849. Five days later he rejected it, adding the insulting comment that he was not prepared to accept a crown from the gutter. Frederick William's grand gesture had the quality of a somewhat grotesque epilogue to the history of the previous year, to the hopes and aspirations placed in Prussia by the revolutionaries. However it made clear to one of the revolution's most critical observers, to Bismarck, the potentially vital power of a strong Prussian monarchy in bringing about the unity of the nation.

Meanwhile the problem of the Elbe duchies of Schleswig-Holstein, which were ruled over by the king of Denmark, had exemplified the dependence of Germany on the great powers. While Holstein's population was almost wholly German, Schleswig had a large Danish minority. The duchies were united in personal rule with Denmark, though Holstein, but not Schleswig, formed part of the German Confederation. The history of the duchies in these years, and that of other national minorities such as the Poles in Prussia, helps later generations to understand why Bismarck's policy

---

* 'Little German solution', that is, Germany without Austria.

of pursuing German unification from strength two decades later, without having regard to the wishes of the great powers, should have been greeted with such uncritical enthusiasm by the vast majority of the German people. In 1848 the Danish blockade of north German harbours and British diplomatic support for the Danes persuaded the Prussian king that the war could not be won, although his own troops had won some military successes in Schleswig. He signed an armistice with Denmark on 26 August 1848, brusquing the authority of the Frankfurt Parliament and the new Reich government in so doing. The Parliament first rejected the armistice and then attempted unsuccessfully to take the duchies with federal troops. These were defeated and in mid-September the deputies voted to accept the armistice after all. The response of the Democrats was immediate and violent. Anger and frustration, the sense that events were passing the revolution by, that the historic moment was being lost of unifying the country and liberalising its institutions, caused violence to erupt on the very streets of Frankfurt. In Baden yet another social revolt led by Struve broke out.

v) *The autumn crisis and the counter-revolution*
The cohesion of the revolutionary movement began to show dangerous signs of disintegrating. Sharp differences of opinion between moderates and extremists, vilification by the radicals of their opponents, incitement by them of the populace, led to attacks on the persons of the deputies. The Reich foreign minister, the Hamburg lawyer Heckscher, was beaten up, the colourful Austrian delegate, Prince Lichnowsky, was brutally murdered in Frankfurt along with his Prussian companion, Hans von Auerswald. The Prussian and Austrian garrison troops from the nearby federal fortress at Mainz were called in to restore order. The Frankfurt Assembly never recovered its prestige or indeed its unity or purpose following the fateful weeks. By and large the politically articulate responded to the new outbreak of violence with disgust and fear. Fanny Lewald, the militant champion of democracy and women's rights, declared contemptuously that anyone with property had come to long for a return of the absolutist system, right down to the last gendarme. All they wanted now, she said, was to be able to promenade once more in peace along the Berlin boulevard Unter den Linden. There was much truth in the allegation. The beginning of the counter-revolution was accompanied by the tacit approval of most of the populace outside Vienna. Yet it was in Austria that the

first moves against the revolution began in October. Prince Windischgrätz, who had suppressed the Czech uprising in June, was made commander-in-chief of the counter-revolutionary forces. On 4 October Nestroy's '*Freiheit in Krähwinkel*', a brilliant satire on the revolution, which had played to capacity audiences in the Viennese Carl Theatre since its premier on 1 July 1848, was performed for the last time. Two days later, in response to the command to the Vienna grenadiers to depart for the Hungarian front to suppress the revolutionaries, the Vienna populace lynched the war minister and stormed the arsenal. However, with the aid of the Croatian leader, Jellačič, Vienna was surrounded, and by 1 November Windischgrätz was master of the city. The Austrian authorities wreaked a bloody revenge on the insurgents, executing many, including the popular and foolhardy Saxon delegate from the Frankfurt Parliament, Robert Blum, who had fought on the barricades in Vienna and who, in vain, pleaded parliamentary immunity. The execution of Blum showed the Austrian authorities' supreme and brutal disregard for the claims of the Frankfurt Parliament to authority and indeed their clear disregard of the national revolutionary movement as a whole. One month later Windischgrätz's able brother-in-law, Felix Schwarzenberg, had the young Archduke Franz-Joseph supplant his epileptic uncle Ferdinand as Emperor, thus cutting across plans of the Imperial Regent to unite in his own person the regency of the German Confederation and the Imperial Crown of Austria.

The counter-revolution in Berlin was less violent and its agents less vindictive than in Austria. True, the radical Prussian National Assembly was transferred from the capital to Brandenburg, where it was finally dissolved on 5 December. A constitution was imposed by law on the same day. 'It is always a bad thing', mused Fontane with pertinent understatement, 'when freedom and such like starts with something being imposed on people.' The Assembly based on this constitution met in February 1849, but its considerable talents were too much for the king and he dissolved it in April, substituting in the following month the three-class indirect Prussian franchise, which remained in force until the fall of the dynasty in 1918. As in Vienna, the army had been used to restore order and prevent rioting. The caustic slogan coined by a Prussian civil servant* in 1848 was frequently reiterated in the months and years to come: '*Gegen Demokraten helfen nur Soldaten*' ('only soldiers can help against

---

* Wilhelm von Merckel, a friend and patron of Th. Fontane.

democrats'). Under the command of General von Wrangel, veteran
of the Schleswig-Holstein war, and, in his youth, a friend of
Heinrich von Kleist, troops entered Berlin in December 1848.
However, no blood was shed, and a gesture by Wrangel, completely
in keeping with the paternalist traditions of the pre-March era,
seemed to distract and reassure the populace: despite the
emergency, he declared, he was giving official permission for the
traditional Christmas market to be held in the city.

The German revolutions did not end with the forcible suppresion
of revolt in Austria and Prussia. The National Assembly continued
in Frankfurt until the constitution was finally ready for promulgation in 1849, but the power to effect political change had
clearly been lost to the revolutionaries. Meanwhile, the economic
and social developments of the revolutionary years, and their
consequences, were beginning to make themselves felt.

vi) *Economic and social problems in 1848*
Very early in the revolution, the adverse economic effects of the disturbances began to make themselves felt, in Austria and Germany,
as in France. The loss of business was widespread by the early
summer of 1848, trade lagged, credit tightened and a run began on
savings accounts in banks. This in turn led to a hoarding of gold and
silver, with dire consequences for employment, production,
consumption and trade, both domestic and foreign. Prominent
Rhenish businessmen had been the natural leaders of liberalism in
Prussia in the years preceding the revolution, and a number
received ministerial posts in the new governments of March. Yet
only weeks later political organisations were being set up by the
bourgeoisie in the Rhineland and Westphalia to 'ensure freedom
and order'. By late June, after the Paris workers' rising had taken
place and been suppressed by General Cavaignac, business circles
in Germany were far more frightened by the possibility of anarchy
than by authoritarianism. These fears communicated themselves to
other social groups during the summer and autumn, including
many who had originally supported the revolution.

The most important social cause of the revolution had been fear
of proletarianisation. The exacerbation of a difficult economic
situation was bound to alienate support for the revolution among
those who had property or status to lose, especially once the initial
excitement had worn off. Above all, the feeling of 'where is it going
to end?' became widespread by the late summer of 1848. The

restoration of confidence in the traditional authorities was cemented by the fact that economic recovery was both rapid and sustained immediately after the suppression of the revolution. This was especially striking in heavy industry in the Customs Union area. To take one example, between 1848 and 1857, the amount of iron ore produced increased by an extraordinary 300%, while the number of works and those employed in them went up by 40%. A further factor in drawing the propertied middle classes over to the side of the old establishment was fear of the potential power of the industrial working classes to challenge their position and interests. The activities of the Communist League, Marx in Düsseldorf, Engels at Elberfeld, Moses Hess in Cologne, had in fact involved few workers, but their potential aroused anxiety among employers, especially when these were faced with sporadic strike action which erupted in the early 1850s. The Confederation was to win support from the bourgeoisie after the revolution by its energetic measures to suppress all political organisations of working men and to restrict association to those founded for purely educational purposes. It was not only the factory owners and big businessmen who reacted thus, but the master craftsmen as well, who distanced themselves from liberal politics during the revolution. The masters' efforts to retain exclusive control of their trade and to exclude the journeymen and apprentices during the Frankfurt Craftsmen's Congress during the summer of 1848, had been answered by the setting up of journeymen's congresses. Moreover, many of the radical craftsman apprentices continued to play a prominent role in the demonstrations, street-fighting and barricades. This was particularly evident at the autumn crisis of 1848; later they threw in their lot with workers and intellectuals who were behind the rising of May 1849 in Dresden, the capital of Saxony, or with south German Jacobin elements in Baden and the Palatinate. The extraordinary success of the Democratic Workers Associations, under the tenacious leadership of the journeyman printer, Stephen Born, who organised the first nationwide strike in the printing industry in April 1848, was a further source of anxiety to small employers and strengthened the instinctive loyalty to the traditional order of this naturally conservative section of the population. Such instinctive responses to the course of the revolution, and to the changes it seemed to be bringing about, by the propertied classes in Germany were significant because they survived and hardened into long-term political attitudes.

The Revolution and its Consequences

In fact, the political constellation of German domestic politics in the latter half of the nineteenth century was largely determined by the experiences of 1848–49, insofar as the bourgeoisie came to accept the power basis of the old feudal aristocracy in the interests of maintaining security and order. In time, the representatives of big business interests and finance entered into a political alliance with the traditional ruling classes, the principal aim of which was to block the advance of organised labour. For they remembered, as did politically-committed working class men and their leaders, that the origins of German socialism lay in the 1848 revolution. The revolutionary year had witnessed the first beginnings of a labour movement in Germany. Working-class organisation was, on the whole, largely concerned with self-help. It was distinguished by an idealistic commitment to humanity in general, the desire, as a cabinet maker's apprentice put it in a letter to the Central Committee of Worker Fraternisation at Leipzig, asking for teaching materials, 'to assist the whole of human society on to its feet'. The revolutionary potential of the brotherhood of workers had been clearly demonstrated in the revolution. The hostility between the German petty bourgeoisie and the organised labour movement belongs to the later history of the Second Empire, but it is undoubtedly a heritage of 1848. The leaders of petty bourgeois democracy provided most of the victims of the counter-revolution, but they left behind them no organisation to defend their former supporters. These remained without political representation in subsequent decades. Despite the brief resurgence of popular democratic pressure groups in the 1860s, centred especially on a number of small states and free cities, such as Hamburg and Frankfurt, Karlsruhe and Gotha, this most populous section of German society failed either to make an impact on domestic politics or to create organisations to look after their interests. When the age of mass politics dawned in Germany with the introduction of universal suffrage (1867–71), no party emerged to represent the *Kleinbürgerum*. The politically active of these people tended to turn either to the Right or to the Left; a certain section eventually joined the Socialist Party, and indeed, in the early years, provided an important number of their leaders, but the majority remained politically apathetic and, in times of economic crisis, gravitated to the right-wing of the conservative parties. The paternalist state had long been the protector of these largely pre-industrial social groups, and by and large it was with the nation-state that they identified themselves in the decades after the revolution. Gradually the ideals of nationalism and dynastic loyalty claimed their support, and by the last decades of the century their political attitudes were as conservative, their commitment to the status quo and their opposition to liberalism, and especially socialism, as adamant, as those of the neo-feudal groups.

The revolution of 1848, then, gave members of the public at all social levels a taste of political activity. Even those who had played no direct role in the deliberations or in the struggles, were drawn into participation by the media, notably the broadsheets and posters published at so many centres in Germany: at Frankfurt, at Karlsruhe, at Offenburg and Berlin, at Leipzig and Magdeburg, at Hamburg and Düsseldorf. Some were preposterous and grotesque, but most were savagely witty in their vindictive persecution of popular bogeymen. The age of mass politics was still a generation away but the overall effect of *das tolle Jahr* was to change the people from being mere objects of government administration to potential agents of political activity. In particular, the potential of the masses as demonstrated during the French revolution of 1848 and its aftermath, made the ruling classes in the German states acutely sensitive to this fact, and in the latter half of the nineteenth century these showed themselves much more 'modern' in their approach to power politics than the liberals, or their supporters, in Germany as a whole.

The effects of the 1848 revolution in Germany on the subsequent history of the country are such that it must be regarded as one of the most crucial events of her recent history.

The achievements which survived were not very impressive, given the intelligence and energy, the dedication and enthusiasm of the revolution's spokesmen. The most important political and social achievements were the emancipation of the peasantry from all feudal dues, the abolition of patrimonial jurisdiction, and the introduction of constitutional government to Prussia, though not to Austria. The king of Prussia abrogated the liberal constitution in the spring of 1849, which he had imposed in the previous December and replaced manhood suffrage with a three-class system, designed to ensure the preponderance of rank and wealth in the government of the state. In January 1850 a new constitution was promulgated. The Austrian authorities affected to disregard or rescind the constitutional achievements of the revolutionary year and in December 1851 the 1849 constitution was withdrawn. Under a neo-absolutist regime, her new leader, Prince Schwarzenberg, initiated a reform of the administration, especially of the finances, which brought a widespread prosperity to Austrian society. He and his advisers acted on the somewhat cynical calculation that most of the articulate members of society were now convinced of the truth of Alexander Pope's dictum:

> 'Of forms of government let fools contest,
> What e'er's administered best is best'.

Of those who had supported the revolution, many were driven into exile, executed or imprisoned; the Austrians were in fact much more vindictive in their pursuit of the ringleaders than Prussia or indeed any of the other German states. A large number of Germans chose to emigrate after 1848 mainly to America – 80,000 from Baden alone, though the majority of German emigrants were driven to do so for economic rather than political reasons. Only a minority of those who remained in Germany continued to be active in pursuit of their political goals. The response of the intellectuals to the failure of 'their' revolution was particularly revealing. Resignation rather than protest was a characteristic response. Their tendency to withdraw from political discussion and activity was described by Fontane in a letter dated January 1851:

> All one can do is to escape with one's mind into the past and one's heart into one's circle of friends and the family ... I've tried the right, the left and the middle; the craziness of the extremes and the pusillanimity of the 'juste milieu' is equally repulsive ...

The economic liberalism, which was characteristic of the Prussian administration in the years of political reaction which followed the suppression of the revolution, proved an acceptable distraction to many professional people. Indeed educated Germans and particularly Prussians in the 1850s came round to the view that living under a constitution, however deficient it might be, was actually a major step forward, a justification of their belief in the progressive character of history in their age. Thus, the liberal civil servant, Hans Viktor von Unruh, who had been president of the Berlin National Assembly at the time of its dissolution by Prussian troops, wrote about the atmosphere of the post-revolutionary scene many years later. He declared that 'a liberal, or indeed a conservative, unless he were an out-and-out reactionary, could only feel a sense of relief at having been freed from the arbitrary tyranny of government and bureaucracy of the pre-revolutionary years'. In general, and for reasons which will be discussed more fully below, the response of most politically-minded Germans to the failure of the revolution was tempered with relief that at last political upheaval and commercial uncertainty were at an end. Businessmen, financiers, traders, householders and the general public showed a confident expectation, soon to be confirmed, that strong government would restore the economy.

In the sphere of domestic politics perhaps the most important short-term consequence of 1848–49 was the changed relationship of Austria and Prussia within the Confederation and the growing public awareness of this. Austro-Prussian dualism had been a vital strand of German history for almost a century. The greater consequence of Austria in the first half of the nineteenth century was reflected in her ruler holding the key position of President in the Confederation; her superiority was openly recognised as such by Prussia. Austrian hegemony was attributed to what had been the Danube monarchy's traditional role in German affairs for centuries, and was accepted as right and necessary by the European great powers. However, the course of events in 1848–49 caused Germans to ask some searching questions about the basis of justification for Austrian hegemony, both on political and – this was new – on economic grounds, During and after the revolution Austria experienced growing difficulties in reconciling her involvement in German affairs with the increasing complexity of administering her multi-racial empire. During 1848–49 Austria demonstrated by her high-handed attitude towards the Frankfurt Parliament and towards issues such as the Schleswig-Holstein affair, and her apparent concessions towards the Slav minorities in her territory at the (inevitable) expense of the German, that she could have little sympathy, either now or in the future, with German nationalist aims. Austria's decision to call in Russian help to suppress the revolution in her territories, and particularly the vindictiveness shown by the authorities towards the revolution in Vienna, was contrasted with the relative absence of bloodshed during the counter-revolution in Prussia. Admittedly, the Prussian army was intensely unpopular for its part in suppressing the Prussian National Assembly in Berlin and the Frankfurt Parliament, and the spring and summer uprisings of 1849 in Saxony and Baden. Yet, because the desire and the need for some form of unified state became more pressing as the country advanced economically in the 1850s, people began to distinguish between the present administration of Prussia under Frederick William IV and his advisers, the so-called Camarilla, and the Prussia which his brother, William, would one day take over. Moreover, in certain circles, notably the upper middle class, one of the lessons learned from 1848 and the failure of the Frankfurt Parliament to implement the national programme, was that this needed a military arm. This knowledge did not assuage the feelings of hostility towards the Prussian army, either in Prussia itself or in Germany as a whole. Nevertheless, it was an important element in conditioning influential sections of the public to accept the Prussian army's role in the process of national unification between 1864 and 1871.

A further vital experience of 1848 for Germans was that it gave them a new perspective on the problems of nationality. Now it no longer was seen, as it had been, in terms of a struggle against the princes, but rather in terms of a successful assertion of one's own nationality against the conflicting claims of other cultures and ethnic groups. It is no doubt an over-simplification to put it in such terms. One should rather say that the observation of the political scene during the revolutionary year, especially the experience of the Polish question in Prussia, where the existence of over one million Poles constituted a potentially serious problem for German nationalists, and to a lesser extent the claims of the duchies of Schleswig-Holstein, conditioned Germans to see that state power might offer the only successful method of bringing about the unification of their country. Bismarck was one of these, and he realised clearly from his observation of the course of the revolution that national patriotism was eminently compatible with the monarchic order and could in fact be used, as Marx was equally quick to appreciate, to buttress an authoritarian state.

6
The National Movement

Germany changed character in the decade 1840–50, and contemporaries, whatever their political loyalties were or whatever modifications these had undergone, were thoroughly aware of the fact. The failure to achieve national unity in the recent revolution was to remain a source of bitterness for a generation to come, and for those who remained faithful to their liberal beliefs, for very much longer. But the sense of German nationhood, which (prior to 1840) had been characteristic of particular social and regional groups only, was by the 1850s something to be taken for granted by all who were in the least politically minded. Moreover, in a very few years Germans had ceased to regard national sentiment, as they had still done in the late 1830s, as a shared experience of European peoples. Instead they increasingly came to see it as something whose quality and worth was determined by its exclusively German character.

The events of 1848 and their impact on the German public mind thus provide a useful perspective for considering the character and development of German nationalism in the century as a whole.

Origins

The vital force which gave birth to the national movement in late eighteenth century Germany lay not in the field of politics, but in the realm of ideas. The writings of German poets and philosophers helped to create a sense of national identity based on a shared awareness of Germany's cultural traditions. For all the peculiarly German character of the work of her great classical writers, Lessing and Herder, Kant and Humboldt, Goethe and Schiller, the framework within which they wrote was a European one. The development of the creative personality to its fullest potential, which was the ideal of the late eighteenth-century German humanists, was the very opposite of that national exclusiveness which later came to be associated with German patriots. The efforts of those writers to make their fellow countrymen, Bavarians and East Prussians, Silesians, Thuringians and Rhinelanders, aware of their common national identity, were aimed primarily at releasing them from the provincial obscurity, to which political divisions had condemned them for so long. And provincial Germans did indeed respond to such ideas. Discussion groups and literary circles sprang up in towns scattered across the country, especially in the northern part, to discuss and speculate upon aspects of nationhood, the role of the citizen, the function of the aristocracy in the modern state, and the contribution which the educated burgher might make in government and administration. The cosmopolitan character of early German nationalists owed much to their conviction that the political divisions of Germany, the traditional multiplicity of sovereignties, constituted the most effective obstacle to the liberation of the burgher from feudal bonds. The formulation of their ideas was often quaint, a mixture of ponderous sincerity and flights of fantasy. Thus, in the 1790s, the members of the Literary Society of the quiet town of Oldenburg in north-west Germany, styled themselves:

> Members of the German Parnassus!
> Authors of Germany!
> High minded citizens of the world!

The effect of the French Revolution and the wars of the 1790s on the French people, the tremendous energy released by the new national ardour, greatly impressed Germans who witnessed them; this was especially true of the young intellectuals, members of the early Romantic movement who had been born in the late 1760s or early 1770s, such as Beethoven, Tieck, the Schlegels, or Kleist, born in 1777. Some hoped that the revolution would come to Germany, destroy the old feudal order, and unite the German people: the French nation seemed in their view a model to be imitated rather than a danger to resist. Even after the French troops invaded Germany and annexed the left bank of the Rhine, even after Napoleon's conquests, his abolition of the Holy Roman Empire and reduction of the majority of German princes to the status of vassals, and subjection of Prussia in 1806, the German national movement lacked a political dimension. The presence of the French as an occupying power in much of Prussia, the erection of the Kingdom of Westphalia under Napoleon's uncharismatic brother, Jerome, even the levies of soldiers which German states had to put at Napoleon's disposal, took a long time to provoke active resistance. Comments generally took the form of exasperated or satiric depreciation of the German national character: the poor German, *der deutsche Michel*, will put up with anything. Thus the political commentator Joh. Gottfried Seume could observe in 1807:

> The Germans have a phrase they are always using: 'I can't put up with that!' and yet there simply isn't anything evil, irrational, stupid and base which the Germans haven't put up with in the last 500 years and more especially in recent times, either from each other or from their neighbours.

The Napoleonic era

It was the gradual accumulation of grievances over a period of years, as well as the glimpse of possible release, which created a political national movement in Germany in the years 1810–13. It is understandable that it should have erupted in Prussia, which by 1813 had endured the humiliations of occupation and attendant ills for nearly seven years. Prussia provided the forum for Napoleon's most tenacious German opponents, though few of the actual leaders were themselves Prussians. It was in Berlin that Fichte, a philosopher of the Romantic movement, had held in 1807–8 his notorious '*Addresses to the German Nation*', whose powerful rhetoric excited and inspired his listeners, where the dramatist Kleist had introduced a new note of vituperation into the efforts of intellectuals to foster a sense of nation by his '*Catechism of the Germans*' of 1809; it was here too that Baron Stein of Nassau had introduced the pioneering reform programme of Prussian society in 1807, including the emancipation of the peasants and self-government for the municipalities. His dismissal by Napoleon in 1808 made him an important figure in Germany, his strong personality and vision of the future nation, his much-quoted statement, first made in a letter in 1811, 'Ich habe nur ein Vaterland und das ist Deutschland', ('I have but one Fatherland, and that is Germany'), all contributed to helping Germans to glimpse a genuine alternative to the old ways in their country. Another significant event of a different order, was the founding in 1810 at Berlin of a new university, a fitting symbol of the moral regeneration of Prussia, which the king had promised in the hour of defeat in 1806. The intellectuals responsible for initiating this great project, such as Humboldt and Fichte, Schleiermacher and the jurist Savigny, aroused the keenest interest among contemporaries. Close personal friendships or relationships linked them with zealous patriots – thus Schleiermacher was the patriotic poet Arndt's brother-in-law; together they inspired enthusiasm for the cause of German liberty in those around them.

As is usually the case in human affairs, it was not until people were personally affected in their private lives by the war and the occupation that they became receptive to the ideas of men such as Arndt and Fichte. But this happened with increasing frequency as the French occupying forces increased their demands on the population, until 1813 saw the emergence of a genuine nationalist movement committed to the expulsion of the French.

Although the ideas of a number of the leading exponents of nationalism in Germany at the time of the wars of liberation, 1813–15, were strongly influenced by the French Jacobins, the kind of popular national feeling experienced by those who fought as volunteers in the war or supported it in their writings, was christian and monarchic in sentiment. The very vocabulary of nationalism in Germany was largely derived from Pietism, a religious movement within the eighteenth century Lutheran church, which stressed inwardness and an emotional experience of the Divine presence in the world. In Prussia the king used the eloquence of his clergy to preach a kind of crusade against the 'godless' French. It might seem surprising that the princes, who had shown varying degrees of servility in their accommodation to Napoleon's wishes, should have been absorbed into the national movement so easily. At the time, the leaders of the resistance to Napoleon were perfectly aware of the value of the local monarch as a rallying point of popular nationalist sentiment. Thus, Baron Stein and the generals, Scharnhorst and Gneisenau, authors of the pioneering reform of the Prussian army after 1806 which was ultimately responsible for the defeat of Napoleon in Germany, and the bluff soldier Blücher from Mecklenburg, and the philosopher Schleiermacher, directed their energies to persuading the recalcitrant Prussian monarch, Frederick William III, to put himself forward as the leader of the national resistance to Napoleon. Of course the heady atmosphere of the wars of liberation, as the philosopher Henrik Steffens told so graphically in the last volumes of his memoirs, was especially infectious to the young and the idealistic; there was indeed a great deal of romantic idealism about the whole affair, but it was not really a mass movement. The death of the unreliable but dashing royal Prussian prince, Louis Ferdinand, in battle against Napoleon

in 1806, the valour of the duke of Brunswick who was killed at the
battle of Auerstädt on the same day as Jena, and the careful
fostering of the myth of the young and lovely Queen Louise of
Prussia, who died in 1810, allegedly as a result of the privations
suffered in consequence of the French occupation, provided the
country at large with evocative symbols of princely love of country
and even martyrdom, which effectively conditioned public opinion.
The accounts of such contemporaries recalling these days in their
memoirs, written in the 1830s and 1840s, speak rather of the 'shame'
their princes endured at Napoleon's hands, of his heedless oppression of 'anointed heads', than of the rank opportunism which
characterised the behaviour of so many of them. The princes in their
turn, their numbers sharply reduced but the territories of many,
especially in the south, much increased, found the national
movement of only limited usefulness in achieving the aim of
restoration of order in Germany.

After Napoleon's final defeat and exile, not only were the wishes
of the patriots overruled, but individual monarchs tried to 'doctor'
the legend. In the last twenty-five years of his long reign
(1797–1840), Frederick William III of Prussia, for example,
steadfastly refused to permit the expression *Freiheitskriege* (literally,
'wars of freedom') to be used. He insisted instead on *Befreiungskriege*
or 'wars of liberation'. Others, such as Ludwig I of Bavaria, were
genuine and somewhat naive devotees of German cultural
nationalism, though they were determined to dictate the forms
themselves. Ludwig was mainly interested in creating a role for
himself in the Confederation as a counterweight to that of the
Prussian king. In the pursuit of his ambition he rebuilt Munich as an
imposing capital city and attracted as much talent as he could to
'Athens on the Isar'. However, his many idiosyncracies, including
his fondness for writing bad verse, and the pious hopes he nurtured
for his hall of fame, Valhalla, erected on the banks of the Danube
with the avowed aim that '*teutscher der Teutsche aus ihr trete, besser als er
gekommen*' (that 'the German may emerge from it more German and
a better man than when he entered'), made him the subject of much
gleeful parody. Certainly few themes lent themselves more readily
to Heine's satiric pen than the sentimental nationalist on the
Bavarian royal throne. In a somewhat similar way to Ludwig, the
new king of Prussia, Frederick William IV, who came to the throne
in 1840, tried to direct the ambitions of his people towards the
symbols of national unity rather than the realities of power. Such a
symbol was the completion of Cologne's last medieval cathedral by

subscription, the *Allerdeutschenhaus*, as the publicist J. Görres termed it, and which fired the young Swiss historian, Jakob Burckhardt, with a deep sense of his German heritage, when he travelled to the Rhineland in the early summer of 1841. But 'cathedral fund patriotism', generous as was the response by Prussian Protestant as well as Catholic Rhinelanders, could appeal to only a narrow segment of society, and even then appeared little more than a palliative at a time when a new political awareness made people conscious of the frustrations of tutelage.

The Restoration era

Once the Napoleonic Wars were over, people in general lost interest in politics; as the Frankfurt journalist, Ludwig Börne, put it in 1819, 'The thinking part of the German people returned to its studies. Already it has returned to its recumbent position.' The nationalists remained a tiny percentage of the population but they showed themselves much more sympathetic to other national movements than before. In subsequent years, especially in the 1820s and early 1830s, the efforts of any nation to forward the cause of national independence or liberty in their country could be sure of an enthusiastic response from Germans. For while the philosophers and writers on the national movement in the early years of the century had been solely preoccupied with Germany's national destiny, which they saw in terms of historical necessity, German nationalists in the Restoration era looked to natural law in support of their pleas for a unified, liberal state. The liberal aspirations of their neighbours and of members of other social classes were at least as meaningful as their own. During the 1820s and the 1830s German nationalists, disappointed by the failure of their hopes of a united Germany in 1815, remained true to the cause of national emancipation in Europe, whether of the Greeks or the Belgians, the Irish or the Poles. Popular German novelists wrote about the lure of fighting for the Hellenes against their Turkish oppressors, and Heinrich Laube called his new novel in 1830 not 'Young Germany', but 'Young Europe', and sent his hero dashing off to succour the Poles in their struggle against the Russians. The Young German poets Freiligrath and Herwegh wrote rousing songs of Irish suffering and English oppression and sentimental ditties on emigrants from that country to America. Germans shared with other Europeans a deep sense of outrage at subjects being mere pawns in the hands of statesmen. 'Nothing', wrote a Rhinelander called Weitzel in the early 1840s, 'has done so much to encourage the revolution which so many appeared to dread, than the treaties, peace negotiations, territorial exchanges and cessions of the last forty years.' Accordingly, the aspirations of educated men that their rulers should trust them, if not to govern themselves, at least to comment upon political matters, and that they should have the power to check the arbitrary power of central and local administration, and the ambitions of working men for greater social justice could be subsumed under the general heading, the 'national movement'. The journeymen, who were beginning to experience very considerable hardship in the 1830s and 1840s, and who looked in vain to their local ruler or town council for succour, also helped to disseminate both national and early socialist ideas throughout the Confederation.

Hambach

The revolution of 1830 engendered much excitement but little change in the political or in the social scene. 1832 saw one of the few mass public demonstrations of the popular will in the 1830s, at Hambach in the Palatinate, which belonged to Bavaria. It was typical too of the sociable character of the national movement in southern Germany during these years, that the main body of the 30,000-strong Hambach demonstrators consisted of friends and families supplied with provisions, who came to enjoy the Maytime outing, speeches and banners. Academics played a prominent role, but artisans were well represented. On this occasion and for nearly a decade to come, the authority of the 'professors' was still accepted by those who would have liked to see more action, for the professors and their students provided political martyrs for liberal and national movements. (More than a third of professors and lecturers of German in universities suffered setbacks between 1830 and 1848 in their careers, fines or imprisonment for their political activities.) The opening speech at Hambach was given by the publicist and lawyer, Siebenpfeiffer, and was suitably entitled 'the German May'. The black, red and gold banner of the volunteers against Napoleon, from now on the symbol of German unity, flew from the castle alongside the Polish flag. There were many Poles present, refugees from the recent revolution, and a generous welcome was given them by the Germans. Siebenpfeiffer's rhetoric seems to have been wholly in keeping with his listeners' mood and their general sentiments, at least to judge from memoirs and reports of the event.

'Italia and Germania' by Friedrich Overbeck.

He ended his address with the following highflown appeal: 'Long live a free united Germany! Long live the Poles, allies of the Germans! Long live the French (he called them 'the Franks'), brothers of the Germans, who respect our nationality and our independence!'

Anti-French sentiments

In the 1840s the French created a war scare and were suspected, not without reason, of nefarious designs on the left bank of the Rhine. Their activities called forth a spate of patriotic gestures, among them the popular song, Nikolaus Becker's '*Sie sollen ihn nicht haben, den freien deutschen Rhein*', und Schneckenberger's '*Wacht am Rhein*'. A year later a provincial professor of German wrote the most celebrated of all such songs, '*Deutschland, Deutschland über alles*', while on holiday in Helgoland. In it he tried to express the love of country, the ideal of brotherly love based on common destiny, a kind of

Portrait of Heinrich Hoffmann von Fallersleben by Carl Schumacher.

German equivalent of the '*Marseillaise*', which he and his friends had but a week before been prohibited to sing. Hoffmann von Fallersleben, with his blond curling hair and dandified dress, was no bluff German chauvinist à la Arndt, no coarse-grained vilifier of French ways, as Jahn or the most influential journalist of the early 1830s Wolfgang Menzel (*der Franzosenfresser*) had been. He was a member of the Young German group of writers and used the vehicle of mild satire in his popular '*Unpolitische Lieder*' (1841–42) to persuade Germany's rulers to grant constitutional government and a national parliament. The quality, then, of German nationalism in the period between Napoleon's fall and the mid-1840s was very different from what it became in the second half of the century. And, as in so much of Germany's social and political life, it was the revolution of 1848 and the way in which it made people of nationalist sentiment face up to the implications of their ideas, which provided a watershed.

1848

Initially the outbreak of revolution in the capital cities of many German states in the spring of 1848 was, in part at least, an expression of solidarity by Germans with their brothers in other parts of Europe. Yet the events of early summer showed a clear change of heart, both among the spokesmen of the revolution, and in the general mood of the country. The brutal suppression of the Czech revolutionaries in June 1848 by the Austrian field marshal, Windischgrätz, evoked no reproof from the Frankfurt Parliament, but rather the reverse, and during the debates in July on the national question, Prussian delegates showed themselves quite unwilling to concede the rights for the Poles which they claimed for Germans living under foreign powers. The writer Wilhelm Jordan, declared in a speech on July 4 in the Frankfurt Parliament:

> All who live on German soil are Germans, even if they are not German by birth or language. We decree that they are Germans, we accord the term 'German' a sublime meaning, and the term 'Germany' will from now on be a political concept.

However, the ineffectiveness of the Frankfurt Parliament or of liberal ministries to assert the claims of the nation against the European powers in the Schleswig-Holstein affair, brought home the lesson that fundamental changes in Germany's political status must come with the support of the German princes, not in opposition to their wishes. Furthermore, the behaviour of the Austrian authorities after the suppression of the revolution left little hope that support from that quarter would ever be forthcoming. People had lived so long with the fact of Austria's being part of Germany that it was difficult to envisage the possibility of her being excluded. But in the course of the 1850s German businessmen, academics and politicians came to accept the term *kleindeutsch*, i.e. Germany without Austria, first formulated in the revolutionary years, and by the end of the decade *kleindeutsch* parties and a *großdeutsch* party were arguing the merits of their respective cases. The liberal politician from Baden, Bassermann, wrote to his friend, the historian Droysen, urging him to write a history of Prussia, which would demonstrate to the 'nation' the stages of Prussia's progress to being the leader of the national movement. Droysen's celebrated history, '*Geschichte der preußischen Politik*' was indeed written and began to appear in the 1850s, but before the last volume came out in 1886, it was already being overshadowed by that literary and chauvinistic masterpiece, Heinrich von Treitschke's '*Germany in the nineteenth century*' (1878–94).

Increasingly in the 1850s individuals began to transcend the particularist loyalties of their homeland. This was particularly true of the Protestant areas of south Germany. Ludwig Bamberger, revolutionary, banker and liberal politician, recalled in later years (he died in 1898) that he had won his first electoral victory in Hesse-Darmstadt by enlisting Protestant middle class sentiment in favour of closer links with the north. The same was true of the merchant and industrial classes of Saxony, despite the natural antipathy of this state towards its more powerful neighbour Prussia, and true also of the Thuringian states. For all the idealistic language in which much of the speculation and commentary on Germany's situation was couched, the years between the revolution and the wars of unification in the 1860s were characterised by the increasing preoccupation of German businessmen with practical necessities: both German and foreign commentators were fully conscious that German commerce and industry needed a unified state in order to continue to develop. As Friedrich Engels put it provocatively but not inaccurately many years later, in 1895, the preoccupation of mid-century German nationalists with unity was primarily with

> the desire for the removal of all superfluous obstacles which the German businessman had first to overcome at home if he wanted to enter the world market and which all his competitors were spared. German unity had become an economic necessity.

Prussia's impressive performance on the economic front in the 1850s, despite her extremely reactionary government, was of very considerable weight in any consideration of future political policy. Bismarck, when he came to power in 1862, showed himself thoroughly aware of the political power which Prussia's economic achievements endowed her with. The decision of a substantial section of liberal politicians and public figures to support Bismarck's policies in the late 1860s should therefore be seen less in terms of a 'betrayal of liberal principles' or 'rank opportunism' than a calculated option for the best solution in the circumstances. Not that it was a straightforward matter, and there are plenty of testimonies by contemporaries to the apprehension felt as to the outcome of their choice, or to their sheer bad conscience, at allowing Prussia's economic and military success to win their support for her leadership of Germany.

Economic aspects

One must constantly keep in mind the contrast on the economic front between the quarter century preceding the founding of the German Empire and that succeeding it, when considering the temper of German nationalism in the second half of the century. The optimism engendered by the rapid expansion of the economy between 1848 and 1873 not only suffered a sharp shock at the stock exchange collapse in 1873, but the depression which followed lasted for over twenty years, and coincided with a period in Germany's history when very considerable psychological adjustments were demanded of her people. The effect was to stimulate certain and very widespread anxieties. Those anxieties concerned Germany's future status as a great power; people were worried about the centrifugal forces within the state, such as national and religious minorities, and the conflicting ideologies among her political parties, they gave way to fears as to the vulnerability of German society in times of severe economic crises, and the lack of security of the state from envious neighbours. These anxieties were not felt uniformly throughout German society, but they were a marked feature of the ruling elite and were encountered across the broad spectrum of the middle classes. Paradoxically perhaps, they acted as a kind of cement, fostering the creation of a feeling for the new Reich as 'the nation'. The effect of international crises, such as the 'war in sight' crisis of 1875, which was largely the work of Bismarck, and the various successive crises of the 1880s and the 1890s was to promote a sense of national solidarity, which found its most appropriate symbol in the army. There were certainly many critical voices raised in and outside parliament about the special status of the Prusso-German army after 1871, and especially after the liberals' failure to retain any budgetary control of the armed forces in 1874, but one should not underestimate its role as a factor of social integration under the Empire. Moreover, increasing awareness of

The unveiling of the Victory Column on the Königsplatz in Berlin in September 1873.

the competitiveness of modern industry, and the state's clear involvement in supporting German heavy industry and agriculture from 1879 onwards, made Germans see production and export in terms of national prestige. While such knowledge fostered a sense of solidarity in the nation, it also made Germans more aggressive towards the outside world.

Nationalism and the Empire

Up to and about the mid-1860s national feeling among the middle classes of north and central Germany, and to some extent among south Germans also, was predominantly anti-feudal. Scarcely a decade later, this had altered radically; the process is documented with little subtlety but considerable clarity in the novels of Fr. Spielhagen – as for example in his '*In Reih und Glied*' or '*Hammer und*

Amboß', or '*Sturmflut**'. By the mid-1870s, the feudal ruling elite claimed to embody the supreme national virtues, and were widely admired and emulated for so doing.

A considerable propaganda effort on the part of the authorities went into projecting this notion. It was fixed in the public mind by visual symbols – most famous perhaps was Anton von Werner's painting of the proclamation of the Emperor in the Hall of Mirrors at Versailles (cf. p. 135), surrounded by princes and generals, with Bismarck in military uniform as sole representative of the civilian contribution. The Victory Monument in Berlin, which was completed in 1873, and was in every sense of the word a genuinely national monument, is a real revelation of the way in which the national ideal had changed in the course of the last sixty years. The figure of Borussia at the summit represented the Prussification of the German nation and the inscription read '*das dankbare Volk dem siegreichen Helden*' ('to a victorious hero from a grateful people'). The attempt of the bourgeoisie to win titles and patents of nobility, to buy themselves or their sons into good regiments, to marry their daughters into the nobility, characteristic of the so-called feudalisation of the bourgeoisie, was in part the desire to join the ranks of those who were held to be the 'best of the nation', those who held 'true national sentiments'. Criticism of the *kleindeutsch* national state was made to seem a criticism of the nation itself, and this process was reinforced by the creation of a whole series of 'outsiders' or 'hostile forces', which were combated by legislation and police harassment. Among those hostile forces were included the Catholic clergy during the Kulturkampf, the Socialists, the racial minorities, Poles or Alsatians. Methods of discrimination included by-passing individuals in appointments to posts within the state service: thus Catholics or persons believed to hold liberal, not to say radical opinions, or Jews, found it difficult to gain university chairs, or senior legal jobs. The strong democratic element in the national movement, which at least in Hamburg, in central and south-west Germany had been active until the mid-1860s, was thus tacitly consigned to oblivion.

Popular literature played an important role in promoting the provincial chauvinism which was the characteristic form of late nineteenth century German nationalism. Traditional feelings of

---

* Spielhagen's novels are immensely informative about Germany in the 1850s–70s. They are unfortunately no longer in print, but it is not difficult to find secondhand copies in Germany and the *Nostalgie* fashion in the Federal Republic will no doubt soon prompt new editions of the most popular.

inferiority towards Germany's French neighbour were exploited to vilify the recent enemy. A crass, but typical example, was a publication ostensibly by Pastor Oertels (pseudonym for a popular writer called W. von Horn) entitled '*Ein Volksbuch für das Jahr 1872*'. Here the writer purports to show of the French 'how horribly dirty their underclothes are beneath the external show of fine raiment', adding in an appeal to human vanity and base instincts 'the reader knows what I mean'. A spate of popular songs contrasted the simplicity and the virtues of the Germans with the decadence and falsity of the French: but it was symptomatic of the essential artificiality of the new state, that it had no truly national anthem. The Prussian anthem '*Heil Dir im Siegerkranz*' was sung on all occasions where the Emperor or the military were prominent, and they were many, but it was ironic that the nation which used music, especially the brass band, so lavishly in support of national occasions, could not agree on a musical symbol of the nation. Nor indeed was there even an agreed national flag, although the Prussian colours, black and white, were combined with the Hanseatic red and white to form the black, white and red imperial colours. However, in other ways the state's promotion of national feeling was more successful. It became customary to associate the national holiday, the *Sedanstag*, with family or business outings, with song and beer to round off a day in the open. But even here the inappropriateness of it all did not escape the critics: indeed one of the authors of the Second Empire, the great General Moltke himself, asked how it was that the anniversary of the great victory over France at Sedan in 1870, resulting in the capture of the French emperor, should be celebrated on the 2 September, when the battle had actually taken place the day before.

Social imperialism

In the 1890s, the character of German nationalism underwent a further modification, which corresponded to the transition from loyalty to the nation state to national imperialism. What is known as 'social imperialism', the galvanising of the nation's energies towards securing for Germany an equal status with other 'imperial powers in Europe', had the advantage from the authoritarian government's point of view, of directing attention away from the domestic and social problems of the Reich. The Pan-German movement was founded in 1893, and other organisations followed which expressedly underlined the chauvinistic mood of the country. These, though by no means peculiar to Germany, assumed extravagant forms in that country. The navy became a particularly evocative symbol of nationalist aspirations, and the naval programme, which aroused anxiety and anti-German feeling in Britain in the last years of the century, also provoked acute anti-British sentiment in Germany, which is amply documented in the press of the time. Moreover, the chauvinist organisations were regarded by the outside world as representative both of the official voice of Germany and the public mind. Their columnists contributed to daily newspapers all over the country, and the German public was politically uneducated and not discriminating. A typical example of public attitudes at this date is the entry in a local paper for the city of Erfurt in central Germany. On 9 September 1912 the citizens read the following account of the recent meeting of Erfurt Pan-Germans: the President, Baron von Vietinghoff-Scheel, started by reminding his audience in his address of that 'glorious historic moment forty-two years ago', and went on to take a line which did indeed evoke an immediate emotional response in German hearts whether Pan-German or not:

> Since that time our people has advanced in numbers, in wealth, in knowledge and skills, but in latter years our international status has been declining, while discontent spreads itself within the nation.

The President immediately provided a remedy for the nationwide neurosis: the cause of Germany's troubles, he averred, was that her frontiers were 'too narrow':

> What we need to do now is to develop an appetite once more for territorial aggrandisement; we must gain new lands to colonise, otherwise we shall become a people in decline, a dwindling race. True deep love of our country should force us to think of the future of our people and of their children, and to take no notice of those who would accuse us of warmongering and aggressiveness.

A year later, General Keim, founder and president of the so-called 'Defence League' (whose very title pandered to the current myth of Germany's encirclement), declared in the annual assembly of his organisation in 1913 'The *German lad* and the *German girl* must be told in no uncertain terms: *You have a right to hate the enemies of your country.*'

Critical assessments of such speeches were not lacking in Germany and the Peace Movement had redoubtable and highly placed leaders. However, as they said themselves, they were officers without men, and were often denounced as unpatriotic or even traitors. In the years before 1914 the myth of Germany's encirclement gained currency among the nation as a whole, as German economic and military power demonstrably failed to gain her authority in international affairs or indeed win her friends. The growing sense of isolation in Europe felt by Germans inclined many to the view that there was no smoke without fire and that no doubt the Pan-Germans, the members of the Navy League, the Association for the Promotion of Germanness in the East, the Defence League, etc., had sources of information unknown to them. Moreover, the social organisation of the country had conditioned the people for more than two generations in favour of militant nationalism: the average citizen's free time was spent not, as in the 1830s and 1840s, in literary clubs or discussion groups, but in singing and gymnastic associations, in the war veteran groups (still going strong forty-two years after the Franco-Prussian War!), all of which were thoroughly chauvinistic, and numbered hundreds of thousands of members. These and similar organisations devoted themselves, among other things, to collecting subscriptions for national monuments, as for example the famous monument of Hermann the Cherusker of 1913, who, appropriately, was depicted brandishing his sword in the direction of France, or for the three hundred and more statues to 'William the Founder' (the first German emperor), erected by his grandson, the last emperor. The growing sense of isolation and a kind of spiritual disorientation encouraged the tendency to think in black and white terms – people were either 'true patriots' (*Reichstreue*), or 'enemies of the nation' (*Reichsfeinde*). The illiberalism of German institutions and of society was reflected in the intolerance shown to those of different views.

The paradox of German nationalism at the end of the nineteenth century was that, despite signal achievements, she lacked the sense of security which success ought, but does not always, bring. Ludwig Bamberger, who had lived through, and consciously witnessed the various stages of Germany's history from the liberal 1840s to the chauvinist 1890s commented succinctly at the end of his life 'a generation has grown up, for whom patriotism appears in the guise of hatred, hatred for everything at home or abroad, which will not submit blindly to its claims'.

7
The Growth of Prussian Hegemony in Germany 1850–71

From the vantage point of German nationalists in 1900 or on the eve of the Great War, the decade which intervened between the collapse of the 1848 revolution and the wars of unification in the 1860s, seemed totally lacking in character or consequence. Nietzsche once spoke contemptuously of the 'fetid air' (*Sumpfluft*) of the '50s and the nationalist commentators used the patronising phrase 'liberalistic' of the public figures of that time. Yet the 1850s had an importance in determining the future course of Germany's history in a way that was only fully appreciated when the economic factors were given due weight. And the significance of Prussia's economic policies in promoting her position of hegemony in Germany cannot be gainsaid.

The economic background

The period between the re-establishment of the German Confederation in 1850 and the founding of the Second Empire in 1871 coincides with the take-off into sustained industrial growth in Germany, predominantly in the north-west and in Saxony. For nearly a generation Germans witnessed the rapid expansion of heavy industry, especially in the Prussian-owned Rhine-Ruhr areas, the Saar and Silesia, and in Saxony, and the steady rise in exports of German manufactured goods. At the same time a less spectacular but vitally important growth in agricultural production was recorded. That the massive increase in the volume of production and trade did not benefit the population equally, nor indeed the whole population, is eloquently attested in official reports. However, the increase in national wealth had long term implications for Germany's weight in Europe, while inside the Confederation the optimism that was engendered in business, commercial and financial circles reacted positively on public opinion generally. In particular it benefitted Prussia. Despite the unpopularity of her reactionary government in the 1850s and of the new king, William I (1861–88, German emperor 1871–88) and his military advisors during the clash between parliament and the army in the 1860s, the Prussian government found increasing support amongst those whose business prospered, and those whose living standards rose as a direct result of Prussia's economic leadership.

The economic background of Germany's unification provides a key to the understanding of many of the problematical features of her history at that time. Austrian policy in the Confederation was essentially defensive in character after 1850 on account of the structural weakness of her economy. True, for a brief period until his untimely death in 1852, the Austrian prime minister, Prince Schwarzenberg, ostensibly pursued an expansionist policy. Efforts on the part of his able minister of finance, Bruck, to combine Austria's need for protective tariffs with membership of a trading area in central Europe were foiled by the extraordinary dexterity of the economic spokesman of the Prussian government, Rudolf Delbrück. Bruck's initiative failed through the simple fact that more and more members of the German business community were benefitting from things as they were. The growing support among Germans for free trade began to be manifested all over the country in the '50s and '60s. In Prussia, the grain-producing landowners in the lands lying east of the Elbe river or East Elbia, who had built-up a lucrative trade with England after the abolition of the English corn laws in 1846, began to invest in industry, in the railways as well as in agricultural machinery. Similarly, merchants and traders in the ports of northern Germany – such as Hamburg, Stettin, Königsberg, Elbing and Danzig – as well as in the manufacturing towns of central Germany and parts of the south, favoured free trade policies. They supported the movement towards the liberalisation of Germany's trading laws, which the administration in Prussia was known to advocate. Gradually a national movement in support of economic liberalism grew up and in the process spawned a host of organisations at local, regional and national level, of which the mainly commercial Congress of German Economists and the political *Nationalverein* (National Association) are the best known. In these organisations, businessmen, civil servants, professional men and academics avidly discussed ways and means of liberalising the economy and the administration – the two were thought to be necessarily part of the same process. Both the logic of the situation, namely Prussian economic leadership in the Customs Union, and the presence of able and articulate Prussians at these meetings, gradually wore down fears among members of other states of Prussian hegemony and its consequences for them.

There was, however, widespread disquiet in states such as Hanover and Saxony, Wurttemberg and Bavaria, at the growth of Prussia's political influence in the Confederation. This was seen to be at the expense of Austria and had implications for their future, since their status as medium-sized states had always tended to make them prefer to see Austria's influence in the Confederation retained as a counter-weight to Prussia. At the same time, considerations of material advantage carried ever-increasing weight with the member states; as the current phrase put it *'Die Dinge sind immer stärker als die Menschen'*. Austria was clearly not going to be in a position to join the Customs Union under the conditions prevailing in the '50s but she had to be a member before she could hope to offer an effective counter-weight to Prussia. Besides, whatever her minister of finance believed was right for Austria, Austria's industrial pressure groups had the ear of the Austrian emperor and were determined to retain protective tariffs for their own industrial products. The financial weakness of Austria was strikingly demonstrated in the early months of 1859, a year which witnessed a new liberal regime in Prussia. In 1859 Austria was embroiled in a war with France over Italy and, following her defeat, Austrian state bonds fell on the Frankfurt stock exchange from eighty-one and a half on 1 January to thirty-six on 29 April. By contrast, the political implications of Prussian economic bargaining power became evident in the negotiations leading up to the trade agreement between Prussia and France, which was eventually signed in 1862, and to which the member states of the Customs Union acceded. This agreement gave a substantial part of Germany direct access to the west European free trade area, including France, Britain and Belgium. Prussia's negotiators consulted the other member states of the Customs Union before proceeding to negotiate with Napoleon III, but threatened to leave the Union when these hesitated to join. The decision of the majority of these states to accede to the French trade agreement was a vital preliminary option for the *kleindeutsch* solution to German unification (H.A. Winkler). Political unification under Prussia was neither a direct nor immediate consequence, but the trade agreement provided a major barrier between the Customs Union territory and Austria, and one which was likely to increase rather than the reverse. At the time, the

Austrian ambassador to Württemberg reviewed the developments in Prussian policy over the previous quarter century for his foreign minister, Rechberg. He wrote:

> Through the Customs Union (*Zollverein*) the royal Prussian government increased its influence steadily up to the year 1848 on other German governments; by the Trade Agreement (i.e. with France) this influence was cemented and the industrial class was won for Prussia, while the German bureaucracy became the servant of Prussian interests. By means of the Customs Union the Prussian government forged the unity of material interests and so promoted the desire for the political unity of Germany in people's minds.

The Constitutional Conflict

It was not only in the power struggle between Austria and Prussia that Prussia's economic liberalism won her major triumphs. It also helped to determine the outcome of a major domestic conflict which broke out early in the 1860s, namely the so-called Constitutional Conflict. This was a trial of strength between the Crown, supported by the Prussian officer corps on the one hand, and the Prussian house of deputies or lower house of the Prussian assembly (*Landtag*) on the other, over the question of budgetary control of the army, and, as a consequence of this, over the role and status of the army in society and the state. The conflict arose out of the financing of an army reform programme. This was the brainchild of the Prussian minister of war, Albrecht von Roon, a personal friend of the king and of Bismarck, and formerly tutor to the crown prince. The lower house of the Prussian assembly accepted the need for the increase to take account of the enormous population rise in Prussia, but members were angered at the proposed abolition of the bourgeois militia as a separate entity, and particularly by the extension of the two years of military service to three. The king refused to accept parliamentary competence in military matters except to rubber-stamp the budget; this led to direct confrontation between the monarch and the *Landtag*. William I, who succeeded to the throne on the death of his brother in 1861, dissolved the *Landtag* in the same year, but it was returned with an enormously increased liberal majority. Again in the following year the king tried to find his way out of the dilemma by dissolving parliament once more and ordering the direct influencing of electors by landowners, employers and pastors. The result however was decimation of the conservative element and overwhelming victory for the liberals. The three-class franchise in Prussia had been imposed in 1849 with the object of keeping the conservative land-owning interest in power. However, in the intervening years, the economic situation of the Prussian bourgeoisie and the free trade politics of a number of aristocratic and bourgeois landowners, especially in East Prussia, who were making large profits out of export trade, changed both the social composition of the *Landtag*, and also their political attitudes. Both parties to the conflict immediately appealed to issues of principle. Roon declared sonorously that 'the destruction of the army will mean the ruin of all orderly social relationships'. For members of the parliamentary opposition, it was not only a matter of constitutional government, it was also a question of the political emancipation of the bourgeoisie. The optimistic mood engendered by the sustained growth in the economy convinced German business and professional men that the political emancipation of their class was only a question of time. Karl Twesten, a leading democratic liberal, voiced the current feeling in an article in the influential scholarly periodical, the '*Preußische Jahrbücher*', in the year 1859 when he wrote, 'Those classes which are the most socially important must inevitably become the political ruling classes also.' The Constitutional Conflict was not in fact a clash between the aristocracy and the middle classes, but rather between the spokesmen of moderate-minded citizenry, the representatives of trade, industrial and agrarian enterprises and the professions, opposed to a pre-industrial elite, whose power and status derived from their traditional function in court and in the army. As again the '*Preußische Jahrbücher*' were to put it in 1862 at the height of the conflict, it was a 'struggle between the bourgeoisie in the widest sense of the term against the Junkers backed by absolutist prejudices'.

Bismarck

In the summer of 1862 an impasse was reached. The government resigned and the king considered abdication. At this point Roon intervened, Roon, whom the Baden prime minister, Julius Jolly, was to describe a few years later as 'a strict systematician, wholly identified with the machine (the reformed army) which he had created'. He telegraphed to summon Bismarck from his diplomatic post in Paris back to Berlin. The king proved reluctant to see him, recalling Bismarck's ultra reactionary stance in the 1848 revolution, 'a Junker stained with blood', as he termed him, and fearing the provocation his appointment as Prussian prime minister might seem to the opposition to represent. However, in a famous interview in the palace gardens, his scruples were overcome by Bismarck's diplomacy, force of personality and charm. Bismarck did not share the king's view on the need for the three year service, and he had the politician's limited admiration for the military, but he accepted the king's views as the price he must pay, as a necessary qualification for high office, and also as a means to preserve the traditional monarchic order in Prussia. He entered his new position with zest, and, justifying his action by a somewhat specious reading of the constitution which allegedly failed to provide for the current situation, he proceeded to govern Prussia for the following four years without a budget. He drew on the buoyant customs and excise revenue and was supported by able advice from banking interests. The seemingly passive attitude of Prussian liberal deputies and those they represented is easier to account for when we recall that the highly unpopular Bismarck government in these years continued to pursue policies in the economic field which corresponded exactly to the wishes of the business community and the progressive ideology of the bourgeoisie as a whole.

In their material interest, both liberals and capitalistic Junkers were at one. In 1863, the Berlin stock exchange registered 'sustained expansion' and despite feelings about Bismarck on a personal political level, they recorded 'confidence in the prime minister'. There was another reason too, why Bismarck's provocative policies did not result in open warfare. So many of the liberal leaders, Twesten, Waldeck, von Unruh, had direct experience of 1848–49 and feared isolation between the right and the left, if violence were to break out. More important was the awareness of Prussian liberals and also of liberals generally, that their political ideology, if one can term it such, represented primarily a class rather than a national interest. Moreover, as the East Prussian spokesman of the Progressive Party in Prussia (see p. 150), von Hoverbeck, put it, Prussian liberalism simply lacked 'a firm social basis in the country'. A number of the Prussian military leaders ardently desired a show-down during these years. Plans for a coup d'état lay sealed in the Berlin headquarters for just such an emergency. Bismarck recognised the paramount importance of the economic factor in the struggle and instinctively appreciated that the common interest of the propertied and educated bourgeoisie in the Prussian authoritarian state, was greater than the former as yet supposed. For a time, from 1863–64 he appeared to have considered forming

Bismarck in 1871 by A. Weger.

an alliance between the ruling classes and the new industrial
working classes against the liberal bourgeoisie; this would in fact
have been an extension of traditional Prussian paternalism, but in
the end it did not come about. It was, however, the nationalist issue
which enabled him to resolve the conflict more or less on his own
terms.

Otto von Bismarck held the position of Prussian prime minister for
twenty-eight years from his appointment in 1862, and in time he
added the posts of Prussian foreign minister and chancellor of
Imperial Germany. To his contemporaries and for at least two
generations after his death in 1898, Bismarck was 'the arbiter of the
national destiny' – 'the architect of the Fatherland': a nineteenth
century Siegfried hailed in countless rhymed tributes on numerous

state occasions. One can still re-capture the aura of his person in the magnificent statue of the Iron Chancellor in Berlin, which still stands, flanked by Roon and Moltke, a little back from the *Siegesallee* and a few hundred metres from the Brandenburg Gate, but which now, suitably perhaps, is half-shrouded by trees. A recent bibliography lists over 6,000 works on Bismarck, and for many years all accounts of the struggle for national unification in Germany were written in terms of Bismarck's biography. However, modern historians have made us much more aware of the underlying structures in Germany's political, economic and social history, as determining both the timing and the form of Germany's unification. Some of them, notably Helmut Böhme, have gone so far as to reduce his stature to 'one force among many'. But Bismarck was much more than that. Bismarck's unique stature as a historical personality lay in his awareness of these structures, an awareness which was compounded of observation and rational calculation on the one hand, and instinctive response on the other. It was not just his precise gauging of the temper of national feeling in Germany, but also his extraordinarily dexterous exploitation of economic interests and pressures which helped to establish Prussian hegemony in Germany and to unify the country in the Second Empire.

The wars of unification: The Danish War

The unification of Germany was the direct result of three wars, the Danish war in 1864, the war with Austria in 1866 and the Franco-Prussian war of 1870–71. The Danish war broke out over the vexed question of the Schleswig-Holstein duchies. On this occasion, in contrast with 1848, decisive victory was won by confederate troops, especially the Prussians. The war ended with the cession of the duchies by Denmark. In considering the effect of the military victory over the Danes, one should remember that for those who were in positions of responsibility and influence in public life and the professions in 1864, Schleswig-Holstein had been a highly emotive issue, a symbol of German nationalism, and the federal defeat in Denmark in 1848 through the intervention of the great powers a source of national 'shame'. Bismarck's handling of the Schleswig-Holstein issue, as well as the success of Prussian armies in defeating Denmark in 1864, did not conciliate the many critics of the regime in and outside Prussia, but it certainly helped to condition their later response. Austria's contribution to the war was successfully

played down and Bismarck managed to make the joint administration of the duchies into a *casus belli* between Prussia and Austria
only two years later.

The Austro-Prussian War

Following so closely on the Danish war of 1864, and preceded as it
was by intense diplomatic activity by Bismarck, the war between
Prussia and Austria of 1866 seems both a natural and obvious
sequence of 1864 and a necessary preliminary to unification in 1871.
It was these things, but it was very much more besides. From a long-
term point of view, it resolved the age-old dilemma of
Austrian/Prussian dualism in Prussia's favour. In the short-term it
led to the establishment of *Kleindeutschland*, that is, Germany
without Austria.

1866 was truly a historic date, more far reaching in its
consequences than 1806, the year of the abolition of the Holy
Roman Empire. From now on Austria was directed south-
eastwards, to concern herself primarily with the problems of her
multi-national empire. Prussia on the other hand, who had led the
Confederation economically for half a generation, found herself
fighting the whole Confederation as well as Austria in 1866: most of
the medium states in the Confederation, including Hanover,
Saxony, Bavaria and Württemberg, fought and were defeated by
Prussia in the 1866 war, as allies of Austria. In territorial terms,
Prussia was able to annex the duchies of Schleswig and Holstein as
part of the peace settlement, and, in addition, the territories of
Hanover, Hesse-Kassel, Nassau and the city of Frankfurt. The
territorial aggrandisement of Prussia established beyond doubt her
hegemony in Germany, but for the moment unification was neither
desired nor attempted by her. Bismarck formed the so-called North
German Confederation in 1867, which lasted until the establishment of the Empire in 1871. But it was the effect on the internal
history of Prussia, which was the most vital aspect of Prussia's
military success for future German history. The response of
Bismarck's liberal opponents in Prussia to the extraordinary and
decisive success of the Prussian armies over Austria and the
confederate states, revealed the dilemma in which it had placed
them. Liberals in Germany had long been wedded to the cause of
national unification, both for its own sake and because they believed
that it would make the process of liberalising the administration an
easier one.

Karl Twesten, who represented the left-wing side of Prussian liberalism, had spoken of liberalism as being the means to win for the German people a position of power and influence which corresponded to their intellectual and material development and one which could represent the nation's real interests and provide a sense of security against outside intervention and aggression.

The establishment of the North German Confederation made it abundantly clear that Prussia had taken a mighty step forward towards realising this aim. Accordingly the ideological justification of the Liberals' position was not long in coming. Prussia's victory was presented in terms of Prussian Liberal triumph over the obscuranticism of Catholic Austria, qualified admittedly, but maintained nonetheless. 'Even if we have not got a democratic ministry at the helm', wrote a correspondent in the '*National Zeitung*', the organ of Prussian right-wing Liberals, on 30 June 1866, 'Prussia undoubtedly represents vis à vis Austria the rights of the people, just as the rigid Lutherans and Calvinists represented freedom of conscience at the time of the Thirty Years War': or, as a speaker at an election rally in Berlin, just before the elections to the *Landtag* in early July 1866 put it, 'North Germany is about to be saved from the Jesuits and from economic ruin.' The fact that the Prussians went to the polls on 3 July, the day on which the historical battle of Königgrätz, which decided the war in Prussia's favour, took place, is one of German history's most extraordinary coincidences. News came through on the electric telegraph in the early afternoon of 3 July from the front, and caused a swing in the electorate against the Liberals in favour of the crown party. The realisation of how tenuous their hold on the electorate actually was persuaded a majority of Prussian Liberals to modify their attitude towards Bismarck.

Outcome of the Constitutional Conflict

In the course of 1867 a compromise over the Constitutional Conflict was reached between Bismarck and some of his opponents in the Landtag, who were joined by those new members of the house who came from the recently annexed states of Hanover, Schleswig-Holstein, Hesse-Kassel and Nassau. The former prime minister of Hanover, Rudolf von Bennigsen, became the leader of a new liberal party, the so-called National Liberal Party (see p. 150) which decided to accept Bismarck's compromise. Bismarck compromised in the so-called Indemnity Bill, by accepting that he was wrong in law while maintaining that he had been right in fact; events justified his stance. The Prussian Diet therefore voted by a majority of 230 to 75 in favour of Bismarck's Indemnity Bill. On the crux of the matter, budgetary control of the army, a compromise was reached, setting the amount of money available for military spending at a fixed ratio in proportion to the population. In 1874 this was renewed as a so-called *Septennat*, that is, it was automatically

Portrait of an officer.

granted for seven years. Later the seven year period was reduced to five years (*Quinquennat*). In fact parliament hereby lost its most vital power – annual budgetary control. Neither the discussions, the conflict, nor the compromise solution had dinted the certainty of the Prussian king and the military that parliament had no rights at all in military matters. The military command, vested in the king of Prussia and thereafter in the German emperor, implied, in the view of the commander-in-chief, William I, and the officer corps, an absolute divorce of the civil and military spheres. That this theory and constitutional practice were not always in harmony in the Empire seems an obvious enough conclusion to later generations. However, there was very much less resentment of the privileged status and political role of the army in Imperial Germany than might have been expected, particularly in view of the unpopularity of the Prussian army as an agent of reaction in 1848–49, and of its character as an obstacle to constitutional reform at a later date. Bismarck himself made an important contribution to the army's claim to be outside the control of parliament. He did this both in his successful defence of the crown's rights against those of an elected parliament, and also in the manner in which he institutionalised the special rights claimed by the Prussian king over the army in the constitution of the North German Confederation which was later adapted for the Empire. But more important for public opinion at large was the association in the mind of the nation of the special role of the army in bringing about the unification of Germany, or, as the emotive contemporary term had it, the *Nationwerdung*: the becoming of a nation. The brilliance of the Prussian army's performance in the 1864, 1866 and 1870 campaigns was seen as a

Proclamation of the Emperor in Versailles 18 January 1871. Painting by Anton von Werner. Note the absence of civilians; even Bismark is wearing uniform.

direct result of Roon's reforms, which had precipitated the Constitutional Conflict.

The Franco-Prussian War

The Franco-Prussian war not only confirmed many people's belief in the validity of the military position, it also, through the direct participation of so many Germans in what was made to seem a kind of crusade against a traditional and vile enemy, made people identify the army with the nation. Thus the outbreak of the Franco-Prussian war in 1870 took place against a very different background of events on the domestic front in Germany. Now, instead of domestic conflict, there was evidence of growing prosperity and a mood of public optimism, a sense of self-confidence, which was a new feature in Germans. At the same time popular chauvinism was widespread, reflected in speeches and gatherings and also in music and literature and painting. During the war the same popular sentiment found expression in song and anecdote very early on in the fighting, which, recalled in later years on innumerable social occasions, helped to substantiate the notion that the Prussian-led troops constituted the 'nation under arms'.

In the years between 1866 and 1870, an increasing number of influential persons in Europe had begun to be convinced that war between France and Prussia was well nigh inevitable. In Bonapartist circles in France there were many advocates of the idea of a preventive war to check Prussian expansion. Notable among these was the Duc de Gramont, whose appointment as foreign minister in May 1870 persuaded observers, not least in Prussia, that France was in fact contemplating an aggressive policy towards her eastern neighbour. News of the acceptance of the candidature to the Spanish throne by a member of the Hohenzollern family broke on Paris early in July. That the candidate, Anton Karl, was not a Prussian but a member of the south German Catholic branch of the ruling Prussian house, could make little difference to the impression the news must have on the French government. Four days later de Gramont declared that the French nation would do its best to prevent the candidature and indeed would administer a severe diplomatic humiliation to Prussia for her alleged attempt to upset the European balance. In warlike terms he called for '*révanche pour Sadowa*' 'the French name of Königgrätz). But the French proved no match for Bismarck's diplomatic sophistication, and he exploited the opportunity offered him both for foreign and domestic political

German unity. Contemporary caricature.

ends. For Bismarck, while affecting to be utterly uninterested in the political future of the south German states (who were not included in the 1867 North German Confederation), had long appreciated the logic of events in Germany since 1864 and was convinced that unity was but a matter of time. However, the form in which it was brought about, the mood in which it was created, would, he knew, be of vital importance for the future of both Germany and Prussia. Bismarck knew that Prussia could not afford to be seen to force or even to manipulate Germany into unity under her hegemonial leadership. For one thing, this would invite foreign, especially French intervention; for another, it would ensure a permanent sense of grievance, among the southern states, especially Bavaria. The mishandling of the situation by Napoleon's government in July 1870 enabled Bismarck to cast Prussia in the role of champion of 'German liberties' in the face of French aggression. Even after Karl Anton renounced his claim to the Spanish throne under pressure from France, it seemed as though Napoleon was determined to win 'compensation' in the form of German territory and that only united resistance on the German part could stop him. A tremendous surge of patriotic enthusiasm in favour of war with France swept across Germany. Even Th. Fontane, who referred to this mood on 19 July as *'unendlich viel Blech'* ('so much bombast') confessed himself deeply moved, as so many were, by the dignified appeal of the Prussian War Lord, the seventy-three-year old king William I of

Prussia, to all Germans to make common cause against the ancient foe.

On a superficial level it seemed that what Marx referred to in contemptuous terms as 'south German beer patriotism' lay behind the response of Bavaria, Baden, Württemberg and Hesse to the image of the Fatherland in danger. In fact the future course of south German history became virtually inevitable, once Prussia, having associated the south German states with her in the Customs Union, had expelled Austria from the Confederation. To resist the inevitable, wrote the Bavarian king, Ludwig II, to his brother in 1870, would be a political impossibility, since the people and the army would strenuously oppose such a decision. The four southern states had signed a secret military agreement with the North German Confederation in 1868 which provided for their defence by Prussia in case of attack: in such a case the south Germans would put their army contingents under Prussian command. Moreover by the summer of 1870 their representatives had close personal contacts with Prussians. They had been sitting in a national German Customs Parliament based in Berlin for two years, their task being to help legislate on commercial matters for north and south.

So when the French declared war on 19 July, some 260,000 Frenchmen found themselves facing an army of 450,000 men, led by an experienced and able command. The equipment of the Prussian-led German army, their exploitation of the railway system ('a nomadic invasion by train') as Fontane called it (5.8.1870), made a formidable war machine. By early August the Germans were on French territory, in a region which for years Prussian officers, disguised as amateur painters, had studied with just such a conflict in mind. Within little more than a month, after bitter fighting in Alsace and Lorraine, Napoleon was defeated at Sedan on 1 September 1870 and taken prisoner, on the following day he capitulated. The Napoleonic Second Empire collapsed, but the war went on, largely on account of the Prussian insistence on the cession of Alsace-Lorraine as a preliminary to peace. Less than six months later another, the German, Second Empire was proclaimed in the hall of mirrors at Versailles. On 18 January 1871 King William I of Prussia was proclaimed German Kaiser and ten days later an armistice was signed by the French and Prussian commands.

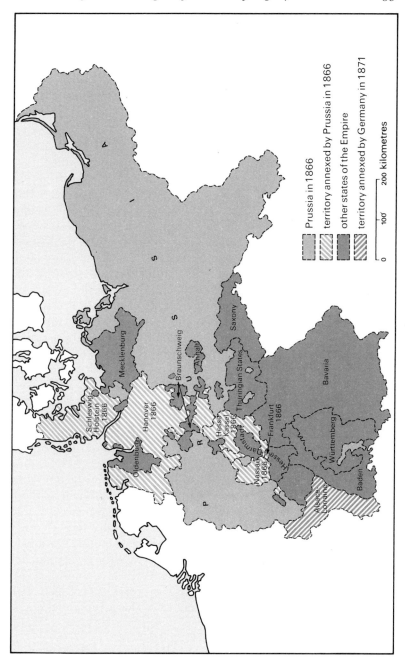

The Evolution of Bismarck's Germany

The South German states

Protracted negotiations had been going on since September 1870 between Bismarck and the south German representatives.* Baden, ruled by the Prussian king's cousin (and son-in-law) was the first to accede to the Federation, Württemberg, 'crowned Switzerland', as it was called, on account of its democratic traditions, followed suit, as did Hesse. Bavaria proved difficult, but Bismarck's well-tried blend of enticement and threat (expulsion from the Customs Union) proved successful yet again.

Low taxes, little industry or militarism and, on the whole, a liberal administration, made life in southern Germany an agreeable affair. Many people were apprehensive at the possibility of Prussian domination in the new Germany, but the bourgeoisie believed firmly in the necessity of a united nation, and the visible successes of German arms provided a subtle form of persuasion. Bismarck conceded certain regalian rights to a number of the rulers of the southern states on agreeing to enter the Empire, as he did to the king of Saxony. But the subordination of south Germany to Prussia was an intrinsic feature of the new state, and one which individual Bavarians, and less frequently citizens of the other southern states, were made painfully aware of in future decades. Yet in general Germany south of the Main continued its somewhat provincial existence for many years to come, not least because the lack of industrial centres, the older commercial traditions and fairly stable rural conditions meant that society was much less mobile than was the case in the north. However, south Germans were undoubtedly affected by the national chauvinism of the Empire. Hans Thoma, the popular Bavarian painter (1839–1924), recalled the quality of this in his memoirs. With wry humour he described the reaction of the inhabitants of the small town of Prien in southern Bavaria to the news that the imperial chancellor (Bismarck) would be passing through by train. While carefully insisting on their disdain and even dislike for Prussia, they flocked enthusiastically to the station at the appointed hour to catch sight of the great man. But in many ways south Germans preserved a certain critical detachment from the main sources of tension in the new Reich, such as militarism, the neo-feudal character of the aristocracy, Social Democracy etc.

---

* That part of Hesse-Darmstadt, whose territory lay north of the Main, had already been incorporated into the North German Confederation in October 1866.

Unification

For Germany's internal history the Franco-Prussian war played the supremely important role of bringing about the '*kleindeutsch*' unification of Germany, that is, Germany without Austria. However the foreign political consequences were even more considerable. The defeat of France, which brought to Germany Alsace and parts of Lorraine along with a war indemnity of five milliards in gold francs, changed the balance of power in Europe. For centuries, France's rulers had been concerned to keep Germany disunited and had not hesitated to invade and despoil her territory more than a dozen times in pursuit of this aim. The permanent power vacuum in Central Europe, which had been the source of endemic conflict throughout the preceding three centuries, was filled in 1871. 41 million Germans, whose economy was booming, who were united in a sense of common achievement and destiny, formed one of the great powers alongside England with 32 millions. The current political witticism, coined by a member of the British House of Commons, that Europe in 1870 had lost a mistress and gained a master, suggests that contemporaries were well aware of the significance of the events they were witnessing.

The entry of the victorious troops into Berlin in June 1871 (one of the first snapshots of such a public event).

It is hard for us today to have sympathetic insight into the 1871 situation. As a result of the attempt to explore the historical origins of the Third Reich, which are seen to lie in the nineteenth century, post-war German, British and American historians have caused us to focus our attention almost exclusively on the nationalist passions and propaganda which the victory over France and the long awaited unification created. However in the opinion of most European governments and most nations of the time, except the French, the solution of the German question offered by the founding of the Second Empire seemed one of the more positive achievements of the nineteenth century, a genuine contribution to the overall stability of Europe. And in international relations Bismarck did his best in the years that followed to reassure them that this was indeed the case.

8
The State, the Parties and the Army after 1871

Bismarck's Germany

The unification of Germany in 1871 did not bring with it centralisation of government and administration in Berlin, although the general trend in subsequent decades was indeed towards increasing concentration of power in Prussia, while at the same time the influence of Prussian tradition and habits of mind gradually pervaded all levels of German society. German unification was in fact a compromise with German particularism, especially with the traditional rights of the princes. Twenty-five states existed within the Empire. These were made up of four kingdoms, Prussia, Bavaria, Saxony and Württemberg, six grand duchies and five duchies, seven miniscule principalities, the largest of which, Lippe, had an area of merely 469 square miles and only 111,135 inhabitants, three free cities, Hamburg, Bremen and Lübeck, and the so-called Imperial Territory of Alsace-Lorraine.

The king of Bavaria, Ludwig II, had been most reluctant to accept the Prussian king as sovereign head of state. After tenacious negotiations, which included the effective threat to expel Bavaria from the Customs Union, he accepted William as 'German Emperor', that is, *primus inter pares* in a confederation of territorial sovereigns. In return Ludwig retained certain sovereign rights over the Bavarian army in peacetime, and, in common with Württemberg, control of the state postal system. All these states, with the exception of Alsace-Lorraine and the two Mecklenburgs (M.-Strelitz and M.-Schwerin), had their own representative assemblies, although the composition of the houses differed widely. In south Germany with its more democratic traditions virtually all citizens who were direct taxpayers were represented in these

Germany's population

States of the Empire	Area English Sq. m.	1871	1875	1900	1905	Density per Sq. m. (1905)
Kingdoms:						
Prussia	134,616	24,691,433	25,742,404	34,472,509	37,293,324	277.3
Bavaria	29,292	4,863,450	5,022,390	6,176,057	6,524,372	222.7
Saxony	5,789	2,556,244	2,760,586	4,202,216	4,508,601	778.8
Württemberg	7,534	1,818,539	1,881,505	2,169,480	2,302,179	305.5
Grand-Duchies:						
Baden	5,823	1,461,562	1,507,179	1,867,944	2,010,728	345.3
Hesse	2,966	852,894	884,218	1,119,893	1,209,175	407.6
Mecklenburg-Schwerin	5,068	557,897	553,785	607,770	625,045	123.3
Saxe-Weimar	1,397	286,183	292,933	362,873	388,095	277.8
Mecklenburg-Strelitz	1,131	96,982	95,673	102,602	103,451	91.5
Oldenburg	2,482	314,459	319,314	399,180	438,856	176.8
Duchies:						
Brunswick	1,418	311,764	327,493	464,333	485,958	342.5
Saxe-Meiningen	953	187,957	194,494	250,731	268,916	282.2
Saxe-Altenburg	511	142,122	145,844	194,914	206,508	404.1
Saxe-Coburg-Gotha	764	174,339	182,599	229,550	242,432	317.3
Anhalt	888	203,437	213,565	316,085	328,029	369.4
Principalities:						
Schwarzburg-Sondershausen	333	75,523	76,676	80,898	85,152	255.7
Schwarzburg-Rudolstadt	363	67,191	67,480	93,059	96,835	266.7
Waldeck	433	56,224	54,743	57,918	59,127	136.5
Reuss-Greiz	122	45,094	46,985	68,396	70,603	578.7
Reuss-Schleiz	319	89,032	92,375	139,210	144,584	453.2
Schaumburg-Lippe	131	32,059	33,133	43,132	44,992	343.4
Lippe	469	111,135	112,452	138,952	145,577	310.4
Free Cities:						
Lübeck	115	52,158	56,912	96,775	105,857	920.5
Bremen	99	122,402	142,200	224,882	263,440	2661.0
Hamburg	160	338,974	388,618	768,349	874,878	5467.9
Imperial Territory:						
Alsace-Lorraine	5,604	1,549,738	1,531,804	1,719,470	1,814,564	323.8
German Empire	208,780	41,058,792	42,727,360	56,367,178	60,641,278	290.4

assemblies. In Prussia a restricted franchise, the three-class franchise introduced in 1849, remained unmodified until 1918. A similar franchise was introduced into Saxony in 1896 in place of a more liberal one in an attempt to check the progress of the Social Democrats in that state. The three-class system allowed representation according to the amount of tax paid, but the rigging of the electoral districts in favour of the rural areas ensured the dominance of a minority group – namely the Conservatives. The Mecklenburg duchies remained politically and socially in a pre-1789 feudal world; nowhere were peasants more oppressed. Up to the end of the Empire, the local nobility (*Ritterschaft*) sedulously and effectively repressed all efforts of liberals and of the dukes themselves to modify the state assembly, which was composed of delegates of the rural nobility and the few towns. In Germany as a whole the state governments and assemblies continued to be responsible for matters such as direct taxation, education, transport etc.

The Reichstag

The actual government of the Empire lay in the hands of the emperor, assisted by the fifty-eight members of the *Bundesrat* or Federal Council, representing the governments of the twenty-five states, and the imperial chancellor. The emperor, together with the upper house of *Bundesrat* and the *Reichstag* or Imperial Diet, exercised legislative power. In 1871 the Reichstag had 397 members elected for a five year term, on the basis of universal male suffrage (for those aged twenty-five and over). Ostensibly a concession to democratic opinion, universal suffrage was in fact severely curtailed in practice. Payment of members was expressly forbidden by Bismarck, to ensure the election of men of substance and ideally of conservative politics. Payment was belatedly conceded in 1906. Furthermore he hoped that the election of men such as landowners, industrialists and merchants, who had their own livelihood to attend to, would make for short sessions and would prevent the emergence of professional politicians. Ideally he would have liked the Reichstag to meet in some provincial town, far from Berlin and thus prevent journalists from attending sessions and reporting them regularly. Secret ballots were also successfully opposed by Bismarck and others in order to maintain the authority of landowners and employers over their dependents in this, as in other matters. Moreover, the actual powers of the Reichstag were restricted in such a manner as to question the right of the German Empire to be called a genuine constitutional state. No political party could aspire to form the government of the Empire, nor could parliaments appoint or dismiss the imperial chancellor. Contemporaries used the word *Reichsleitung* (Reich leadership) rather than the normal German word for government, *Regierung*, thus emphasising features of the anomalous character of the German set-up. No imperial ministers were responsible to the Reichstag, because apart from the chancellor there were no imperial ministers, but only permanent secretaries (*Staatssekretäre*) of the relevant government departments: in other words, civil servants. True, there were Prussian ministers of foreign affairs, of war etc., testifying to the factual predominance of Prussia in the Empire, but either their powers, as in the case of the war minister, were curtailed, or their authority by-passed by the Crown's special powers in military matters, or, as in the case of the foreign minister, the office was actually combined with that of imperial chancellor by Bismarck.

The actual constitution of the Second Empire was that of the North German Confederation (1867–71), adapted to serve the unified state. It was clearly an ad hoc arrangement, designed by Bismarck, despite those measures reflecting the economic liberal climate of the late 1860s, to perpetuate the traditional rights of the crown and the special powers of the military and bureaucracy. Only a few years after the founding of the Empire, Bismarck determined to arrest the growth of liberal institutions in the state. Senior civil servants of liberal convictions were eased out of office – Rudolf Delbrück, responsible for Prussia's extremely successful economic policy in the 1850s and 60s, who resigned in 1876, was a case in point; liberal junior civil servants were passed over for promotion. The anti-Socialist law of 1878, protective tariffs introduced in 1879 to bolster up the position of feudal landowners in the eastern provinces, a so-called 'civil service reform' by the new arch-conservative Prussian minister of the interior, von Puttkamer, introduced in 1878, were all part of a wider programme to ensure the continued dominance of the conservative establishment. In 1890, the year of his fall, Bismarck was engaged in a scheme designed to abolish universal suffrage, which had demonstrably failed to perform the function envisaged by the Iron Chancellor. He and others even envisaged using repressive measures to provoke civil disturbances, which would be countered by a coup d'état. The reorientation of Bismarck's domestic policy in 1878–79 after less than a decade of the founding of the Empire, the subsequent concentration of real power in the hands of individuals and elitist

The Emperor William I reviewing the troops. Engraving of a drawing by
E. Hosang.
'Good morning, grenadiers.' 'Good morning, Your Majesty.' (1881)

groups, is frequently referred to by modern German historians as *die innere Reichsgründung* (internal foundation of the Empire). As a formative influence on the domestic policies of German governments between 1878 and 1918, it is indeed a crucial date.

Parliament and the parties

It is therefore understandable that parliament, although attracting much interest and comment in the daily press and satirical journals between 1871 and 1918, could not be considered the hub of political life or the centre of the decision-making process, nor, apart from the Socialist Bebel or the colourful leader of the Progressives, Eugen Richter, or the dwarf-like figure of the Centre leader, Windhorst, did it attract the kind of gifted and charismatic individuals likely to provide the nation with future leaders. However, the development and changing fortunes of political parties in Bismarck's administration, and in the Germany he designed for his successors, clearly reflect structural changes taking place in the political and social life of the country. The composition of bourgeois party leadership changed under the Empire from being primarily local notables, who determined both party policy and organisation, to the spokesmen of political and economic pressure groups. Indicative of the evolution of political attitudes of the bourgeoisie was the decline of liberalism as a political creed; the amoeba-like behaviour of the Liberal parties, fragmenting, coalescing under a new name, to split yet again, was a seemingly inexorable accompaniment of this process. The Conservative parties also witnessed a decline in electoral support from the late 1880s onwards, although the electoral system ensured that their percentage of seats at national (*Reichstag*) and state (*Landtag*) level remained generally well in the excess of their percentage of the vote. Splinter parties, such as the Antisemites, which appeared under a variety of names, including Christian Socialist, benefited to some extent from this situation – the Antisemites won 4% of the Reichstag seats in 1893 and again in 1907. However the chief beneficiary of changes in the voting patterns was the Socialist Party. From a mere 3.2% of votes in 1871 and 0.5% of seats in the Reichstag, the Socialist party increased its share to 23.3% of votes and 11.1% of seats in 1893 and 38.8% and 27.7% in 1912. A steady percentage of both votes and seats continued to be held by the ethnic and other minority groups throughout the Empire. Their share ranged from 4% of votes and seats for the Poles to about 0.5% for the Danes (North Schleswig).

The Alsace-Lothringians' share declined from about 4% in 1874 to approximately 2% in the three elections between 1903 and 1912.

Origins of political parties

It is important to remember when studying the anomalous character of the German state after 1871, that, when her political parties were formed, they grew up alongside a bureaucratic and military establishment, whose origins lay in the former absolutist states of the late seventeenth and eighteenth centuries. In south Germany, which had had some form of constitutional government since the early nineteenth century, political groups, roughly analogous to the later party divisions, were already in existence in the pre-March era. In the north, political parties were not constituted until the 1860s, although the 1848 revolution had seen the growth of liberal, democratic, Catholic, labour and conservative groups in the Frankfurt Parliament and other assemblies. Such groups disintegrated immediately after the suppression of the revolution and in the reactionary climate of the 1850s no opportunity existed for party political activity. By contrast, the climate of the early 1860s was buoyant, the political situation at home and abroad fluid. To contemporaries, the age seemed to be rich in potential, the opportunity seemed to be at hand in which public-spirited men would have the chance to steer German politics in a new direction. The optimism engendered by an expanding economy, by the fluidity of the international situation, especially in countries contiguous to Germany, together with the known liberal sympathies of the new Prussian crown prince, (later Frederick III), born in 1831, seemed to point in the direction of a new Germany. The new Germany would, it was confidently believed, resemble a western European constitutional state, rather than the semi-absolutist one which she had long been.

All over Germany organisations in the late 1850s and 1860s had been formed with the specific aim of winning the support of public opinion, and indeed the participation of the general public, in the goals of national unification, genuine constitutional government and liberal economic policies. Some of these organisations, such as the liberal *Nationalverein*, which was founded in 1859 under the patronage of Duke Ernst II of Saxe-Coburg-Gotha, brother of the English prince consort, Albert, and which included prominent citizens such as the historian Mommsen and the engineer Werner Siemens, or the conservative Prussian *Volksverein* (1861), were the

forerunners of national political parties. The early 1860s also saw
the meteor-like career of the Silesian lawyer, Ferdinand Lassalle,
as champion of the working classes. In 1863 he founded the first
German Labour Party which had its basis of support in the cities of
Berlin, Frankfurt and the Rhineland. The Constitutional Conflict
in Prussia (1862–67), which was essentially a power struggle
between the feudal Hohenzollern monarchy and parliament over
budgetary control of the army, aroused a vigorous response among
bourgeois circles in Germany generally. At the same time petty
bourgeois democratic organisations, centred principally on
Karlsruhe, Hamburg, Frankfurt and Coburg, sought to involve the
broad spectrum of the middle classes in political decisions, and
included small-town tradesmen, farmers and professional men.
Mass public meetings in the south and central Germany in the
spring of 1866 were called in protest against Prussia's aggressive
policies over Schleswig-Holstein, and drew astonishingly large
crowds. The vigour with which political issues were discussed in
public and in the journals during these years, suggested that the
traditional character of German politics was changing radically. In
fact the numbers of the politically active or even politically
conscious in the 1860s were never very high. The *Nationalverein*, the
largest pressure group, never exceeded 25,000 members, and
Lassalle's working class movement not much more than 1,000. Even
the newspapers and journals with a reputation of genuine
popularity, rarely had a circulation of more than about 5,000. The
decisions taken on the battle-field of the Austro-Prussian war of
1866, determined that the character of German political parties
would be that of associations of bourgeois and upper class notables,
rather than mass political parties.

The Liberal parties

The first modern political party in Germany was the Progressive
Party (*Fortschrittspartei*), which formed a distinctive group among
the liberal members of the Prussian lower house at the height of the
Constitutional Conflict, and which led the opposition to Bismarck.
In 1867, after the formation of the North German Confederation,
Bismarck offered a compromise solution to the Conflict, and
brought a split in the party. Many joined the new National Liberal
party, formed from those Prussian liberals who were prepared to
accept Bismarck's solution and from representatives of the recently

annexed principalities, such as Hanover or Electoral Hesse, who had not been involved in the conflict. For the next decade the National Liberals under their leader, the former Hanoverian prime minister, Rudolf von Bennigsen, became something of a government party in Germany, collaborating with the chancellor on an impressive body of liberal legislation, which included emancipation of the Jews, standardisation of the currency, weights and measures etc. However, the National Liberals were not successful in gaining the all-important concession of ministerial responsibility to parliament, nor budgetary control of military expenditure, which in fact accounted for something like 90% of the imperial budget. At the height of their electoral success, the National Liberals won under 30% of the votes, while the Progressives rarely captured more than 20%. The incisive leaders of the latter party, Eugen Richter and Eduard Lasker, recognised very clearly the implication of Bismarck's refusal to concede ministerial responsibility, and it was thanks to their strenuous and dexterous opposition that a few important concessions were wrested from the chancellor.

Despite the diverging roles played by the two parties in parliament, both the National liberals and the Progressives, as well as the later splinter-groups in the Liberal movement, regarded themselves as part of the 'Liberal Political Party', and frequently campaigned for each other's candidates in elections. A party apparatus was not developed by the Liberals until very much later. In fact in the 1870s and even in the 1880s the party, apart from parliamentary representatives, virtually disappeared between the elections. The process of selecting candidates or even checking their views, was, to say the least of it, haphazard. Indeed it was particularly characteristic of. the liberal party or parties, that the local member largely determined the political line taken. Towards the end of Bismarck's administration, and particularly from the 1890s onwards, the dynamics of a modern industrial society began to have its impact on the political parties, which then developed from collections of notables to pressure groups representing sectional interests. The dividing line between the right and left wings of the liberal movement, between National Liberals and Progressives, grew more and more apparent, both to members and to their supporters. For all intents and purposes the National Liberals, who increased their share of the vote in the 1890s, were by that time a conservative political party, drawing their support from those engaged in the consumer industries, from north German merchants and from large farmers in central Germany.

The Conservatives

At no time between 1871 and 1900, or even 1914, did the Conservative parties in the German Reichstag enjoy a support of the electorate comparable to that given to the Liberals. In 1871 they gained 23% of the vote, in 1881 23.7%, in 1893 19.2% and in 1912 a mere 12.2%. However, this is less an indication of their ineffectiveness as a factor in the political life of the nation, than the lack of effectiveness of the Reichstag. The powers of the Reichstag were indeed limited. Many of the crucial issues of domestic policy continued to lie within the competence of state governments and assemblies. In Prussia, which after 1871 comprised three-fifths of the population in the area of the Second Empire, the Landtag came to be increasingly dominated by the Conservative interest. In the Reichstag there were three, later two, Conservative political parties. The *Reichspartei*, generally known as the Free Conservatives in Prussia, led by Wilhelm von Kardorff, who founded the Organisation of German Industrialists in 1876, and representing mainly heavy industry, drew support from Lower Silesia, Berlin and the Rhineland. While the Conservative Party represented the landowning interest in the eastern provinces of Prussia and in Mecklenburg, a third Conservative faction, a nationalist group, disappeared after 1874. The Conservatives relied even less than the Liberals on a party apparatus. Instead, the local nobility and the (Protestant) clergy brought pressure to bear, where necessary, on tenant farmers and workers to vote as their masters wished. The attitude of most German Conservatives could be interpreted with some over-simplification thus: constitutions, elections and parliament were seen by the majority of the great landowners and magnates as a necessary evil of modern society. They regarded it as part of their responsibility to future generations to ensure the preservation of their culture, by seeing that their dependents voted for the Conservative party. The commitment of these people to what they chose to identify as 'the Prussian tradition'; the preservation of a social structure and hierarchy, of habits of mind and a kind of life which was totally that of a pre-industrial society, was absolute. It was invariably presented in moral terms. Deviation from the pattern was regarded as an affront. Hence the tremendous moral outrage in Conservative circles when a member of one's family or connections or one's dependents, voted for one of the Liberal parties, or worse still, gave their support to the Socialists. The decision by the local teacher whose appointment depended on local patronage, or a rural labourer, to vote for the Democratic, Liberal or Socialist candidate was tantamount to inviting dismissal from employment and home.

The Centre

The third major party in German parliamentary life was something of an anomaly among western parliamentary institutions. This was the Centre Party, destined to play a prominent role in parliamentary politics for the next three generations: it was a purely confessional party. It emerged as a movement in the late 1860s, formed and led by Catholic noblemen from the Rhineland and Silesia, and was founded as a party in the year 1870. It represented both the propertied and the professional classes, and the smallholders of south and west Germany, as well as the Catholic farmers and the urban working classes of the western regions. The Centre party played a supremely important role in developing political awareness among German Catholics in a period in their country's history which was largely unfavourable to them as a community. Prussia's defeat of Austria, who had been a natural protector of the Catholic interest since the days of the Holy Roman Empire, seemed to imply a threat to their position, although Prussia treated its Catholic minority, some 40%, with reasonable fairness. But particularly during the early years of the Second Empire, when German nationalism was presented as a compound of Prussian military achievements, Protestant fervour and Liberal philosophy, none of which they could identify themselves with, German Catholics felt isolated and defensive. Moreover, the *Kulturkampf* (1872–88), which was an attempt on the part of a Liberal secularised state to break the control of the Catholic Church over marriage and education of children, encouraged a siege mentality among them. Yet at the same time it greatly increased the homogeneity of the Catholic community, despite the very different character of its members' social and regional background. Despite the hierarchical organisation of the *Zentrum* (from 1911 the *Deutsche Zentrumspartei*) under its traditional leaders, despite the rigid class barriers which kept intelligent and critical workers out of the leadership, it still retained the support of the Catholic community all over Germany, in the forty years or more after its foundation. In common with the Liberal and Conservative parties, the Centre party was slow to develop a modern party apparatus. However, in the Catholic press, in the annual *Katholikentag*, or gathering of German Catholics (from 1868 onwards), and in the various Catholic associations formed for charitable or social purposes, it possessed effective agencies for promoting Catholic awareness among constituents and directing their support to the party. Most Centre party candidates were expected to have prior experience in these associations before presenting themselves for selection. The most prominent of these was the *Volksverein für das katholische Deutschland*. This was founded in 1890 and was particularly important for the way in which it took over mass agitation and retained the loyalty of the Catholic urban vote, at a time when the policies of the leadership favoured the agrarian interest at the expense of industrial workers.

In the loyalty of its supporters to the party and its policies, in the sense of community within the wider organisation of state and nation, and in the defensive mentality which to a certain extent was thrust on it by the ethics of the Second Empire, the Centre party undoubtedly bore a resemblance to the German Social Democratic party. But in most other aspects of its history the Centre party was distinct from anything else in the Second Empire. Indeed one could go so far as to suggest that this remarkable party was a unique institution of German political life.

The Socialists

Even more striking was the rapid rise and development of the German Socialist Workers Party into being the largest and best organised labour party in Europe. The movement's beginnings lay in the 1840s, and it emerged as a national party in the 1860s; by 1913 the German Socialist party had almost 1,000,000 members, employing fifty regional and one hundred district secretaries, and owning more than ninety daily papers and sixty-two printing presses. The cohesion and unity of the party, sustained through many decades and many vicissitudes, owed a very great deal to the dedication and the ability of its leaders, among whom the most notable was August Bebel (1840–1913), who represented it for forty-two years in the Reichstag. Other important factors, which helped to create a sense of proletarian consciousness among workers of widely differing skills and trades, were the rapid industrialisation in the last decades of the nineteenth century and the response of both the authorities and society in general to the emergence of a dynamic Socialist movement.

It is true that many regions of Germany and many areas of

working class life remained immune to the appeal of Social Democracy. The largest area of potential support was the rural labour force, some 60% of the population in 1871 and still around 30% in 1913. For a variety of reasons, the party made few converts here. The most important of these were the difficulty of direct propaganda in the still feudal social structure of many agrarian regions, and the lack of interest envinced by doctrinaire Marxist Socialists in what Marx had chosen to regard as a dying race. Other areas where support was minimal included many of the Rhenish and Westphalian industrial towns. Here young priests worked to provide the Catholic working class with their own organisations and were surprisingly successful in retaining the loyalty of their people. As early as 1877, the Centre party's first labourer deputy, a turner, was elected to the Reichstag to represent Essen. Christian trade unions and the so-called Hirsch-Dunkersche or Liberal unions were set up as part of an effort to offer workers an alternative to Socialism; by the end of the century they could still command the loyalty of nearly one sixth of all organised workers.

But on any reckoning, and especially given the immense variety of German society and her economy, and the massive changes which occurred in the size, distribution and occupation of her working class population, the achievements of the German Socialist Party were truly remarkable.

i) *Origins*

Recent scholars have stressed the links between the organisations of working men which emerged both immediately before and during the 1848–49 Revolution and the Socialist parties of the 1860s. One of the most important features of the second wave of revolution in the autumn of 1848 was the realisation among workers' leaders that their interests were at variance with, or indeed opposed to those of bourgeois liberals. The repressive policies of German state governments in the 1850s – the Federal Diet ordered them to proscribe workers movements in 1854 – led to the disappearance of all but educational associations of working men in Germany. But the experience of 1848, and the issues which had animated the discussions of revolutionaries in Germany, helped to provide the stimulus to the founding of political parties to represent the urban working classes in the more liberal climate of the 1860s.

The first German Socialist party, the *Allgemeiner Arbeiterverein*, or General Workers Association, was founded at Leipzig in May 1863 in the presence of delegates from eleven German towns: Leipzig and

Dresden in Saxony, the free cities of Hamburg and Frankfurt,*
from Hanover and Homburg, and five Rhenish towns including
Cologne and Düsseldorf. This was the first explicitly national
workers party, and the first to renounce any association with
bourgeois liberalism. Its founder, Ferdinand Lassalle from Breslau
believed that the state should and could take over the role of
protecting its workers against the egoism of the bourgeoisie. It was a
view which made sense to the skilled or semi-skilled craftsmen, who
for many years to come would provide the backbone of the German
labour movement. The interests of the left-wing liberals and the
workers associations, which had been similar or seemed even
identical in the 1848 revolution, began to diverge as industrialisation gathered momentum in the following decade (i.e.
1863–73). The phrase *unzeitgemässe Arbeiterbewegung* ('ill-timed
labour movement') became current in Progressive party circles in
the 1860s, and was offensive and revealing of the Liberals' determination to use their patronage of working class associations for
their own political advantage.

However, Lassalle's party, for all the publicity it attracted both
then and later, was anything but a mass organisation; by 1864, the
year of Lassalle's death in a duel, it numbered not much more than a
thousand members. Five years later, at Eisenach in Saxony, a rival
organisation was founded, the Social-Democratic Workers Party. Its
authors were the journalist and veteran of 1848, Wilhelm
Liebknecht, and August Bebel, a master turner and son of a
Prussian NCO. The new party was democratic and opposed to
Prussian militarism and nationalism. The amalgamation of the two
groups was delayed by the opposition of Bebel and Liebknecht to
the Franco- Prussian war, which lost them electoral support and
earned them prison sentences of nearly two years. At Gotha in 1875
unity was finally achieved under the new name of Socialist Workers
Party of Germany. The party fought in the 1877 election and
attracted nearly 10% of the votes but won only twelve seats. Not
least among the factors contributing to its success was the violent
suppression of strikes and the impact of the depression of the 1870s
on industrial workers.

ii) *Anti-Socialist Law*
The growth of the Socialist vote and the implications of universal
suffrage for its future progress, as well as the need for a national

---

* The free city of Frankfurt was annexed by Prussia after the Austro-Prussian War.

scapegoat in the new reactionary orientation of his domestic policy, persuaded Bismarck to move into the attack. Exploiting the coincidence of two assassination attempts on the emperor's life in 1878, he introduced the Anti-Socialist Bill into the Reichstag. The measure was eventually passed by the Conservatives and the Centre, and gained the support of the majority of the National Liberal party. The Socialist party as such was not prohibited but all working class associations were proscribed and meetings forbidden. All but two of the fifty-one party papers were suppressed. This not only hampered the activity of the movement: it constituted serious hardship for the many who earned their livelihood in journalism and hit at vital sources of party funds. (Since members of the Reichstag were not paid, Socialist deputies were especially dependent on such funds.) The police, above all in north Germany, responded with alacrity to the authorities' demand for vigilance against known or suspected Socialists. In the twelve years in which the measure was in force, some 900 labour leaders were expelled from their place of domicile by the police, and some 1500 served prison sentences. The Socialists showed impressive energy in dealing with the emergency. The leading Socialist paper, the '*Sozialdemokrat*', was printed in Zurich and smuggled in by Julius Mottek, 'the Red Postmaster'; families of imprisoned or expelled members were helped; congresses were held abroad in Switzerland and Denmark, despite the efforts of the authorities to prevent the passage of Socialist leaders. Certainly, the *Kampfzeit* or period of struggle, as it came to be called, fostered a sense of solidarity and awakened the political consciousness of working men. The party extended its area of support from Saxony and Berlin into the Rhineland and south Germany in these years. By 1890 it commanded just under 20% of the vote. But the years of persecution also helped to isolate the party from the state, and to aggravate relations between working men generally and the police, the military and the lower ranks of officialdom.

Social welfare legislation

The palliative offered to the German working classes by Bismarck in the 1880s in the form of a programme of social legislation did not succeed, as he intended it should, in weaning workers away from Socialism. However it represents an important pioneering effort in the context of the time, when few state governments in Europe or elsewhere felt called upon to involve themselves in the physical welfare of the nation's workers. In 1883 sickness insurance was introduced, the cost being borne equally by employers and employees. Bismarck had wished the workers to contribute nothing in order that, as he put it in a speech to the Reichstag some years later, 'the common man might learn to regard the Empire as a benevolent institution' (18.5.89). In 1884 accident benefit was introduced, in 1889 old-age insurance and invalid benefit followed. The scheme was extended in subsequent years and by 1900 some five and a half million German workers were insured, and five milliard marks had been paid out in benefits to them (in 1910 the sum was ten milliards). Although Bismarck failed to win the workers away from their allegiance to the Social Democratic Party, his policy did create a split in its ranks between the former supporters of Lassalle on the one hand and the Marxists on the other. However, by 1887 Bebel succeeded in restoring the ideological unity of the party on a Marxist basis.

The parties and the state

In contrast with the fate of the Socialists, the relations between government and the majority of members of the bourgeois parties of the opposition, the Liberals and the Centre, became more harmonious at the end of, or immediately after, Bismarck's administration. In the late 1880s the *Kulturkampf* or conflict between the state and the Catholic church in Prussia was at last laid to rest. (With fine tact Pope Leo XIII, (1878–1903), commissioned the well known painter, Franz Lenbach, to paint Bismarck's portrait.) Accordingly, the natural conservatism of Catholic voters was shown in their support for a rapprochement between the Centre party and the state in Germany. At the same time, the right wing of the National Liberal party drew closer to the Conservative interest; when in 1893 the powerful agrarian interest in Prussia formed its own pressure group (*Bund der Landwirte*), many National Liberal deputies and their constituents, particularly among large and medium farmers in Hesse and in Hanover, gave it their active support. In the 1890s and early 1900s, turbulent years in German domestic politics, the dynamic developments of modern industrial society began to have an impact on all her bourgeois parties, changing them from so-called *Honoratiorenparteien*, to political pressure groups, whose leaders relied on extra-parliamentary pressures to defend what were primarily economic interests. On specific issues the Centre party leaders associated themselves with the democratic wing of the Left Liberal party (formerly the Progressives, now known as the *Freisinnige Vereinigung*) and the Socialists against the government. In general however, in the years before 1914, the pressure was strong on dissident elements to support the establishment in face of what seemed an international situation fraught with peril for Germany, and, as has been said, even the Socialists proved their ability in local administration and in the state parliaments of the southern German states. But in the Reichstag, and in the Prussian and Saxon assemblies, the prevailing suspicion of opposition, which was one of Bismarck's legacies, and the well-known rigging of the electoral system in favour of the ruling classes, made it extremely difficult for chancellor and cabinet after Bismarck's fall, and even given good will, to create a cohesive and consistent basis of government support among the parliamentary parties.

The chancellor Bismarck at the laying of the foundation stone for the new Reichstag, 1884. (Contemporary engraving.) Note Bismarck's dress.

The army and the state

The nineteen years of Bismarck's administration witnessed no change in the special position enjoyed by the military in the German Empire; if anything the reverse was the case. The constitution laid down the peacetime strength of the German army as a fixed proportion of the population, namely 1%. Similarly the amount of money per soldier was fixed at an annual 225 marks payable from the imperial or Reich budget. There was no limit set on the duration of this arrangement known, suitably enough, as the 'Iron Budget'. As far as the Prussian king, William I, now German emperor, was concerned, parliament had no rights over the army and he was very reluctant even to concede the rubber-stamping of the military budget by the Reichstag, seeing in this an infringement of his royal prerogative. That the Iron Budget made nonsense of the budgetary rights of the legislature is clearly evident when one considers that even in peace-time almost all the revenue of the North German Confederation (1867–71), under which this arrangement was first introduced, was spent on defence: in 1868 some 88.8% went to the army and 10.7% to the navy.

In the event the semi-absolute powers of the Hohenzollern ruler in military matters were even greater under the Empire than they had been in Prussia prior to 1867. William I's powers as commander-in-chief of the imperial army were derived not from the fact that he was German emperor, but were exercised by him in his capacity as king of Prussia. Yet the constitution extended all Prussian military laws, ordinances and instructions to apply to the contingents of other member states. There was no imperial minister of defence, only a Prussian minister of war. As time passed even the Prussian minister's powers were curtailed by the existence of the military cabinet, and by the emperor's belief that the minister of war was much too deferential to parliament. The chief source of influence of the military cabinet was its closeness to the monarch; the personality of its head was thus of crucial importance since he, with his colleagues, advised the commander-in-chief on all matters relating to army organisation. The emperor himself exercised supreme authority over the imperial army with regard to armaments, command structure, organisation and training. At the same time the general staff of the army, which in the early years of the empire was headed by Helmut von Moltke, hero of the wars of unification, gradually emancipated itself from the control of the

Prussian war ministry and as such from control by the civil authority.

The special position of the army in the state could be accepted, if reluctantly, by parliamentarians of liberal persuasion after 1871 because of the aura attached to it after the recent successes in war. True, the Progressives voted solidly against the military clauses of the constitution in the debates of 1866–67 and their leader, Eugen Richter, who was probably the best-informed parliamentarian on military matters, proved a doughty opponent of the military establishment in subsequent decades. However, the strength of the Progressives had declined steadily after the heady days of the Constitutional Conflict; members of other Liberal groups hesitated to be seen to be 'anti-national' by criticising the armed forces. In the 1880s and 1890s the hostility of the Social Democrats to the special status of the army in the state made it impolitic for other, more 'respectable' parties to associate themselves with them.

Undoubtedly the Prussian army enjoyed unprecedented popularity in the years following unification. Family magazine stories and popular novels presented a stereotype brave, handsome and noble officer for the delectation of the reading public. Military parades continued to play a role in the social life of people long after the much reproduced victory parades of 1871 had passed into myth. The delights of the military band, the superior regard enjoyed by the uniform over civilian dress, became part of the lifestyle of the Second Empire. German chancellors wore military uniform in parliament, Bismarck that of a Prussian general. When Bethmann-Hollweg first became chancellor in 1909 he held the rank of major and was therefore forced to sit below generals and colonels at court banquets. When the news reached him of his promotion to general, he showed himself moved and delighted.

Military service consisted of three years for every man fit to serve – apart from those who had passed the Abitur or school leaving examination or spent an approved number of years at secondary school, and who might serve as volunteers for one year. Military service was followed by four years in the reserve and five in the militia. It was widely regarded as being a necessary part of training for 'citizenship'. As the writer of one military manual put it:

> It (military service) will be a school to inculcate blind obedience to those in authority as well as to foster monarchic sentiments in the citizen.

Much play was made of the 'Prussian' virtues of order, discipline, absolute subordination to those in authority over one in daily life, in school, in the office or workshop and even in the family too. Indeed 'the soldier's values and concept of honour, his ideas and attitudes pervaded the whole of society' (H.-U. Wehler). The survival of that relic of feudal days, the duel, among army officers and those of noble birth as an honourable solution to quarrels and conflicts was a characteristic instance of this, part of what contemporary historians of Germany today term 'social militarism'. Readers of Fontane's novel '*Effi Briest*' (1895) will remember that Effi was ostracised by society for the rest of her life for her adultery with Crampas, an army major, which was discovered by her husband six years after the event. Her husband, a former officer, challenges and kills Crampas; six weeks later he is allowed to appear again in society, sufficient time having been deemed to have elapsed since the event for him to have 'expiated' the killing of a former comrade and married man.

The attitude of the officer corps towards society changed significantly in the course of nineteenth century Germany. A crucial event in this context was the 1848 revolution. In the course of the year 1848–49 troops were used to quell disturbances and subsequently to disband popular assemblies and to crush revolutionary uprisings in Baden and Saxony. The revolution served to make the Prussian army politically aware in a way that had not been true prior to that event. The clash between the crown and parliament in Prussia in the 1860s only served to increase the militancy of the officer corps. Under Bismarck's administration the army came to be regarded and to accept their role as guardians of the peace against internal hostile elements, rather than against a foreign foe. The exemplary character of the Paris Commune was something in which politically conscious soldiers believed without question. It was a not infrequent practice on the part of the authorities in the German empire to use the army to break strikes, as for instance the Ruhr miners' strike of 1889; the army's potential as the means of striking a preventive blow against Social Democracy came to be regarded by the upper classes and by the bourgeoisie as one of the positive, because socially reassuring, features of their state.

The 'Praetorian Guard' character of the Prussian officer corps in the last decades of the century was diluted by the expansion of the army in the years immediately preceding the outbreak of war in 1914.

The German Army 1880–1914

Strength of the German Army 1880–1914

Year	Total Strength	Officers	Ranks	Of these NCOs	Total Strength as a Percentage of Population
1880	422,589	17,227	401,659	48,531	0,937
1881	449,257	18,128	427,274	51,586	0,989
1887	491,825	19,262	468,409	55,447	1,035
1891	511,657	20,400	486,983	58,448	1,028
1894	584,548	22,534	557,112	77,883	1,138
1900	600,516	23,850	571,692	80,556	1,065
1905	609,758	24,522	580,158	82,582	1,006
1910	622,483	25,718	589,672	85,226	0,959
1914	800,646	30,739	761,438	105,856	1,181

Strength of the Navy 1880–1910

1880: 11,116	1894: 20,498
1881: 11,352	1900: 28,326
1887: 15,244	1905: 40,862
1891: 17,083	1910: 57,374

At least this was the view of senior officers who were becoming vexed at the difficulties they were experiencing in finding sufficient men of 'the right calibre' into the service. Noblemen continued to dominate the higher ranks and the better regiments – in 1913 80% of the cavalry, 48% of infantry regiments were noblemen as were 30% of all officers (in 1865 the figure for the last had been 65% in Prussia). By contrast there was not a single professional officer of Jewish faith in the imperial army in the years 1878 to 1910, and even the bourgeois applicants were thoroughly screened for their 'suitability'.

The special position of the army in the German state and in imperial society was not seriously or effectively challenged by any state government, political party or pressure group between 1871

and 1913, apart from the efforts of the Socialist deputies in the
Reichstag or state assemblies. Certainly many south Germans
disliked and derided the militarisation of society associated in their
minds with the overweening influence of Prussia in the nation at
large, but their displeasure did not make itself felt actively. When,
however, in 1913 the so-called Zabern Affair occurred, scandalising
public opinion right across the country, critics of the system were
soon forced to acknowledge their impotence to challenge the
political and social supremacy of the military. A young Prussian
lieutenant, aged only twenty, submitted the townsfolk in the
Alsatian garrison town of Zabern to humiliating language. The
military responded to the local protests by overriding the civilian
authorities, proclaiming a state of siege, and subsequently arresting
large numbers of Zabern citizens. The emperor William II
intervened personally in the dispute on the side of the military,
choosing to see the affair as belonging to the sphere of his royal
power of command, and actually refusing to receive the Governor of
Alsace. At a subsequent military court the officers involved in the
affair were acquitted. The impotence of the Reichstag, where
stormy scenes broke out, to make any headway in gaining justice for
the people of Zabern involved, the arrogance of the military and the
clear case in law against a number of officers, made the scandal of
the Zabern Affair an exemplary illustration of the constitutional
weakness of the German Empire and the apparently impregnable
position of the army in the state.

9
Politics, Government and the Masses (1890–1914)

Bismarck's heritage

Bismarck resigned office at the request of the emperor on 18 March 1890. For the next two decades and more, Germans became involuntarily aware of the degree to which Bismarck had stifled the growth and functioning of political institutions in their country. Bismarck had not only held the reins of power in his hands for almost a generation, but he had used his resources of men and material to try and perpetuate the power structures which he had created. Nearly seventeen years of Bismarck's nineteen-year term as German Reich chancellor, from 1873 to 1890, had coincided with a protracted industrial recession in that country. Furthermore, from 1876 onwards, a severe structural crisis in agriculture revealed itself. The unfavourable economic climate accounts in great measure for the pessimism which characterised these years in Germany (Wehler), for the genesis of a sense of *Angst* about the future (F. Stern) in the new nation, which had a negative effect on people's attitudes to the outside world. Bismarck's own natural misanthropy affected those around him. As the years went by he was visited by visions of catastrophe. which would destroy his life's work after he had gone. Although the Bismarck cult was still vigorous in the late 1880s and was to be artificially nurtured after his fall, through demonstrations and loyal addresses on his birthday and national holidays, there was a widespread feeling by 1890 that Bismarck had become somewhat of a dead-hand, and that his departure offered the possibilities of new and vigorous policies. Many Germans hoped for more harmonious relations between classes and economic groups in the future. Bismarck was seen to bear responsibility for social tensions consequent on the anti-Socialist legislation which he had introduced in 1878. His determination to extend it in a more severe form had in fact been a principal cause of his dismissal, and the legislation was repealed in 1890. This did not, however, prevent official and unofficial harassment of the Socialists and of working-class organisations in Germany thereafter, even of those without political connections. The public, or rather the mass of articulate political opinion, approved of this measure. But Germans in 1890 were much more concerned with external relations than with domestic questions: their primary concern was that their country should make an impact as a world power. Bismarck, it was commonly felt, was too much bound by age, origin and political experience to merely European horizons. Germany's opportunities and Germany's security, it was believed, lay most surely overseas. Imperial expansion, which was what was envisaged, was described at this time by the influential liberal thinker, Friedrich Naumann, to be but the natural 'urge of the German people to extend its influence across the globe'.

In thus distinguishing between the old-fashioned 'Europe-centred' policies of Bismarck, with his carefully structured alliance system, and the modern 'world-political' outlook of the new generation of policy makers, Germans were guilty of a misconception. Bismarck was not the reluctant exponent of colonialism for Germany, as his celebrated aphorism might suggest: 'I do not', he once observed in the Reichstag, 'wish to resemble the Polish nobility, whose fur coats conceal the fact that they cannot afford a shirt'. He appeared suspicious of colonial adventures in the early 1880s, but he came to appreciate the possibilities of such activities, as distracting from the increasing problems and tensions of contemporary domestic politics in Germany. There was undoubtedly a marked change in the style of German politics after Bismarck's fall in 1890, and this was particularly apparent in Germany's relations with her neighbours. However, the central aims of Germany's rulers remained fundamentally unchanged, namely to preserve intact the power structures of imperial Germany, and, by satisfying the nation's need for material and social security and for prestige, to maintain the general acquiescence of the governed in the status quo. A further difference in style and in degree, though not in substance, of politics after 1890, was occasioned by the increasing politicisation of the masses. Political and economic pressure groups began to play a dominant role in the next decades. In some cases, these acquired a majority influence on decision-making, by-passing or pressurising constitutional institutions, such as the Reichstag or even the imperial chancellor. In others, they were more social in character, a substitute for participation in political decision-making, absorbing and distracting those concerned, by giving them importance and status in their community and region.

William II and his chancellors

William II succeeded to the throne at the age of twenty-nine in June 1888 following the death of his father, Frederick III, of cancer after only ninety-nine days of rule. Less than two years later the new emperor requested Bismarck's resignation. The real object of this decision was, in William II's own words, that he should 'rule as well as reign' and his strategy, if one can call it this, was to appoint those who would be accessible to his ideas. Bismarck's reluctant successor was von Caprivi, a professional soldier who had most recently served as chief of the Admiralty. Caprivi showed more initiative than his master expected or desired, and was eased out of office only four years later. He was perhaps the only one of William's four chancellors between 1890 and 1914 who faced the realities of Germany's transformation from an agricultural to an industrial state, and tried to legislate for this situation. The greatest political problem for Germany in these decades was that of modernisation, and Caprivi was bound in any case to encounter enormous difficulties, quite apart from those occasioned by his own upright, inflexible character, and his lack of political experience. His efforts to reform tariff policy in the interest of the German manufacturing industry and urban consumers, and his hopes of conciliating Germany's minorities, all called forth bitter opposition from vested interests. Most notable among these were the great landowners of East Elbia, who angrily dubbed their fellow nobleman 'the Knight without ear of corn or blade of grass', for Caprivi had no private means and owned no estate. The fact that a brief upswing in trade in 1889–90 was followed by a sustained recession until 1895–96, made the task of Caprivi's government even more difficult. He did succeed in lowering agrarian tariffs; this both helped the consumer and opened the Russian frontier to German industrial export trade, which had virtually come to a standstill over the earlier imposition of German tariffs on Russian grain. But his success stimulated one of the most vociferous interest groups in Germany, the East Elbian landowners, to organise themselves in defence of their privileges. In 1893, the so-called Farmers' League (*Bund der Landwirte*) was constituted and became a major force in subsequent years.

Including among its members farmers from most regions in Germany, it was dominated by the East Elbian landowning interest, whose powers derived from the fact that family members held key posts in government ministries, particularly, but not only, in Prussia; at the same time the rigging of electoral districts and the three-class voting system meant that their supporters dominated the Prussian Landtag. The implications of Caprivi's strictly limited attempts at conciliating dissident opinion in post-Bismarckian Germany were clearly evident to the ruling elite. This elite, consisting of the landowners, the military, the upper echelons of the bureaucracy and the captains of heavy industry in Germany, such as Krupp or Stumm, determined to offer collective resistance to constitutional government. Under Caprivi's successor, the elderly Hohenlohe, (born 1819, only four years after Bismarck), these forces attempted, with the support of the Emperor, to by-pass state institutions and to create corporate bodies, which would wield real power in Germany.

A mediatised prince, Hohenlohe, who had been Bavarian prime minister and governor of Alsace-Lorraine, headed the government from 1894 to 1900. The first three years of his regime saw a series of minor crises which were associated with the successful attempt by the emperor and his close associates to replace relatively independent-minded ministers and state secretaries with more pliant ones. By 1897 this process was complete. The key ministries in the Prussian government (Prussia occupied some three-fifths of the territory of the German Empire), and key posts as state secretaries of the imperial administration, were held by nominees of the emperor, among them the new secretary of state for the Navy, Admiral Tirpitz. The new set-up seemed in every way to be a victory for William II's personal rule, and the emperor certainly saw it in this light. But although his personal power was truly immense, his political substance was too slight for him to rule in any genuine sense. This situation created in fact a power-vacuum in domestic politics, which was a prime source of Germany's instability over the next decade and a half. The powers behind the throne, the 'strategic clique' Wehler, wielded effective power in the years to come and determined the oligarchic character of German government in the decade and a half before the First World War. Initially, the key figures were Johannes Miquel, former mayor of Osnabrück and of Frankfurt, now secretary to the Reich Treasury and Prussian minister of finance, Bernard von Bülow, 1897–1900, secretary of state for foreign affairs and 1900–1909 imperial chancellor, Philip von Eulenburg, confidant of William until the early years of the century, and the Prussian minister of the interior, Posadowsky-Wehner.

'Sammlungspolitik'

The policy of successive governments in the years between 1897 and 1914 was not to deny the massive changes in contemporary German society, but to try, by a mixture of manipulation and repression, to make the unorganised masses into active supporters of the status quo. Miquel gave his name to the contemporary slogan *Sammlungspolitik* (colloquially translated as 'a policy of together-ness') which was also pursued at certain periods under the chancellorship of Bülow. It was aimed at conciliating the Conservatives by tariff concessions and by authoritarian domestic policies, while the bourgeois parties were to be won by imperialist policies overseas and by domestic peace. The bourgeoisie on the whole believed that *Sammlungspolitik* indicated the German government's intention to adhere to the constitution; only the military were mindful of the plans for a coup d'état, as an eventual option against radical or allegedly radical forces in German society. Essentially, Bismarck's provocative division of Germans into *reichsfreundlich* or *staatserhaltende* elements and *reichsfeindliche* elements was maintained.

Pressure groups

The fact that the urban wage-labourers were organised by the Socialist party and the trade unions and that the *Volksverein für das katholische Deutschland* came increasingly to be regarded as the spokesman of the German Catholics since its foundation in 1890 made the establishment see these two very substantial minority groups as beyond the reach of organised consensus politics. Hence they were widely assumed to be hostile to the status quo. Although the attitudes of the authorities to political Catholicism were modified towards the end of the 1890s, the deep and strident anti-Catholic prejudice of the emperor and his consort was a further influence on the anomalous position of some 40% of his subjects. Prejudice was made evident in active but secret discrimination against Catholics, as also against Jews or those of Liberal opinions. The new activist consensus policies were aimed primarily to win support from the so-called *mittelständisch* groups, namely middle and lower officials, white-collar workers, craftsmen, small-business people, traders and also farmers. These people combined a pride in Germany's achievements with complex and deep-seated fears for their own position and status in society, for the future of their own particular livelihood, which found expression in a collective consciousness (Wehler). These groups proved readily accessible to political agitation, either by producing self-styled leaders of economical and political pressure movements, or through direct and indirect government propaganda.

From 1897 to 1902, with the active help of ministers and state secretaries close to the emperor, the powerful representatives of heavy industry in Germany, the so-called *Centralverband der Industriellen* (founded in 1876), won direct influence on government policy by their presence in the recently instituted *Wirtschaftlicher Ausschuß* or 'Economic Council'. This was an extra-parliamentary government advisory body and it also included representatives of the manufacturing industries, the *Bund der Industriellen*, although they were much less influential. The association between heavy industry and the East Elbian grain producers, which dated from Bismarck's early days as imperial chancellor was revived at this time. What one Rhenish industrialist had called in 1885, 'the long recognised solidarity of interests', persuaded the spokesmen for heavy industry, especially the steel industry, to agree in 1902 to the restoration of the heavy tariffs on grain imports into Germany. The aim of such support, which was bound to attract bitter criticism from their own employees and all those forced to pay more for their food, was to gain the landowners' support for what these had termed 'the ghastly navy'. With this restored alliance between 'corn and iron', the *Bund der Industriellen*, founded in 1895 to represent the export-orientated manufacturing industries, found itself excluded from influence on government policy. As regards society as a whole, it must be said that the much vaunted 'solidarity of interests' was primarily negative in that it was directed at excluding from power those social groups which the rapidly expanding industrialisation of the country and a population growth of nearly 900,000 per annum, was making preponderant in numbers.

The Navy

An apt illustration of the character of domestic politics in Germany during this period was the Navy League, founded by the secretary of state for the navy, whom William II appointed in 1897, Admiral

Tirpitz. The issue of the navy in imperial Germany is also an apt illustration of the interaction of domestic politics on Germany's relations with her neighbours. Tirpitz, convinced by his own eloquence and bedazzled by the success of his organisation, pursued the specious 'risk theory' of equipping Germany with a massive battle fleet, in order to make war unlikely for the simple reason that it was too dangerous. The emperor gave backing to what was for him the prestigious symbol of his mighty empire. The German ruling elite, however, was at least as concerned with its palliative influence on the internal situation, as with the significance of the naval programme for German's security and expansion.

> Without seapower, Germany's influence in the world will be like that of a mollusc without any shell.

wrote Tirpitz in his memoirs. Tirpitz, to use a quotation from another context, 'played like a virtuoso on the well-tempered pianoforte of middle-class German ambitions'. How well he made himself into the mouthpiece of German neuroses when he talked of *unser geschichtliches Zuspätkommen* ('the historic fact that we came on the scene too late'), but pointed to the unique ability of a great Navy to overcome this 'unfair' situation. In 1895 in a letter to a former head of the Admiralty, Albert von Stosch, he wrote evocatively: 'in my view Germany will sink rapidly in the next century from her great power status, unless these marine interests are pursued systematically and energetically, without further loss of time.' Moreover, he added, such a policy would provide a real 'immunisation against educated and uneducated Social Democrats'. The alternative to the fleet programme and an aggressive imperialist policy, he averred, was nothing less than a return to earlier policies of emigration to the United States and elsewhere, 'leaving the world to the Anglo-Saxons and the sons of Jehova'. The sentiments and resentments which Tirpitz invoked – xenophobia, especially against the British, anti-Semitism, anti-Socialism and resentment of all forms of emancipation or indeed of modernisation, illusions of grandeur, all these were characteristic features of the political climate of these years in Germany. Germans responded to such propaganda with alacrity. Tirpitz encountered initial objections among the ruling oligarchy and especially in parliament to his ideas, but by 1900, the naval programme had begun to proceed apace. However, developments in the international scene gave a lie to Tirpitz's and the emperor's confident assertions about 'Germany's growing influence in the world'. To be sure, after 1896, her economy began

Das englische Schwert

„Oh wäre es doch ‚made in Germany, dann hätte es sich gewiß
besser bewährt!“

'The English sword.'
'O if it had been 'made in Germany' it would have lasted better!'
Drawing by Th. Th. Heine from *Simplicissimus*.

to boom again and production figures rose rapidly. Her population was increasing all the time, from 49.5 million in 1890 to 60 million in 1910. But the very success of industrial production made the problem of markets and supplies of raw materials even more acute, especially to a generation which was persuaded by Social Darwinistic arguments that the supply of both materials and outlets to market products must decline, as industrialisation brought ever more competition on to the scene.

International relations

On the international front, German policy from about the 1880s onwards, was characterised by a persistent restlessness. Bismarck had been deeply aware of Germany's exposed geographical position and had attempted to off-set this through his alliance system, based on the Dual Alliance in 1879 with Austria, the Triple Alliance with Bulgaria, the Quadruple Alliance extended to include Italy in the 1880s, and on the controversial Re-insurance Treaty with Russia of 1887. In broad terms, he had hoped that Germany would be needed by all the major powers and they would be prevented from forming coalitions hostile to Germany. Germany, in his view, was to be 'the indispensable centre of things' (Waller), at least in continental Europe. But Bismarck, like his successors at the helm of German government after 1890, placed too much trust in power and too little in fostering genuine goodwill in international relations. He was wedded to a policy of containing Russia, though he did not share the strong anti-Russian attitude of his younger contemporaries. He was aware of the grave structural weaknesses of Russia and feared the temptations for her of Pan-Slav imperialism. His support of colonial politics in the mid 1880s was prompted, among other things, by his desire to reduce German foreign investment and trade with Russia and eastern Europe and to divert it to other parts of the world.

Bismarck's successors did not renew the Re-insurance Treaty which lapsed in 1890, partly because a secret protocol of the treaty actually ran counter to commitments undertaken towards Austria by Germany, in the Dual Alliance. But relations with Russia had in any case worsened sharply even before Bismarck's fall, and by 1893, Russia and France, Germany's neighbours to the east and west, were for practical purposes in alliance with one another. Germany now began to pursue a policy of trade agreements with politically weak states, such as Serbia or Roumania, whom she wished or believed she could dominate politically. The notion of *Mitteleuropa,* a central European trade area, providing both a market for German industrial goods and a source of raw materials, fascinated many Germans, particularly among the middle classes, in the 1890s. Representatives of the export industry, and Liberals generally, hoped thereby to provide a counterweight to the reactionary agrarian party in Germany itself, and a 'safer' colonial policy than the overseas one might offer. However, the concerted power of the 'Iron and Corn League', of heavy industry and the agrarians, proved stronger, and *Mitteleuropa* did not materialise. On the other hand, the new high tariffs on grain imports imposed in 1902 antagonised Russia still further. By this date, however, increasing numbers of middle class Germans had transferred their interest to the alternative imperialist dream, which was being provided for Germany in the form of the fleet, and which was seen as the means of securing and protecting overseas possessions and trade.

Both Bismarck and his successors, as has been said, placed too little reliance on genuine good relations between states, especially those based on mutual trust. Bismarck was too much of a misanthrope to be really convinced of the possibilities of such an approach, too haunted perhaps by deep-seated doubts about the future of his life's work. German governments after Bismarck were influenced by his practices and too restricted by the rigidity of their concept of the German state and the egoistic principles on which it was based, to be capable of a novel approach. What is often referred to as the 'Byzantinism' of the imperial court, which in time affected those who lived and worked in its atmosphere, and the lack of exposure to other cultures besides their own, prevented German leaders from a fresh approach to their political situation. How often indeed had Bismarck been abroad since his ambassadorial days in the 1850s and early 1860s? How many makers of policy in the 1890s and 1900s, such as Johann von Miquel, or advisors of ministers, such as Friederich von Holstein, or indeed the chancellors Hohenlohe or Bülow, had genuine links based on personal friendships with foreigners? Hohenlohe had a Russian wife, Bülow an Italian, but in their case personal shortcomings prevented their redressing the imbalance in their governments. Of course it is also true that the British had little genuine understanding of foreigners and little desire to acquire such understanding, but they had the self-confidence and detachment which an island kingdom and possession of a vast empire conferred on them. Germans were instinctively aware of the potential weaknesses of their position but lacked confidence and patience to pursue 'informal' imperialism – i.e.

penetration by German banking and industrial investment overseas, which might have provided a relief to domestic tensions, as well as satisfying what were felt to be vital economic needs.

Domestic implications of foreign policy

The special and urgent role reserved for a demonstratively successful foreign policy to act as a 'palliative' on the domestic front, made the emperor and successive cabinets constantly prefer the short-term gain to the less spectacular long-term understanding. Bülow declared roundly in 1897 that 'only a successful foreign policy can succour, conciliate, soothe and reconcile', but little progress was made anywhere after 1890 in terms of territorial expansion or security. Germany's determination to dictate terms, to have other nations depend on her will, not only injected a permanently unsettling element into interstate relations, but progressively isolated Germany in Europe. Bismarck's Russian policy in the last years of his administration had undoubtedly contributed to the Russian-French rapprochement, although, because of the diverging natures of their regimes, this had always seemed highly unlikely. By 1904 another 'permanent factor' in Bismarck's and German political calculations was proved wrong; England and France settled their many differences and came together in the Entente Cordiale. Two years later, Germany's isolation and her diplomatic ineptness were demonstrated at the conference of Algeciras, while in the following year, Russia's joining the Entente demonstrated the failure of German diplomacy. Moreover, it gave credence to the myth or belief beginning to be current in the nation, that Germany was becoming a victim of a conspiracy, of a planned encirclement, and that a preventive war might well prove to be the only possible solution open to her. In that same year, 1907, the German decision was finally taken that, in the case of war, Belgian neutrality would have to be violated in order to win a quick victory over France before Germany would turn to fight Russia. Since Britain was a guarantor of Belgian neutrality according to the 1839 Treaty, the risk of war with Britain was clearly faced at this time. This option was a natural consequence of an attitude which had been pursued since the 1890s. On the 30 April 1897, Friederich Holstein, a senior official in the foreign office had observed to the then secretary for foreign affairs, Kiderlen, 'success can only be expected as the result of a European war', or through 'the acquisition of territory outside Europe'. That

DEUTSCHE IM AUSLAND

So sahen Herr und Frau Schmidt aus, als sie nach London reisten, um sich die Krönung anzusehen.

Und so sahen sie aus, als sie nach acht Tagen als Mr. und Mrs. Smith zurückkehrten.   TH. TH. HEINE

Germans abroad.
This is what Herr and Frau Schmidt looked like when they went to London to have a look at the Coronation. And this is what they looked like when they came back a week later as Mr and Mrs Smith.

such options were a gamble was clear to him, for he went on to describe them somewhat portentously as 'a world historical game of chance'.

German historians have tended in recent years to discuss the 'will to war' in the years before 1914 and the enthusiastic response to the decision to go to war in that year, as something particularly and perniciously German. The Hamburg historian, Fritz Fischer, declared categorically in 1965, that among the European nations only in Germany did there exist a genuine desire for war and a belief in its effectiveness. And it is true that war had a peculiar appeal to both government and nation at that time. The deep pessimism among Germany's ruling classes in these years immediately preceding 1914 and the spectre of revolution evoked by the sudden downswing of the economy from the spring of 1913 onwards, were all factors which influenced the trend. By contrast with the domestic front, the notion of a nation at arms had a certain visionary appeal. As one contemporary writer put it in fulsome words, the declaration of war was 'a great and unforgettable moment, the ringing opening chord of an immortal song of sacrifice, loyalty and heroism'. In other countries too, it must not be forgotten, in Britain, France, Russia, Austria-Hungary, war offered emotional release to the people and perhaps a solution to or at least a distraction from bitter and harassing domestic problems: for Austria-Hungary, the problem of the nationalities, for Russia, the seemingly unsuperable problems of modernisation and even perhaps for Britain the problems of Ireland. However, a consideration of the course of domestic politics in Germany since Bismarck suggests that, while the July crisis of 1914 and the declaration of war brought a sense of relief and even release to governments and nations in Europe, in Germany there was a different dimension to the situation. Here, war had the nature of a deliberate gamble, taken to ward off a greater evil.

Internal problems of the empire

Germany's greatest problem was that its social and political structure was being carefully preserved intact, fossilised, one might even say, at a time when the enormous industrial and democratic changes taking place demanded a highly flexible and adaptable system. Bismarck's Reich was not a modern state. It was a federation of twenty-five states, and, in order to guarantee the traditional liberties of the ruling princes and the preponderance of

Das alte Märchen

Der Hafe und der Swinegel wollten
miteinander um die Wette laufen,

und da legte der Hafe los.

Aber wie er nach Paris kam, war der
Swinegel schon da,

und da lief der Hafe, was er nur konnte.

Aber wie er nach Rom kam, da war der
Swinegel schon da,

und da lief der Hafe furchtbar.

Aber wie er nach Petersburg kam, da war
der Swinegel schon da.

Und da faß der Hafe erschöpft auf dem Feld
und war glänzend isoliert.

Skit on William II's love of travel and his ineffective efforts to outdo his uncle
(Edward VII) in popularity among the European nations. Drawings by
O. Gulbransson from *Simplicissimus*.

Prussia within the empire, Bismarck had set severe limits to the evolution of a central government of Germany. This created complex problems for the chancellors and their governments after Bismarck, particularly as regards finance. According to the constitution the imperial budget was set at a certain sum, and revenue, from whatever source, exceeding this was paid back to the states on the basis of population. The strains on the budget became considerable once the state began to take over increased responsibility for the social welfare of its citizens, as was the case from the 1880s onwards. Yet a variety of vested interests vigorously opposed any modification of the financial system, and deficit budgeting for the empire was a problem facing successive imperial governments in the years before the war. This had the further implication of imposing restrictions on monies available for social welfare benefits, at a time when Germany was seen by all its inhabitants to be a rich and ever more prosperous country, yet with pressing social problems resulting from industrialisation. But it was a fundamental axiom of policy in the establishment, as represented by the agrarians, military, captains of industry, upper bureaucracy, that the system then obtaining should remain unchanged. This meant keeping direct taxes to a minimum; demands for an increase of revenue had to be made from indirect taxation, namely on the consumer. However, every increase in indirect taxation inexorably led to a rise in the Socialist vote and, though to a lesser extent, to increased support for the Left-Liberal parties, both of whose leaders constantly exposed the blatant injustice of the tax system in parliament. The fleet programme in its early years was financed by indirect taxation. At the same time the Prussian and imperial governments were paying considerable sums by way of subsidies to the great landowners in the form of tariffs, export premiums, cheap transport for their goods, subsidies on those industries which were based on the land estates, such as sugar, distilling etc. The tariff increase raised the price of food for just those classes who paid the bulk of the indirect taxes. By the end of the decade 1900–10, the fleet could no longer be financed in this way. The agrarians offered obdurate and powerful resistance to any increase in direct taxation. Redundancies in the shipbuilding industry suddenly seemed imminent, with all the expected social and political consequences. The rise in the cost of living, particularly from 1911 onwards, after a prolonged period of rise in real wages, was a further serious problem.

The 1912 elections added to the anxiety of the government and the establishment. The Social Democrats attracted more than one third of all the votes cast and became the largest political party in the Reichstag; there seemed no reason to suppose that their vote would not increase progressively. In fact the effectiveness of even the most numerous and forceful opposition in the Reichstag was limited, as long as the three-class franchise in Prussia and Saxony excluded the vast majority of the population in those states from influence over their internal affairs. Hopes of a reformed franchise diminished rather than increased in the pre-war years, simply because the power of the Conservative interests rested in their domination of the Landtage or state assemblies, and in their power to make senior official appointments. To surrender these privileges would be to destroy their own power base. The electoral victories of the left-wing parties at Reich level only increased the determination of the ruling classes to resist reform in any guise. Yet among their opponents, the knowledge of the limited effectiveness of political opposition affected both Liberals as well as Socialists. It encouraged them to concern themselves increasingly with the pursuit of the economic rather than the political interests of their supporters, at least up to about 1909. The exclusive concentration on fiscal matters inevitably affected the character of the Reichstag, which found itself being progressively reduced to not much more than 'an expanded Customs Parliament'. (G. A. Ritter.)

Political parties

Having said that, the point should however also be made that the development of the political parties, at Reich and at state level, between Bismarck's fall and the end of the Empire is of considerable significance and interest for what it has to tell about the politicisation of the masses in this period. It throws light on the peculiar character of domestic politics in pre-war Germany by illustrating the way in which party, and other affiliated organisations at national and local level, gave Germans a sense of political identity, in spite of the fact that the 'neo-feudal' government system effectively excluded them from a real say in public issues. The year 1890 provides a certain watershed in the history of German political parties as in other spheres too, although it remains true that the party system in Germany changed very much less in its aims, organisation and activity in the Second Empire as a whole than one might have expected. Those parties which were not identified with sectional interests (i.e. workers and Catholics) experienced growing tensions after 1890, particularly in view of the tremendously rapid growth of the Social Democratic vote. This is especially true of the bourgeois Liberal parties, who found it more difficult than Conservatives, Socialists or Catholics, to create a mass organisation, which would assure them a steady section of electoral support in an age of mass democracy.

The parties of the Right

The response of the Conservatives and the Catholic Centre to the change in character of politics in what was now a capitalist society, provides an interesting example of how long traditional social attitudes and barriers remained operative in German life. In the Conservative parties, a certain strain between the urban and rural areas became evident in the early 1890s. The so-called 'Berlin Movement', associated with the name of the Court preacher and anti-Semitic agitator, Adolf Stoecker, appeared briefly to challenge the dominance of the East Elbian agrarian interest, but from about 1893 onwards, the traditional rural leadership asserted itself again. Much more than that, the newly founded pressure group, the *Bund der Landwirte* or Farmers' League (1893), was permitted to take over the task of propaganda and agitation in support of the Conservatives. Forceful, highly organised and well-funded, and covering a wide area, the Farmers League provided the Conservatives with a mass organisation. Its propaganda reached right into the smallest villages and, more significantly, it won a firm footing in originally Liberal areas of Germany, the north-west and the south-west, which were far removed from its own power base. It is not without interest that in the late years of the Weimar Republic this element of Conservative support deserted en masse to the Nazis; the Prussian Conservative voters, on the other hand, remained loyal to their traditional party, then known as the German National Peoples Party. By 1912, the Farmers League had over 300,000 members. The organisation had for the Conservative party leadership the signal advantage that, as a spokesman put it, 'One now had a mass basis of support, without having to give it any influence'.

The Centre Party, whose early history had been dominated and its solidarity immensely strengthened by the *Kulturkampf* of the 1870s and 1880s, grew from 1890 onwards increasingly aware of its vulnerability to economic and political pressures. In particular, the party stood to lose the support of Catholic workers and the urban middle classes. However, with the founding of the *Volksverein* in

1890, which took over the task of education and agitation among the Catholic masses, the party continued to be led by its traditional leaders and to provide central organisation and policy. The Centre's traditionally tactical role in German politics, the 'balance-wheel' as it was called, made the leadership determined to retain its oligarchic character. Despite the deep anti-Catholic prejudice of influential circles in Germany, the Centre Party came to be regarded as loyal to the sovereign and state, as well as retaining the loyalty of the vast mass of the Catholic population. It was perhaps surprising, in view of their recent history, that German Catholics should be so loyal to the state and the emperor. This can be understood through their natural affinity with paternalist forms of rule. While an element of ghetto existence remained characteristic of Catholic political life right down to the end of the Empire, the sense of unity and their concern for the needs of individual and very different social groups continued to be strong. The annual *Katholikentag* was important, both as a form of party conference but also as a kind of public relations day for Catholics from all regions of Germany.

The bourgeois parties

The Liberal parties, as already has been said, found it difficult to provide a similar type of grass-roots support or its equivalent. True, despite numerous divisions and tensions within the various groupings, there was a resilient commitment to the liberal ideology at regional level, which assured a certain stability in voting patterns. But from 1890 onwards, Liberalism was clearly on the decline in Germany, and the efforts both of the right-wing National Liberal and the Left Liberal parties, to provide a more comprehensive structure and to draw more people into participation proved to be abortive. Among the National Liberals, the rural elements began to play a more active role than hitherto, especially between 1893 and 1906, in part to counter the agitation of the Farmers League. Regional loyalties remained strong but it proved impossible to reach beyond the traditional sources of support for the parties – the pre-industrial notables such as judges, communal officials, academics, lawyers, editors etc. A number of craftsmen and teachers voted also for the Left Liberals, but attempts to make conquests among urban working classes, by way of workers educational associations or the Liberal trade unions, proved ineffective. In the years just before the war, a Young Liberal movement in the National Liberal party seemed to offer an alternative to a fossilised political system – they formed Liberal associations throughout the country which numbered 2,007 by 1914–15, and gained a quarter of a million members. Keenly imperialistic and anti-clerical, but committed to social and domestic political reform, it was to such an association that the young Gustav Stresemann, foreign minister of the Weimar Republic, owed his rapid rise in the party. Liberals did succeed in winning some support among the so-called new *Mittelstand*, white collar workers in industry and the service industries. They introduced a generally dynamic element into a lethargic group. Certain charismatic figures came into political life in the process, most notably the Lutheran clergyman, Friedrich Naumann, on the left wing of the Liberal movement. Naumann's support among intellectuals and professional men in Germany (including the first President of the Federal Republic in 1949, Theodor Heuß), gave evidence of a genuine search for alternative policies to the current system. In fact, however, there was too little consensus of opinion among the bourgeois parties as a whole, for such a search to have had any real chance of success.

The Socialists

Bismarck's fall and the repeal of the anti-Socialist legislation in 1890 and signs of a more constructive attitude on the part of state governments towards the industrial workers seemed to presage a new role for the Social Democratic movement in Germany. The young emperor cast himself in the role of *Volkskaiser*, the harbinger of social peace and justice. Such hopes were not destined to be fulfilled. Governments pursued a zigzag course (G. A. Ritter). Legislation to ameliorate the lot of workers was extended, but the authorities refused to accept the legitimacy of the Social Democratic Party, as it was now called, and the trade union movement as the bona fide representatives of working class interest.

Socialism and Society

Harassment of Socialists and those suspected of Socialist interest continued, not only by the uniformed representatives of the state, but by landowners and employers. In north Germany it proved virtually impossible for Socialists to get on to school boards (*Schuldeputationen*), or town councils; the three-class franchise to state parliaments in Prussia and Saxony operated to the signal disadvantage of the urban wage labourers. The official policies of the Social Democratic Party were not, if understandably not, calculated to make relations more harmonious. At the party congress in Erfurt in 1891, revolutionary Marxism was formally adopted as the official ideology of the party. It did not matter that the actual behaviour of party members was anything but revolutionary, that anarchism had no success in the German labour movement; little account was taken in establishment circles that, in the period of national prosperity between 1895 and 1913, the aspirations of working men were directed ever more towards a share in bourgeois possessions and indeed towards emulating bourgeois life styles, rather than the overthrow of the state. The Socialists' leaders, who had endured the hardships of the *Kampfzeit*, such as August Bebel, Wilhelm Liebknecht, Karl Kautsky, believed that a breach in the policy of steadfast opposition to the current system must imperil the unity of the movement. The so-called Revisionist doctrine, formulated by Edward Bernstein and calling for a policy of gradual integration of the proletariat into bourgeois society, was regarded by most party leaders with dismay. Bernstein was moved by his own deep concern for his fellow workers and by his belief that Marx' analysis of the development of society under capitalism was not in fact proving to be a correct one. The great debate between the Revisionists and the orthodox party leaders preoccupied German Socialists for years. As the sage and experienced party secretary, Ignaz Auer, pointed out to the somewhat headstrong Bernstein, it was not really surprising. 'Do you really think it possible' he asked him, 'for a party with a fifty-year-old literature, an organisation going back nearly forty years and a tradition which is even older still, to make such a right-about-turn at a moment's notice? ... one doesn't decide on such a matter, one doesn't talk about such a thing, one just gets on with it.'

Given the implacable hostility of the environment, in which the movement had grown strong, unity based on ideological purity seemed of primary importance. But was the hostility of society absolute and permanent? The history of Socialism in south Germany in the latter years of the nineteenth century suggested that it was not. In fact, the fortunes of the Socialist party there offers evidence of how it might have developed into a genuine popular party at national level, rather than a class party. For in the years 1877–90 Socialist votes in the south German states had increased, relatively speaking, even more than in the Reich as a whole. Thus in Bavaria it rose from 3.7% to 13.9%, and in Upper Bavaria, which of course included Munich, from 3.77% to the astonishing figure of 24.35%. In Baden the percentage was 1.52% to 13.9%, in the Grand Duchy of Hesse 8.72% to 20%, Alsace-Lorraine 0.0% to

10.72%. In the south, Socialists served on school and municipal councils, and there were even a number of Socialist mayors. By 1910, according to an estimate by Bernstein, there were some 100,000 Socialists active in some area of public life, in 1913 some 320 sat in state parliaments. Such fraternisation evoked bitter criticism from Bebel and other northern Socialists, who were not familiar with the different political traditions of the south and did not really try to make the effort to understand them. The Bavarian Socialist leader, Georg von Vollmar, was a genuine man of the people, a powerful speaker, and despite Bebel's attacks, the Bavarian Socialist party continued to expand under his genial leadership. In many ways the south German Socialists, notably the Baden leader Ludwig Frank, were closer to those of other European countries such as France, Austria or Belgium than to their northern comrades. Frank demonstrated that it was possible to collaborate fruitfully with the Liberals in parliament and indeed in all south German states Socialists achieved a modest measure of success in reform legislation at state level. The rigid stand of the party's national leaders and their preoccupation with ideological questions brought forceful criticism from brother Socialists abroad. At Amsterdam Jean Jaurès baldly declared that the attitudes of the German Socialists suggested that they were simply covering up their own inadequacies in the cause of working class emancipation. Indeed, in the last years before the Great War the leadership of the labour movement seemed to be passing more and more into the hands of trade union leaders. Present day historians suggest that the electoral success of 1912 represented a saturation point for the party; by comparison the Free Trade Union movement, which in 1890 had numbered under 300,000, had 2.5 million members in 1913. Their numbers were still growing, their involvement in the process of emancipation of the working class was dynamic, and to the young and active Socialists, they stood in sharp contrast with increasing bureau-cratisation and rigidity of the party.

The parties and the state

German political parties, apart from the Social Democratic party, were deeply affected by the prevailing national ideology and by the concerted opinion that Social Democracy was anti-national. The fact that all parties had an ideological rather than a tactical base made it difficult for leaders and voters to accommodate policies to a changing social and economic situation. They showed an unusual stability in terms of European history between 1871 and 1914, indeed until 1928, but it was not a healthy stability:

> The German party system was essentially the expression of structural conflicts which already existed before the Empire was formed, hence they remained anchored in politically mobilised ideological groups, where the conflicts themselves became ritualised. (Lepsius)

Thus the party system in Germany tended to perpetuate the autonomy of the various milieus in Germany, which were regional, confessional and social. This in turn impeded the democratic process and the integration of these milieus into modern society.

Pressure groups

i) *Representatives of the propertied classes*
Another related aspect of this feature of German political and social organisation was the existence of pressure groups. The years 1870 to 1914, especially the period 1893 to 1914, saw a rapid growth in the numbers and influence of pressure groups in Germany. Economic pressure groups are a characteristic feature of industrial society. What was peculiar to Germany in these years was the commitment of the majority of such organisations to resisting either evolutionary modification or revolutionary challenge to the status quo. The existence, activities, numbers and percentage of the articulate population involved in these organisations, were in striking contrast to the limitations imposed by the German constitutional system on the political participation of its subjects. Thus the Free Trade Unions, or *Freie Gewerkschaften*, increasingly came to be regarded as the spokesmen of the workers, yet the workers party, the SPD, the largest party in Germany, was in fact excluded from any hope of government. Large and powerful pressure groups such as the *Flottenverein* (Navy League) and the *Hansabund* agitated successfully in favour of imperialist policies without being held in any way responsible for the consequences. Moreover, the two most powerful sectional interests, heavy industry and the agrarian party, managed to win a preponderant degree of influence on legislation and other administration through the activities of their pressure groups, the elitist CDI, (*Central-Verband deutscher Industriellen*), founded in 1876, and the Farmers League, which had developed from a smaller organisation known as the *Volksverein für Wirtschafts – und Steuerreform* (Popular League for economic and tax reforms), founded in 1876. The impact of these organisations grew in the years preceding the

On the Charlottenburg Chaussée in Berlin.

First World War, and their importance was reflected both in the variety of the groups and the astonishing numbers who joined them. In a recent article, the German historian, Wolfram Fischer, spoke of the 'ever more closely woven network of large and small associations' and went on to observe that 'there was hardly a sphere of public interest in which the 'official' representatives of such interest, whether government, parliament or administration, did not run up against organised citizen associations, which were attempting to make their influence felt'. Some, such as the representative organ of heavy industry, the CDI, had few members. Their weight derived from the standing, connections and wealth of their members, or the firms they represented. Others such as the Free Trade Unions, had over a million members on the eve of the war, while in 1878 they had counted a mere 77,000. Some represented ideological and religious issues, rather than economic ones, some both. The *Volksverein für das katholische Deutschland* represented all three. It numbered half a million in 1906 and 800,000 in 1914, of which half came from the Rhineland and Westphalia. The *Volksverein* was in fact the largest organisation in Germany after the

Social Democratic Party. The Farmers League represented the conservative agrarian interest in Germany and was both economic and ideological in its aim. It grew from 200,000 in the 1890s to 328,000 in 1911. One local group which was indeed conservative but not representative of the propertied classes and which exercised a powerful influence on the awakening political awareness of many middle and lower-middle class groups, was that called the *Deutsche Handlungsgehilfenverband*, for white-collar workers and shop assistants; membership was specifically confined to 'Germans not of the Israelite faith'.

The pressure groups did not see themselves as agents of the government. Rather they treated the state authorities as if they were 'a fortress which must be attacked, conquered and cleansed of hostile elements' (Fischer). Nor were the Conservative ones averse to criticising or even defaming government ministers or secretaries of state in public, whose policies and actions did not accord with their own sectional interests. The Farmers League exercised considerable influence in bringing about the fall of three successive Reich chancellors, namely, Caprivi, Hohenlohe and Bülow, and the resignation of Miquel. All such organisations invariably identified their own vested interests with the national good, coining emotional slogans, which anticipated Nazi practices, in order to put across this idea. Typical of such slogans were 'protection of national labour' (which meant in practice discrimination against foreign workers), 'securing the basis of food for the nation', in effect protective tariffs and subsidies for grain producers, which greatly increased the cost of the nation's food, or 'guaranteeing Germany's defence' – this implied special protection for heavy industry (at a cost to manufacturing industry etc.). The more powerful pressure groups, such as the Farmers' League, financed candidates for parliament, who agreed to support their programme. Such was its success that in the 1898 Reichstag, there were 118 such candidates, while in the 1904 Prussian Landtag, 220 out of 420 candidates were controlled by the Farmers' League. By comparison, the CDI could only muster 120 deputies in the 1912 Reichstag.

ii) *The trade unions*
The relationship between the trade unions and their parties was different again. The Christian Trade Unions were based mainly in the Rhineland and Westphalia and though, as in the case of the Free Trade Unions in the Socialist party, their members voted solidly for their own party, they were by no means uncritical of the leadership.

The Liberal Hirsch-Dunker Unions had affiliations with the Left Liberal parties, but represented a fairly small proportion of the movement. The Socialist trade union movement had had relatively little political influence on the Socialist party before the 1890s. The tremendous increase in numbers from the mid-1890s onwards gave increasing weight to their counsels in organised working-class circles, so much so that, to a growing number of labour leaders, especially in northern Germany, the party seemed to be excessively doctrinaire and to be becoming divorced from political and economic realities.

German Trade Unions

The origins of the trade union movement in Germany went back to the 1860s. Thus they pre-dated employers' organisations by a decade, and the agrarian interest group by over a generation. Most trade unions fell a victim to the anti-Socialist legislation of 1878–90 but re-emerged in the mid-1890s as a centralised organisation under Carl Legien's leadership. In the expansion of the economy after the end of the 'Great Depression' (1873–96), hundreds of thousands of workers joined the union movement, so much so that the 1890s earned the name of the 'decade of the unions' (Franz Mehring).

Some two-thirds of all organised workers were brought into a single Socialist movement in the following decade and a half. Steady improvements in terms of employment and earnings over the subsequent two decades gave trade union leaders increasing authority within the working class movement over the Socialist party leadership. A sense of collective destiny had drawn workers together in the years of persecution and discrimination by institutions of state, and it remained a genuine experience after 1890 also. It was kept alive by the tacit assumption common to many middle and upper class Germans that the working man was 'a potential enemy of the state'. This attitude was shared by drill sergeants, who were convinced that the conscripts who came for their military service had to have Socialist sympathies drilled out of them by the army, 'the school of the nation'. Strikes and lock-outs, such as the Ruhr miners' strike in 1889, which involved some 90,000 workers and constituted the largest trade union action in the nineteenth century in Germany, or the 1890 lockout of some 3,000 workers in an attempt to break the union, became part of the common memory of working men. Although in the early 1890s the failure of strike action (in many cases) led to the decimation of membership, the number of unsuccessful strikes taught the trade union leadership to use the strike weapon with greater economy, but also increased efficiency and impact. The energy and militancy of the employers' organisation in the 1890s, which to working-men was a clear demonstration of class injustice in the Empire, stimulated the formation of a more sophisticated organisation. The experience of the early '90s influenced opinion in favour of organisation by industry rather than trade, though in certain branches and concerns the traditional trade organisations remained characteristic. Older trades, such as building, proved volatile in their support for unionisation, the numbers swelling in good, being decimated in bad years.

Membership of the principal Trade Unions in Germany

Year	Free Trade Unions	% of total	Christian	% of total	Hirsch-Duncker	% of total
1869	47,192		—		30,000	
1889	174,608		—		62,688	
1890	294,551		—		62,643	
1894	245,723		Foundation		67,078	
1899	580,473	80.2%	56,391	7.8%	86,777	12.0%
1900	680,427	80.2	76,744	9.0	91,661	10.8
1904	1,052,108	82.0	118,917	9.3	111,889	8.7
1909	1,832,667	82.5	280,061	12.6	108,028	4.9
1910	2,017,298	82.1	316,115	12.9	122,571	5.0
1913	2,548,763	85.0	341,735	11.4	106,618	3.4

Some unions, such as that of the tobacco workers, which was the second oldest union in Germany and at the time of the anti-Socialist legislation, the largest of them all, were thoroughly militant, while other employees, such as the textile workers, proved difficult to organise; here large numbers of women were employed. Others again, such as the metal workers, proved adaptable and efficient in organising both skilled and unskilled workers. By the eve of the war, the metal workers possessed a national organisation of considerable power and militancy, very critical indeed of party leadership and of the moderate stance of trade unionism as a whole.

In the late 1870s the printers, and tobacco workers and other skilled workers with strong craft traditions in medium and small concerns had been the centre of the trade union movement. By 1913, 60% of the whole trade union movement were recruited from the metal, wood, transport, building, factory and textile workers. The skilled workers, generally younger men, remained dominant in the movement's leadership. Increasing mechanisation, as well as the attitudes of state and society, tended to make the sense of a common social group-consciousness more important than skilled traditions. At the end of the nineteenth century the geographical strength of the trade union movement depended largely on the degree of industrialisation. Its centres were Hamburg, Berlin, Bremen, Schleswig-Holstein, which was an old centre of Socialism, Hanover and the Thuringian states. The movement was less strong in Saxony than might have been expected, both on account of the severity of the authorities towards organised labour and because domestic manufacture was still the predominant form of enterprise. It was in the Rhineland and Westphalia that the Christian Trade Union movement had its base; its numbers, together with those of the Liberal Unions, accounted in the years 1900–14 for something between 10 and 12% of the whole. The increase in funds from supporting members was dramatic between 1895 and 1913, from 600,000 marks in the former to 88,100,000 in the latter year. The number of paid trade union officials rose from 269 in 1900 to 2,867 in 1914. The number of members in the Free Trade Unions rose from 52,511 in 1877 to 329,230 in 1896, 680,427 in 1900 to reach 2,548,763 in 1913 (this last figure does not include associations of domestic and rural workers).

In the years before the war, the pragmatism of trade union leaders was an important element in modifying the relations between the urban working classes and the state, especially outside Prussia and Saxony. Tangible benefits came in the form of a rise in real wages, particularly during the first decade of the twentieth century, and the concession in less militant areas of Germany of the eight or nine hour working day. However, the obdurate attitude of employers is well illustrated by the way Robert Bosch (founder of the electrical firm Bosch) was criticised by his fellow-industrialists for his liberal attitude to labour relations. Dubbed by them 'the Red Bosch', he was one of the first to introduce the eight hour day into his Stuttgart-based factory. Bosch's many concessions, based as least as much on his concern for greater efficiency as on altruism, ensured that his rapidly expanding business experienced very little labour trouble before 1913.

A further aspect of trade union organisation which is worth stressing is the social role played by the trade unions. Here Carl Legien played an important role in fostering a sense of collective group consciousness, which the attitudes of society and the defamatory propaganda of state institutions against the urban wage labourers, made particularly needful. Trade union clubs, meeting places, social occasions, which would also include wives and families, provided a parallel or similar organisation to that of the Social Democratic Party, or of the churches in a previous generation. The trade union movement was thus much more than a pressure or interest group, though this remained its primary function.

Political pressure groups

A late arrival, as it were, among the economic and interest pressure groups of the German Empire, was the *Hansabund*, founded in 1909. It was formed and supported by medium and small entrepreneurs, with strong representation from the north German Hansa towns (Hamburg, Bremen, Lübeck). It had a political as well as an economic dimension, in that it was formed as an anti-Conservative cartel. Its leaders aimed to try and break what they regarded as the Prussian Conservatives' stranglehold on political power. For in the last five years preceding the outbreak of war in 1914 various attempts were made by politicians and industrialists, and to a limited extent by journalists, church leaders (as in the Peace Movement) and academics, to bring about a new orientation on the domestic front. The *Hansabund* can be seen in this context. Economic and fiscal matters, such as the tariff question or tax reform, seemed to lose primacy in public debate. Constitutional issues, especially the limited franchise in Prussia and Saxony, which provided the power base for Conservatives, became dominant. Although the *Hansabund* undoubtedly proved less successful in political terms than its promoters hoped, it is interesting as a symptom of the overall trend, characteristic of German politics in this era, namely for pressure groups to provide a kind of parallel political system to the parliamentary parties.

Besides such pressure groups which were identified with a particular stratum or particular strata of society, the latter decades of the Second Empire saw the growth of numerous and increasingly vocal organisations, agitating in favour of national solidarity. The appeal of such associations is seen in their numerical success. The Navy League, founded through the impetus of the industrialist Krupp and Prince zu Wied, in 1898, had in 1913 about a million members and associates (a Navy League in Britain at that time had 15,000 members; the German Social Democratic party 385,000 paid-up members). The Navy League was master-minded by that genius in the field of public relations, Admiral Tirpitz, who so well understood his countrymen's fondness for social occasions with a 'higher' purpose. Tirpitz organised numerous lectures, social evenings, visits to ships, for regional associations all over Germany, and, in his publicity, paid particular attention to the provinces. The element of popular nationalism in the Navy League and in the notorious Pan-German League (*Alldeutscher Verband*) which was founded in 1893, had marked success. It was absent from the so-called HKT organisation, an elitist association, founded, with Bismarck's blessing, by three millionaires, Hansenau, Kennemann and Tiedemann in 1894. The professed aim of this association was to pursue Germanisation of the eastern provinces, where there was a substantial Polish population, in places even a majority, such as Posen, East and West Prussia and parts of Upper Silesia. It throws an interesting light on official attitudes to such matters, to learn that the Prussian minister of the interior encouraged the local administrators, the *Landräte*, to join the organisation. If the HKT indicated by its membership that the government was actually prepared to sponsor active discrimination against its own (Polish and Russian) subjects, another organisation, which bore the name of *Reich Organisation against Social Democracy* (1909), found favour with the highest powers in the land. Many patrons of this organisation among the ruling classes were utterly convinced of the patriotic and altruistic character of their agitation. Although the League's activities were suspended in keeping with the national peace or reconciliation, the so-called *Burgfrieden*, after the outbreak of war in 1914, it says a great deal about official attitudes that someone as near to the emperor as his own aide-de-camp, a certain Caprivi, (not to be confused with the chancellor of the same name) could declare that in 1914 the death of a Social Democrat volunteer in battle was a mere propaganda trick to force concessions for the Socialist party (Riezler's Diary).

Zwei Deutſche

„Na, Bebel, jetzt lernen wir uns doch noch richtig kennen!"

Bismarck and Bebel from *Simplicissimus*.
'At last, Bebel, we've got to know each other properly!'
(Reference to the 'Burgfrieden' between the authorities and the labour movement
on the declaration of war in 1914.)

Germany on the eve of the Great War

These organisations and other similar groups such as the older
Colonial League (1882) the Defence League (*Wehrverein*, 1897) and
the nationwide network of war veterans associations, still going
strong forty years after the Franco-Prussian war of 1870–71,
served the primary purpose of diverting growing political awareness
among the citizenry of the German Empire from the fundamental
problems of the state. The most significant of these problems were
the imbalance between the power of the pre-industrial or, as recent
historians have named it, the neo-feudal leadership, and the
modern industrialised economy. Friederich Naumann, the liberal
politician and social reformer, likened Germany at the beginning of
the twentieth century to a great and ever-expanding factory built in

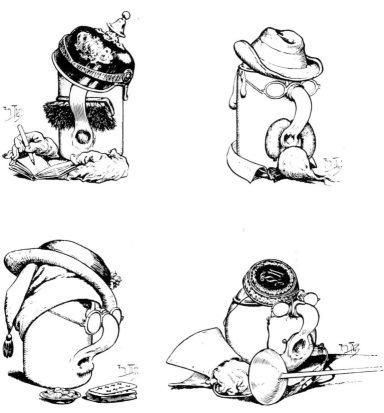

'Tankard types' by A. Thiele.

a barn, its steel girders gradually breaking through the mud-and-wattle walls. The tensions between different social and economic interests, the widespread fear among middle and lower middle class circles of the organised labour movement, despite its general quiescence in the last years of the Empire, were part of this, as was the resentment felt in many regions at the predominance of Prussia in Germany. If political and to some extent religious reasons determined the hostility felt by the less industrialised, socially and politically more cohesive south Germany towards the north, fundamental differences in economic and social structure and in income divided the east and the west. The notion of the unity of the nation as its greatest asset was something that most Germans accepted and believed in. But the gap between myth and reality in this and other respects was in itself a prime source of tension in pre-war Germany.

'*Alles ist sehr alt geworden*', 'everything seems to have grown so old', wrote a sensitive observer of the German establishment, Kurt Riezler, from his position as secretary to the chancellor, Bethmann-Hollweg, in 1914. Whether one supports or rejects the emotional thesis of Germany's war guilt in 1914, there seems little doubt that the decision to go to war was taken with fatalism and in many quarters with manifest relief, as a kind of last option for Germany.

10
The Evolution of German Society 1800–1914

Population

The social history of Germany in the nineteenth century is a record of profound changes, the most striking of which is perhaps the trebling of her population from an estimated 23 million in 1800 to 67.8 million in 1914. This figure becomes even more impressive when one remembers that emigration from Germany continued to be high throughout the century. This was particularly the case during the famine years immediately after the Napoleonic wars, during the 'hungry forties' and in the aftermath of the 1848 revolution. It reached nearly 5% of the population in 1881 and did not sink below 1% until 1894, thereafter to drop gradually to insignificant proportions in 1914.

Germany's population in the nineteenth century
(= population of the territory constituting the German Empire in 1871; it does not include Austria)

1816	24,833,396
1855	36,113,644
1871	41,058,792
1875	42,727,360
1900	56,367,178
1905	60,641,278

High marriage and birth rates prevailed throughout the century, boosted by improved medical facilities and a decline in infant mortality (mainly among legitimate babies) in the last decades of the century. After 1900 the continuing increase in the life expectancy rates was in part counter-balanced by a fall in the birth rate, which, apart from the years between the mid 1930s and the late 1950s, has been a general feature of Germany in the twentieth century.

Scarcely less significant was the change in the regional distribution of Germany's population between 1800 and 1914. In 1800 some 90% of Germans lived and worked on the land, 5% in small and 5% in larger towns. Vienna was the largest city in Germany, numbering about a quarter of a million inhabitants (Paris at that time had about 600,000) and Berlin was the next largest with 170,000. By 1840 some 60%-70% of Germans still depended for their living on agriculture, but by 1907, it was a mere 28.4%, as against 42.4% in industry, 12.9% in commerce and transport, 3.3% in domestic service, and 5% in administration, 5.2% in the army and the professions. On the eve of the war in 1914 Germany had some 13 million industrial workers, 2 million 'white collar' employees (the fastest growing section), 2 million lower and middle-ranking civil servants, and one and a half million traditional craftsmen, of whom half a million were still members of the guilds; there were somewhat under three-quarters of a million retailers and 2 million smallholders. Rural labourers, including women who worked on the land, accounted for about 8.5 million.

The industrial revolution, political unification and a massive growth in national wealth in the late nineteenth century had not brought a general levelling out between regions and classes. By the end of the century there was a marked and growing imbalance between east and west Germany in population, living standards, average wages and general culture. In the year 1907, for example, 2,326,700 of those born in eastern Germany, that is, the provinces of East and West Prussia, Posen, Silesia and Pomerania had moved to other regions, while the region gained only 358,100 by immigration. In the same year, 1,203,700 of the inhabitants of Berlin and Brandenburg (the province in which Berlin is situated) had not been born there. Westphalia and the Rhine province had attracted nearly one and a half million residents from outside, while some 449,400 natives left the region. The average wage in East Prussia, the province in Germany with the lowest average income, was but 63.4% of the national average, Pomerania had 75.2% while Westphalia had 117.4% and Schleswig-Holstein in the north west, although not highly industrialised, had 99.6%.

The growth of the cities heightened the contrast between east and west, and to a lesser extent that of north and south. Certainly Germany east of the Elbe lost virtually all its natural increase to the cities in the years after 1870. The growth in the size of German cities is especially striking in view of the relatively short space of time in which this occurred. South Germany, on the other hand, despite having several medium-sized towns and a few large ones, retained its predominantly pre-industrial landscape well into the twentieth century. Berlin, Bremen and Breslau doubled in size between 1875 and 1910. In the same period Munich, Hamburg, Chemnitz (today Karl-Marx-Stadt) and Nuremberg increased more than three times; Düsseldorf and Frankfurt more than four, Essen and Kiel nearly six times. The number of cities with over 10,000 inhabitants rose from 271 to 576 in those years.

Structural change

The pace of social change was a factor of prime political importance in the second half of the century. Its effect was much more profound than the severe social problems of the years before 1848, including even that of pauperism. In the earlier part of the century, contemporaries did not experience the kind of dislocation and consequent moral disorientation which was a characteristic response to the changes of the last quarter of the century. In the first sixty years or so of the century German society retained its traditional hierarchical character, and so continued to provide both individuals and groups with a sense of identity within the whole. Patterns of behaviour, both in personal relations and in public attitudes, continued to be determined largely by the inherited criteria of each social and professional group, at least until the 1860s. Between 1800 and *c.* 1860 the barriers between certain strata of society became less rigid, as a result of the liberal economic policies of many German states in the early nineteenth century. The dividing line between the nobility and the upper bourgeoisie, for example, became less hard and fast than it had been in the eighteenth century. This did not come about through capitulation on the part of the nobility to the tenets of the west European bourgeoisie, but rather because the nobility absorbed a limited number of energetic bourgeois entrepreneurs into its own ranks. In the middle ranks of society, on the other hand, among academics or civil servants, merchants, craftsmen or small traders, social mobility remained restricted in the early decades of the century.

It was not merely that one married one's own kind, but one tended to dance, drink, take tea or go on excursions with one's own kind. While this was a general feature of European society, the segregation of social groups was even more pronounced in Germany

Beiblatt zum Kladderadatsch.

Berlin, den 9. August 1885.

Halb gepökelt, halb gebraten —
Socialisten, Demokraten —
Stehplatz, Tabakrauch in Masse —
Also fährt man **vierter Klasse**.

Dritte Klasse muß oft schwitzen,
Aber darf auf Bänken sitzen.
Zwar kein Platz für Staatsminister,
Aber gut für Reichsphilister.

Wenn Coupé nicht überfüllt ist
Und zu stark nicht qualmverhüllt ist,
Vis-à-vis auch jung und niedlich —
Zweite Klasse — sehr gemüthlich.

Erste Klasse — welch Behagen
Ausgestreckt durch Welt zu jagen,
Weil in erster Klasse hausend
Nur die oberen Zehntausend.

German society as seen by *Kladderadatsch* 9 August 1885 in its railway passengers.

than elsewhere. At the lower end of the social scale the barriers separating the so-called petty bourgeois from the proletariat became less defined in the economic crises of the post-Napoleonic period. However, the urban wage-labourers grew more slowly in numbers than a superficial acquaintance with the history of the industrial revolution in Germany would suggest. Although industrialisation was rapid after 1850, emigration abroad continued to be a major factor until well into the 1850s, and the great internal migration, 'the flight from the land', did not reach full proportions until the last thirty years of the century. It was not in fact until the 1890s that Germany ceased to be primarily an agrarian country in terms of the percentage of her population employed on the land, and became a predominantly industrial one.

The nobility

At the beginning of the twentieth century, the leader of the German Conservative party, the Prussian landowner von Heydebrand, remarked to a deputy of the Left Liberals: 'The future' he said, 'belongs to you, the *masses* will set themselves to rob us, the aristocracy, of our influence. A strong statesman can only delay the inevitable, but we do not intend to surrender our position voluntarily.' It was a cool appraisal of what, in the context of European history since the French Revolution of 1789, was an extraordinary fact. The German, more particularly the Prussian, nobility, whose political and social influence had rested on the particularist structure of Germany under the Holy Roman Empire, demonstrated in the nineteenth century its ability to survive the demise of the feudal order. Not only did it do so, but its members proved able to preserve and actually to consolidate their power and position in the century of liberalism, nationalism and industrialisation. The German nobility survived the demise of the Holy Roman Empire in 1806 and the revolutions of 1830 and 1848, with its legal privileges abolished but its political influence and social status, if anything, enhanced. It had been able to do this for a variety of reasons. Among the most important of these were the survival of more than thirty sovereign princes in the German Confederation (1815–67), and the traditional policy of royal and princely rulers of giving preferment to the nobility in the army and state service. Under Bismarck's administration, and particularly in the reactionary era from 1878–90, a determined effort was made by the Prussian and the German leadership to appoint noblemen to key

posts in government and administration. At a lower, and as it
proved, vitally important administrative level, the practice in
Prussia of almost invariably appointing a local noble landowner
into the influential position of *Landrat*, who was the representative of
the central government at local level, assured the maintenance of
the nobility's power at grass-roots level. Preferment of the nobleman
over the commoner had long been the practice in the army, even in
Bavaria, where the local nobility had since the seventeenth century
taken relatively little interest in posts in the state service. In an effort
to involve them more the Bavarian ruler created in the 1820s the
institution of royal pages, who were then educated at cadet schools,
as was the practice in Prussia. In Germany in the latter years of the
century, the growth of the German army was not matched by an
increase in the number of aristocratic recruits presenting themselves, but even then the higher posts and better regiments were
reserved for them almost exclusively.

  The vigorous discussion in intellectual and government circles in
the late eighteenth and early nineteenth centuries on the role of the
nobility in German society had seemed to suggest that its abolition
was only a matter of time. Yet bourgeois opposition to class privilege
proved surprisingly·ineffective in subsequent decades. Even in the
debates of the Frankfurt Assembly during the revolution of 1848
there was by no means a consensus among middle-class deputies in
favour of getting rid of the institution as such. Indeed, many self-
confessed liberals continued to believe that it had a role to play in
the future constitution of the state. Survival of the nobility as a class
owed a very great deal to the lack of cohesion in the German middle
class, and especially to the fact that Germany did not possess a west
European type of bourgeoisie in the first half of the century. The
failure of German revolutionaries in 1848 to bring about a
redistribution of political power, contrasts with events in France
after the 1830 revolution and particularly after the 1848
revolution, or in Britain after the introduction of the Reform Act of
1832. Even the emergence of a new bourgeoisie from mid-century
onwards in Germany did not change the situation. The commercial
classes proved much more preoccupied with private economic
concerns and the professional classes with personal status than they
were with political power or privilege. Indeed, in the second half of
the century members of the new bourgeoisie identified themselves
more and more with the reactionary values of the nobility, the pre-
industrial elite. They did this, either because those of academic and
professional backgrounds found themselves in competition with the

nobility for posts in government service, or because fear of organised labour convinced them of the necessity of solidarity. If the preeminence of the nobility had been based merely on social exclusiveness, as in the Latin countries, it would have been easier for the German middle class to ignore it. It was the fact that the majority of German noblemen had to earn their living and therefore occupied important positions in government and administration, which persuaded ambitious bourgeois in the late nineteenth century, that they were more likely to be successful if they emulated rather than challenged the traditional ruling elite. Social and political influence was to be gained by connections with the court, the army and the senior civil service. These could be sought through marriage or personal ennoblement, which could be won by making substantial monetary contributions to the Conservative parties or interest groups. By contrast with Britain, a parliamentary career offered a middle class German little in the way of prestige or personal power.

The nobility could claim little justification for their continued privileges apart from tradition. It was not as if the nobility as a caste had rendered service to the community, either as a social group or through individual members, apart from their association in the public mind as commanding officers of the victorious Prussian armies in the 1860s and 1870s. The example of the British upper class in the same period offers a singular contrast in this regard. There is no comparison, for example, between the moral and political energies of a Wilberforce or a Shaftesbury and their kind, which were generated by the evangelical movement and applied for the benefit of their fellowmen, and the stultifying reactionary influence of religious revivalism among aristocratic families and members of the Prussian royal family in the early nineteenth century. In one case, social need was seen to demand action by the powerful individual, whatever the state did or did not do. In the other, social need was interpreted primarily as representing the danger of revolution, which must be legislated against. Through their control of appointments to church and school on their estates, and the local gendarmes, as in the case of the Prussian landed classes, and through the Conservative political parties in the early years of the German Empire, and the pressure groups, such as the Farmers League in the last years, the German nobility acted as the spokesman and self-styled protector of the rural classes. This is not to say that the rural nobility did not show genuine concern for their tenants. But particularly in the latter half of the century, such sentiments of paternalism were invariably associated with claims to absolute submission on the part of the dependent, to the will and authority of the master, while those who questioned such assumptions were treated as dangerous radicals. A sentimental-isation of their role and a self-congratulatory righteousness, which of course is a common human failing, very often accompanied the expression of a sense of responsibility. In spite of the modernisation of the economy, in spite of the immense increase and mobility of the population, what the great 19th century historian, Otto Hintze, called the 'nimbus of local lordship', disappeared very slowly, particularly in east Germany. The extraordinary authority exercised by the local landowner in Mecklenburg, in Pomerania, Silesia, East and West Prussia, is eloquently, if not always impartially attested, in memoirs of those who experienced it. In other parts of Germany the proportion of land held by noble landowners was very much less, and the more numerous urban and village settlements restricted the power of the local nobility by contrast with the situation in north-east Germany.

In the south, the nobility was generally less privileged than in the north. Württemberg had traditionally curtailed the privileges of its nobility, especially in the political sphere. Noblemen might not be members of the estates of the realm. Personal nobility was another thing and was granted automatically to every staff officer, to every minister and to such figures of the establishment as the rector of Tübingen university. In southern Germany generally the nobility, which included a considerable number of mediatised families who had their estates there, formed an exclusive social caste, marrying and moving within their own rank. However, here the Prussian tradition of service of the nobility to the state was lacking, and although prime ministers of Bavaria and Hesse-Darmstadt, but less generally of Baden, were usually noblemen, the middle classes provided the administrators at both state and local level, and thus had access to court and government in a way which was not true of the north. Moreover in some regions, as in Bavaria, the state loaned the peasantry monies to pay off their obligations to their landlords; in this way the landed classes gained access to capitalist enterprise, which helped to integrate them into the bourgeoisie.

In Germany as a whole the nobility's successful defence of its privileged status and position in the nineteenth century owed a great deal to the political settlement of 1815. The princes and statesmen concerned with the re-ordering of Germany in the aftermath of Napoleon saw in the nobility a vital element of reconstruction. Noblemen were made directly subject to the state, which not all had been before, though this was a feature which was bitterly resented by the highest nobility, the so-called '*Standesherren*' or mediatised princes. However, many *Standesherren* were compensated by being given prestigious appointments in government service, especially in diplomacy. One of them was for many years prime minister of Bavaria, later governor of Alsace-Lorraine and finally (1894–1900) imperial chancellor, Chlodwig von Hohenlohe. Loans enabled others to develop resources on their lands, and noblemen also enjoyed exclusive fiscal privileges. In Prussia, for example, some 50% of manorial land was free of tax in the years after 1815, and the institution of *Landschaften* or provincial estates provided credit facilities only to aristocratic landowners, which enabled the efficient among them to transform their estates into viable economic enterprises in the aftermath of the land reform. Moreover, the influx of well-to-do bourgeois into landownership and their elevation to the nobility injected new expertise and, above all, a capitalistic approach to agriculture. It was this process which gave an apparently moribund social class a revitalised economic basis for its survival and allowed its members to consolidate their influence in society and the state. Thus, after an initial period of adjustment and severe problems on the land, Prussian Junkers, their neighbours in Mecklenburg and the newly ennobled landed proprietors in Saxony, enjoyed almost half a century of prosperity, exploiting the resources of their land. After the abolition of the Corn Laws in Britain in 1846, they pursued a highly profitable export trade in grain abroad, which lasted for thirty years.

A much more serious challenge to the status and function of the aristocracy emerged in the 1870s as a result of economic, demographic and political changes consequent on the industrial revolution. Events over which Germany had no control, such as competition of cheap American and Russian grain, threatened their financial position. It was then that with the dexterous support of Bismarck the Prussian landowning classes demonstrated what Max Weber so aptly called 'their will to power'. They appointed themselves spokesmen of aristocratic claims to special treatment in society. Between the mid-1870s and the early 1890s, the landowning interests organised themselves into powerful pressure groups, winning allies from other groups and appointing themselves leaders of the large and disparate groups of Germans, both in and outside Prussia, whose expectations had not been realised in the new nation. The driving force behind all these dissatisfied groups were the

Prussian conservatives, whose leaders showed their thoroughly sound grasp of modern methods of propaganda and public persuasion. As the modern historian Rudolf Stadelmann once observed, 'Under Frederick Wilhelm IV (1840–61), Prussian Conservatism was a *Weltanschaung* (ideology), under Bismarck, it still represented some kind of spiritual tradition, but under Caprivi in the 1890s, it became purely an economic interest group.' Representatives of the landowning interest became the self-styled guardians of 'pre-industrial values', which appealed to people of very different backgrounds from their own. Thus the farmers of north-west and south-west Germany accepted the leadership of Prussian Conservatives, if rather reluctantly in some cases, in defence of their own economic interests. In common with the leading industrialists with whom the landowners had formed the tactical alliance known as 'Corn & Iron', the Prussian Conservatives laid claim to a monopoly of paternalist values in the society in which they lived and they did so, in a manner which reassured petty bourgeois circles in many parts of the country. The tolerance of the continued influence of the nobility shown by much of the population, from the bourgeoisie to the lower middle class, and by some, if not all of the farming communities, had much to do with the sense of political dislocation in late nineteenth century Germany, consequent on the rapid transformation of Germany from a rural to an industrial state.

The Middle Classes

Civil servants

In 1807, just a year after the overthrow of the old Fredrician order on the battlefields of Jena, Napoleon wrote to his brother Jérome, recently made King of Westphalia, that he thought the effect of the *Code Napoléon* would be considerably more persuasive in winning the loyalty of Germans than all his victories. 'What the German people want more than anything else, is for those who are not of noble birth to have equal rights (on the basis of their ability) to distinctions and positions.' Their recognition of the validity of Napoleon's assessment inspired the liberal bureaucrats in Prussia, and hence in other German states, to introduce a wide-ranging programme of reform. These had a twofold aim; a special category of persons within society was to be brought into direct relationship with the state, and the subjects of the ruler were to be transformed into free and self-reliant citizens of the state. Secondly, encouragement was to be given to private enterprise, in order to increase state revenue. Certain aspects, such as the the introduction of freedom of trade and the abolition of obligations traditionally associated with owning property, directly fostered the rise of a capitalist economy. The consolidation of the civil service into a kind of semi-independent class, did much to help Germans of middle-class origin identify with the state in the Restoration era. State service was made open to competition in Prussia in 1834 and in a number of other German states in the post-Napoleonic period; it attracted large numbers of candidates, both from the middle and upper ranks of society. Not only noblemen, but even mediatised princes had to submit themselves to the same examination as bourgeois aspirants. (This was not the case for the diplomatic service. In Germany, as in other European countries, members of the nobility, and particularly the high nobility, were preferred, for the practical reason that a man's exalted position would give him an easier entry to the 'best society' in the country to which he was accredited, than would be given to someone without such connections.) The personal oath taken by the bureaucrat to the sovereign, the need to conform in public and in private to a certain code of behaviour, the existence of disciplinary procedures and the provision of economic security in case of illness or retirement, all helped to give government officials a sense of belonging to a corporate estate, somewhat comparable to the esprit de corps in the army.

Constitutional states such as Bavaria had special provisions governing the legal rights of their officials, and both Bavaria and Prussia associated the bureaucrats with the nobility. A Prussian cabinet order of 1837 referred to the nobility, the military and the civil servants as 'persons of exalted or educated status'. Wilhelm von Humboldt observed shortly after the end of the Napoleonic wars, 'Only the state officials command respect, and this is why everyone is trying to enter this class.' The status awarded to government service at every level, despite frugal salaries until well after the middle of the nineteenth century, lessened the tensions which existed, for example, in Goethe's youth between the two classes (viz. '*Werther*') and made it largely immaterial whether the official was of noble or middle class origin. Tensions between the aristocracy and the middle class lessened considerably in the Restoration era, by contrast with previous decades. Attitudes of suspicion and resentment were much more apparent between members of local communities, as for example in the Rhineland or south Germany, towards government officials, whether bourgeois or aristocratic, who interfered, as they believed, in the conduct of their own affairs. Moreover, the lifestyle of the Restoration era was itself unmistakably bourgeois. The frugality of German court life, especially in the north, was proverbial, most notably in Prussia, to a lesser extent in Saxony or Weimar. However, the two groups did not merge, and the educated bureaucrats tended to form a distinct stratum in society, distinct from other middle-class groups, a 'titled patriciate' as the historian of the 1848 revolution, Veit Valentin, once phrased it. Towards the end of the Restoration era, a trend developed for noblemen rather than commoners to be promoted to senior posts in administration. This proved to be a long-term trend, although initially it did not include the judiciary, which had several liberal and even radical members of relatively humble origins. In Prussia from Bismarck's time onwards (that is, from 1862), and in the Empire from 1871, bourgeois civil servants found themselves increasingly discriminated against when applying for senior judicial and administrative posts.

The academics
One group of civil servants remained solidly middle class and they regarded themselves as the repository of specifically bourgeois values in the nineteenth century. These were the university professors and grammar-school teachers. In the pre-March period they had been spokesmen of specifically liberal and national values, and they had often suffered for their principles. In the 1848 revolution, academics had seats in parliamentary assemblies out of all proportion to their number in society, indeed the Frankfurt Assembly for a long time was known as the 'Professors' Parliament'. The political affiliations of German academics changed in the second half of the nineteenth century and they became increasingly conservative both in their political sympathies and their public behaviour. They esteemed their status as members of the so-called '*Bildungsbürgertum*', the educated classes, more highly than their income. As the sociologist Theodor Geiger once put it, 'The kind of income one had was less important than the question of who one sits beside in the local inn.' Increasing conservatism among the educated as a class was motivated in part by their wish to defend the elitist position which they enjoyed vis-à-vis other middle-class groups. They became vigorous supporters of chauvinistic nationalist ideals, and towards the end of the century, of imperialism. The academics, and this included also members of the liberal professions – doctors, lawyers, editors – gave active support

to Nationalist pressure groups, such as the Navy League. It is striking that higher civil servants, professors and lecturers, teachers and artists,* constituted some 50% of the membership of the militant Pan-German League in 1901.

The educated elite in Germany had traditionally tended to recruit its members from its own ranks, although a significant minority came from the merchant class and a small number from the artisan class. Similar social origins and academic training (a classical education at a grammar-school, followed by a six-year university training), fostered a homogeneous mentality. Under the Empire this homogeneity was developed further by membership of special institutions, such as student fraternities with their 'old boy' network, and the possession of a commission as officer of the reserve, which helped to identify them more closely with the militarist values of the state in which they lived. Whether they voted for the Conservative or the right-wing Liberal parties in elections, German academics in the late nineteenth century invariably gave their support to the status quo. Even the whimsical Professor Schmidt, hero of Fontane's satirical novel of Berlin in the 1890s, '*Frau Jenny Treibel*' (1894) and the obvious favourite of his creator, shares the same enthusiasm for things as they are with his less attractive colleagues.

The commercial classes

The educated bourgeoisie, in contemporary parlance the *Bildungsbürgertum*, existed alongside another successful middle class stratum, the plutocracy or *Besitzbürgertum*. The two groups had relatively little contact with each other before the last years of the century, and then generally only in regions such as the Rhineland and the smaller towns of southern Germany, where numbers were too small for social barriers to be maintained. In the early nineteenth century the social origin of those who came to represent the propertied middle classes lay in banking, commerce and the retail trade. Social mobility was not generally a feature of the early industrialists. Few were self-made men, though some of the most famous names were sons of craftsmen and traders, as for example, Borsig who made his name in the manufacture of locomotives, and Karl Zeiss who made his in precision optical instruments. The

---

* In Germany successful artists, such as the painters Makart or Lenbach, or the composer Wagner, tended to become much more 'establishment figures' than their counterparts in west or south Europe.

banker Gerson Bleichröder, the first unbaptised Jew to be ennobled
in Germany, came from a family who had been market traders in
the early nineteenth century. Where upward social mobility did
take place, it usually spanned two generations. A feature of the early
German entrepreneur was that he was often different in religion and
life-style from the community in which he lived. Most factory
owners in the Ruhr and Wuppertal were Protestants, the majority
of them Calvinists. The merchants of Aachen and Cologne were
Lutheran, while Jewish businessmen in mid-nineteenth century
Berlin numbered some 50% of the whole. These men had little
contact with social groups other than their own. The close business
links between the more important industrialists and bankers in mid-
century were increased by marriage alliances. Their patriarchal
life-style was not unlike that of the established commercial families
in the Hanseatic cities of Hamburg and Lübeck, frugal in everyday
life, munificent when it was a question of 'representation'. The
energies which early entrepreneurs devoted to building up their
businesses allowed little time for politics or entertainment. The
same still held true at a somewhat later date between about 1860
and 1890 in south Germany when family firms were founded which
grew rapidly, as for example the many breweries in Württemberg or
the electrical firm of Robert Bosch in Stuttgart. First of all business,
then politics, was the rule of another electro-technician, Werner
Siemens, son of a Hanoverian tenant farmer, and from small
beginnings in 1847 his firm grew to employ nearly a quarter of a
million in the early twentieth century.

    The prodigious expansion of business in the so-called *Gründerzeit*
or Promoter's Boom in the late '60s and early '70s, caused Rhenish
and Berlin businessmen to alter their way of life and the same was
true in the 1890s, when the long depression at last came to an end.
While Jewish bankers such as Abraham Mendelssohn, father of
Felix, or Wilhelm Beer, brother of the composer Meyerbeer, had
entertained splendidly within the confines of their home and to a
small circle in early and mid-century, a generation later the
hospitality of businessmen could be positively imperial; in no case
more than that of Bismarck's banker, Bleichröder. In the case of
wealthy Jews, and of captains of industry to a lesser extent,
ostentation no doubt compensated for a continued sense of social
inferiority. It was however, an increasingly common feature of
successful industrialists, especially from the Rhineland, that under
the Empire they sought acceptance by their social superiors.
Economically, the industrialists were a powerful stratum, but they

did not possess political influence in the 1870s commensurate with their wealth, nor the social status enjoyed by the academic classes. The award of titles as *Kommerzienrat* (commercial councillor), of patents of nobility, which occurred with increasing frequency in the 1870s, purchase of landed estates and of commissions in fashionable regiments for their sons, accompanied often by large contributions to the Conservative party interest, not only satisfied the ambitions of the plutocracy, but helped them identify with the political values of the ruling classes. A nice illustration of the status consciousness of the times in general, and of the industrialists in particular, is provided by the anecdote concerning Werner Siemens, who refused the title of *Kommerzienrat*, which he said was not appropriate, since he was a technologist and not a businessman. He did, however, accept with alacrity the title of *Geheimrat* or privy councillor, as it acknowledged the scientific quality of his life's work and brought him into contact with scholars. Middle-class businessmen made valuable contacts by proving themselves useful to the Prussian aristocracy on the stock exchange. Friedrich Spielhagen's novels give accurate pen-portraits of these and other contemporary social types and are very informative on the relations between the different strata of society. Although the narrative is usually presented through an idealised middle-class hero, and the corruptness of the nobility is highlighted through individual characters, the immutability of the social hierarchy is never questioned, either by hero or by narrator. The middle-class types may be the heroes, the nobility (with a few female exceptions), the villains, but an awareness of their own virtues, not social change, much less revolution, is deemed sufficient reward for patient striving and loyalty to king and country.

The impact of the depression of 1873–96 on heavy industry and the potential power of organised labour brought about the tactical alliance already referred to, that of 'Corn and Iron', namely the Prussian landowning interest with those who were already beginning to be dubbed the 'industrial barons'. The two groups shared similar views as to their relations with dependents. The patriarchalism of the old craftsmen and early factory owners was cultivated by some big industrialists such as Stumm and Krupp, who controlled their workers' free time, their opinions and their reading. Siemens spoke of his organisation as an 'industrial dukedom'. Despite their wealth, German businessmen did not see themselves as an independent and liberalising element in politics and society. Rather did they share in the overall tendency of the

Der Herr Commercienrath VOR

und NACH seiner Decorierung

A. OBERLÄNDER

Mr Commercial Councillor *before* and *after* his decoration, by A. Oberländer.

German middle classes in the late nineteenth century to identify themselves with the authoritarian system or even, as in the case of the way they managed cartels and syndicates, to promote the neo-feudal character of imperial Germany. The same overall trend is characteristic of that section of the middle class in Germany, known as the *Kleinbürger*.*

---

* The difficulty of rendering the German term *Kleinbürger* into English is virtually insuperable. It has associations of 'lower middle class', but more important, at least in the nineteenth century, are the sense of rights and duties conferred on a member of this social group by the traditional association of 'Bürger' with being a citizen of a town or local community: hence choice of the English term 'burgher'.

The Kleinbürger or German burgher

Some years ago, before awareness of the dimensions of the Federal Republic's economic power became current abroad, many foreigners' image of Germany, or rather of what they liked to think of as the 'true Germany', was of a country of small idyllic towns and sleepy citizens. Even the stereotype Prussian officer or drill sergeant could not displace the widespread notion that the typical German was a comfortable burgher, sedentary in his ways and equable of temperament. In nineteenth century Germany, the burgher, or *Kleinbürger*, indeed regarded himself as the true representative of his people, the backbone of the nation. Artisans and traders, shopkeepers, innkeepers and publicans, subaltern officials and small to medium farmers, made up the body of this stratum of society. They were particularly well represented in the small communities of south, central and north-west Germany. Because of the relative poverty and political divisions of Germany before the industrial revolution, poor communications perpetuated the tendency to live within narrow communities, with all the accompanying values associated with such traditions. The German burgher was traditionally thrifty and diligent, status-conscious and politically passive. Several factors came together in the course of the nineteenth century to influence his position in society adversely.

In the post-Napoleonic period, the economic situation of craftsmen worsened sharply in many states, as a consequence of the introduction of freedom of trade. English factory-produced goods, particularly textiles, flooded the market at prices much lower than German artisans could afford to sell at. Furthermore, competition increased at home, because of the removal of restraints on trade and on account of the sudden population increase in this particular social group. In Prussia, the population increased by some 50% between 1816 and 1843; the increase in the number of master craftsmen was 80%, craftsmen without a master craftsman's certificate as high as 120%. Yet the majority of artisans were poor. In Berlin, for example, 70% of all artisans in the Restoration era were too poor to pay the trade tax (*Gewerbesteuer*). The guilds had lost their economic power to control production and membership in most German states, but they retained their social functions to care for their members, and this to a certain extent helped to isolate them from other social groups. The problem of widespread pauperisation of the *Kleinbürger* class and its implications attracted the attention of governments, municipal councils and social commentators. In the Communist Manifesto, for example, Marx observed emotively and accurately: 'Those who up to now were members of the lower middle classes (*kleinen Mittelstände*), small industrialists, merchants and rentiers, the artisans and farmers are sinking into the proletariat.' The plight of artisans and related social groups caused many governments to revise their liberal trading laws, though not in Prussia. The problems experienced by these social groups had an important influence on the course of the revolution in 1848, problems which were exacerbated by their own sense of division within their ranks. Many were conscious of their burgher status being under attack, and when appeals to the authorities had produced little result, gave active support to the liberal assemblies in 1848. Others joined popular uprisings in the spring and autumn of 1848, supporting strikes and trade congresses and looked to organisations of the kind envisaged by one of the strikers' leaders, the printer Stephan Born, namely self-help.

Nowhere is the regional diversity of Germany more evident than in the history of her craftsmen. In general, the determined adherence to economic liberal principles by the Prussian government brought former artisans to the factories or to workshops as suppliers to shops and middlemen. Borsig's locomotive factory in Berlin during the 1850s employed over 1,000 men, many of whom were former artisans from the metalworkers guild. In the many regions of southern Germany, despite rivalry from manufacturing enterprises, craftsmen continued to enjoy or actually regained the kind of state protection they relied upon, and thus remained men of consequence, if not of substance, in their community. The fate of the artisans and tradesmen in the industrial revolution depended both on the individual and the craft. Some trades, as for example branches of the fancy goods trade, such as wig-makers or hatters, suffered virtual obliteration. Others, notably metal-workers, and in the second half of the century, workers in the food industry, prospered. In the last decades of the century, craftsmen found themselves in great demand to repair or service products, or to provide specially commissioned articles such as leather or fashion goods. In general then, after the severe dislocation of the Restoration years, German artisans adapted to the changed economic situation and continued to exist alongside industry. Whole groups had disappeared, one-man concerns became fewer, but the role of the artisan both in large and in small communities continued to be deemed necessary. Many former artisans had gone into industry in the 1850s and 1860s. Here they regarded themselves

as an elite among other workers. By the 1870s, however, the
majority were beginning to identify themselves with the wage-
labourers and were drawn to the Socialist movement. The artisan
tradition of self-help survived to find new outlets both in the party
and, especially from the 1890s onwards, in the Free Trade Union
movement.

The self-employed craftsmen and tradesmen, on the other hand,
felt a sense of solidarity with a number of other groups in society,
among them the subaltern officials. It was not uncommon for
craftsmen to keep one of their sons on at school if they could afford
it, to let them sit an examination qualifying them for the lower levels
of state service, as a clerk or even as a primary schoolteacher. The
status and the economic security enjoyed by such a person, however
low the salary, were attractive to them. Another status symbol an
official might enjoy, which was not open to a craftsman on
educational grounds, was honorary office in the community. After
1871 the state began to take on more of the tasks which had hitherto
been performed by individuals or by the community, and the
opportunities for employment as subaltern official were increased
considerably. An instance of this is the state takeover of private
railway lines. The length of state railway lines in Prussia in 1878 was
less than 5,000 km, but by 1890 it was 25,000 km and in 1910,
37,000 km. A further source of employment was the postal service
which from the 1890s onwards included telephones. The state
assumption of responsibility for maintenance of roads, lighting,
drainage, waterways and water supply, and the beginning of
communal help and social services are part of the same process.
Municipal transport also provided employment, and its provisions,
as for example in the case of Berlin, for different and smart types of
uniforms for each form of transport – white top-hats for the cab
drivers etc. – emphasised the notion of status and responsibility in
the mind of both the employee and the public. However, the
unsatisfactory economic situation of subaltern officials even in the
second half of the century, and the fact that the state expected all its
employees to keep up appearances in dress etc., was often a cause of
frustration and bitterness. In the south this was less evident, partly
because of the more settled social structure and because the state,
unlike in northern Germany, continued to grant its employees a
number of perquisites of office such as accommodation, and its
officers of the law in Württemberg for example, a percentage of fines
imposed.

In the last years of the century, the growth of a new social group, the white collar workers in industry, the so-called 'new *Mittelstand*' who generally earned more than the subaltern officials, and on the other hand the growing solidarity of wage-labourers in their various political and economic organisations increased the political awareness of what was called the 'old *Mittelstand*'. Indeed, the 'old *Mittelstand*' came for many Germans to represent the traditional order whose passing they lamented. The widespread rejection of the notion of industrialisation and modernisation by the majority of Germans in the Empire, despite their enjoyment of its many benefits, and the political propaganda of the establishment including the emperor, members of the court as well as of the administration and the army, which attributed to pre-industrial social groups, special 'moral' and 'national' values, all these things nurtured their self-regard and their claims to continued privileged status in the community. While the subaltern officials had been liberal and even radical up to and during the 1848 revolution, as had rural inn-keepers, shop-keepers and small merchants, the course of the revolution had changed this. However, although in subsequent decades they became increasingly conservative by inclination, they had neither a political party nor a pressure group to represent their interests. A certain social envy was characteristic of them at the ostentatious wealth of the bourgeois classes, and a fear of the urban labour force on the other hand. These trends directed very many of their members towards the Conservative political parties in the late nineteenth century, and particularly the pressure groups of the late 1890s. They gave their whole-hearted support to organisations such as the War Veterans Association, the Pan-German League, the Navy League, the Reich League against Social Democracy. In the German Shop Assistants Association, which excluded Jews, one sector of this social stratum formed its own pressure group. A common bond between all such groups, including in general the 'new *Mittelstand*' also, was that their civic virtues of obedience, discipline and diligence put the authorities under a special obligation to protect their interests. The ruling classes sought to reassure these potentially disaffected social groups, by their use of terms such as the phrase '*staatserhaltende Kräfte*', (forces which support and sustain the state) with regard to them, and by such reassurance to win mass support from the nation for their policies.

The workers

Wage-labourers

The social origins of the work force in Germany in the early nineteenth century were very diverse. The majority worked in domestic craft and manufacture, but in some branches of production, especially textiles, the labour force was predominantly female; the women were generally single, widowed or deserted, or the wives of ill-paid or invalid workers, or of former soldiers. Factory workers in the early years of industrialisation were generally former artisans who had not been successful in establishing themselves as masters or whose trade had been destroyed by foreign or native factory competition. A number came from among those landless rural labourers who proved to be the victims of the land reforms. There were further differences in status among individual wage-labourers, deriving from skills and traditions, conditions of work between one entreprise or branch and another, and even within the same concern. Wage differentials were often very considerable; again these existed both between trades as well as within a single factory or workshop. Contemporary terminology in the Restoration period reflects structural differences – *Arbeiter*, usually translated as worker, referred to men with skills, whether they had served their time as craft apprentices or not, and the term *Arbeiterstand*, literally 'the estate of worker', was occasionally heard; the pejorative *Proletarier* or proletariat was used in the 1840s to refer to the mass of unskilled labour, whose origin could be either urban or rural. Alfred Krupp, founder of the firm of Krupp, declared in the 1830s that he recruited his labour force wherever he could get men – 'from the hearthside, from the ploughshare, from unemployed craftsmen'. The Berlin machine tool and metal industries, on the other hand, took most of their workers from among skilled craftsmen. Paper and textile manufacture and the ready-made clothing industry tended to attract principally surplus rural population and a high proportion of women. In line with the diverging social and professional origins was the variety of educational backgrounds among the labour force as a whole, although a number of workers in manufacture and industry acquired skills in their trade and were able to better themselves. These were the exception; for the majority of workers in the mid-nineteenth century, it proved extremely difficult to improve their lot. In the generation which followed, the widespread employment of young children, who worked with the active encouragement of their parents, meant that these had little elementary schooling and less chance of acquiring skills. Educational facilities in the factory were introduced by law but inspection proved thoroughly deficient, and the institution of such inspections has been described contemptuously as 'a fig-leaf designed to conceal the employers' disregard of compulsory education requirements' (Henning). Such neglect remained generally characteristic of industry well into the second half of the century, except in the rare cases where altruistic factory owners founded their own schools.

The wide regional diversity of Germany, the very great differences in the pace of industrialisation between east and west, north and south, make it difficult to generalise about earnings and living standards. In his magisterial work on the situation of the German worker under capitalism, *Die Geschichte der Lage der Arbeiter in Deutschland von 1789 bis zur Gegenwart*, the East German scholar, Kuczynski, demonstrates that, while real wages were relatively stable in the 1820s and 1830s, they dropped alarmingly in the mid-1840s. The (estimated) index of real wages in Germany, taking 1815 as the base-line, averaged 86 in the 1820s, 82 in the 1830s, but only 65 in 1846 and 57 in 1847. At the same time the price of basic food-stuffs rose alarmingly, in response to the last great crisis of the traditional type in Europe, namely famine based on crop failure and potato blight. Wages recovered in 1849, to fall rapidly in the 1850s. Sustained recovery in the '60s was followed in 1874 by the great depression which lasted until 1895, but this affected some branches of trade and industry, notably mining and heavy industry, much more than others. Hardship and exploitation found expression in a series of strikes in the 1850s and again in the late 1880s and early 1890s, which were often crushed with great ruthlessness, particularly in the former period. The over-supply of labour to the factories helped to keep wages down, yet there was little machine breaking in Germany, apart from the isolated instances of the Silesian weavers in 1844, the metal workers at Solingen in the 1850s and a few more such cases. While skilled workmen in mid-century tended to organise themselves in middle-class type organisations, such as educational associations and social clubs, the industrial proletariat was slow to develop a group-consciousness; their attitude seems to have been one of fatalism or hopelessness. As the mid-nineteenth century sociologist W. H. Riehl observed, the vast mass of uneducated or unambitious workers knew 'that their job could be

„Was will denn das Gesindel?" — „Wir möchten nur bei Ihnen lernen, Herr Geheimrat, wie man das macht, wenn man den ganzen Tag nicht arbeitet."

Strikers at their employer's by O. Gulbrasson from *Simplicissimus*. 'What does the rabble want?' 'We only want to learn from you, sir, what one does all day when one doesn't work.'

Der — Die — Das

Der Pöbel

Die Menge

Das Volk

Der- Die- Das-
Der Pöbel – the rabble
Die Menge – the masses
Das Volk – the people
      from *Simplicissimus*

filled tomorrow by a child and the following day by a new handle or screw'.

The hostile attitudes of bourgeois society towards the urban wage labourer, which developed at the same time as the rapid expansion of the industrial work force from the 1860s onwards, helped to bring about a cohesion between the various elements of the labour force. Attempts by workers or their spokesmen to provide political organisation were met with the law prohibiting combinations (*Koalitionsverbot* of 1869). Severe penalties for infringement of this measure were invoked by the authorities even as late as the years immediately preceding the 1914 war. It was symptomatic of current attitudes that the brothers Grimm had defined the term *Arbeiterbewegung* (labour movement), in the first volume of their German Dictionary as *Aufruhr der Arbeiter, Arbeitskrawall* (workers' riot or rioting). The volume appeared in 1854. It was bought by bourgeois householders throughout the century and beyond and was regarded by them as authoritative. The attitude of society and the state thus fostered a sense of social isolation among urban wage labourers, especially under the German Empire, which helped to account for the success of the Social Democratic movement and the militancy of their programme.

The appeal of the labour movement in Germany was all the greater since immigrant workers in northern Germany had largely lost contact with their churches. This was not, however, the case with Catholic workers in the Rhineland, who had their own trade union movement and who voted solidly for the Centre party throughout this period. Socialism provided not only a political programme but an ideology for its members and one which was orientated towards the future. It also provided a variety of cultural and social activities, which tended to diminish the revolutionary ardour of the masses, if not of their leaders, in the years of active persecution (1878–90) and of discrimination in the years which followed. An intelligent and ambitious workman who joined the Social Democratic Party had every chance of becoming a person of consequence in his locality; indeed after 1890 at a national level also, when the number of paid officials began to rise rapidly. While school and military service – the later styled 'the school of the nation' – were designed to imbue patriotic attitudes into the urban as well as the rural working class, this often had quite the opposite effect and made workers and intellectuals thoroughly militant. In general, however, most politically minded workers felt a dual but not necessarily conflicting loyalty to 'Kaiser and Bebel'. However genuine their patriotism might be, urban wage labourers were treated as second-class citizens and were constantly made aware of the fact. Yet in the years 1893–1914 workers became aware of their own power, while at the same time they experienced a gradual improvement in their material standards. Spectacular electoral success for the Social Democratic party and huge increases in trade union membership were recorded in the same period. A steady rise in real wages also helped to foster a more pragmatic approach between spokesmen of German labour and the authorities. This however was scarcely acknowledged by employers or by society as a whole, especially in the north. In south Germany, Socialism, as has already been seen, was less militant, for here a Socialist was not a bogey man, known only from reports or caricatures in the paper, but somebody you might find yourself sitting beside in the *Landtag* or at a town council, or even at the next table to your own in the local inn.

However, labour organisations by no means claimed the allegiance of the whole of the German labour force. The members as well as the leaders of labour organisations remained predominantly skilled urban workers, although the semi-skilled became more prominent in labour movements in the years immediately before the war.

The employment agency for domestic servants. Engraving, 1889.

The vast mass of rural labourers remained without contact with the movement and lacked organisations of their own. The same was true of domestic servants, who in this bourgeois age remained a substantial though declining numerical group. Servants did not feel any sense of class solidarity in a political sense; for one thing they moved about far less than did workers in industry. 'Great importance will be attributed to how long domestic servants have been in their former posts' advised Frau Davidis, a kind of German Mrs. Beeton, in her much reprinted manual for housewives. Another important factor was the growing percentage of women over men – by contrast with earlier times – as well as the tendency of servants to identify with the 'family'. Exploitation of domestic servants was a widespread phenomenon in Europe generally, and little of it was recorded in German literature or memoirs. It did not lead to rebelliousness, both because of the relative social isolation of servants, and because of the serious disadvantages of their legal position. The prevailing *Gesinderecht*, or the law or laws relating to domestic servants and their employment, was heavily weighted in favour of the employer. Moreover, the poor educational background of most servants prevented them from asserting themselves, while the kind of reading material provided for female servants and avidly consumed by them was designed to foster their

Servant girls pass the Royal Ulans. Painting by H. Huisken.

native conservatism. However, many servants were aware of the advantages of their position. Country girls, often daughters of rural or small-town tradesmen, such as inn-keepers or café owners, went into service in bourgeois households to learn skills and refinements; after marriage into their community, they would work in their family or a neighbour's business. Service was also considered to improve a girl's chance of marriage, at times above one's station, while the opportunity at market or in one's free time to air grievances or express aspirations no doubt acted as a stabilising factor on the consciousness of this most conservative social sector.

Rural workers

The largest social group in German society until the 1890s was that of the rural labourers and small-holders, numerically greatest in north-east Germany and in the so-called *Realteilungsgebiet* of the south-west, where farmland was equally divided among all the heirs. The agrarian legislation of the late eighteenth and early nineteenth century, one of 'the most incisive and far-reaching events of modern Germany history' (Lütge), had had a profound effect on the inhabitants of rural areas. For those at the bottom of the social scale, legislation robbed many a household of their traditional use of common land, that for grazing and fuel. However, the change-over from a natural to a money-economy, especially in the manorial states of eastern Germany, created a demand for their services as day-labourers, which to some extent catered for their needs. In north-west Germany, a long tradition existed of small-holders renting a plot of land and a cottage from a local farmer and working for him. The same was true of agricultural labourers in Westphalia, who might also ply a trade at home, such as linen weaving.

Among the rural labourers and small-holders in the Restoration era, the enormous, and to contemporaries frightening, population increase was particularly marked among rural labourers and small-holders. While the impressive policy of land-reclamation in nineteenth century Prussia, which increased the area under cultivation between 1807 and 1864 by 100%, went a long way towards providing for the surplus population and preventing the kind of catastrophe suffered by Ireland in the 1840s, conditions of life for rural workers remained hard and in times of crisis, grim. This is evidenced by the number of emigrants to the United States, especially from the north-east and the south-west. Between 1820 and 1860 two million Germans left the land to migrate to the cities or to emigrate to the New World. In the last decades of the century, the flight from the land was on an even greater scale. The increase in the number of bourgeois capitalists, who bought up estates of the nobility in the early decades of the nineteenth century also affected the relationship between landowner and tenant. Capitalist farming did not foster the kind of sense of responsibility for the physical welfare of the rural labourers on which Prussian noble landowners prided themselves. Moreover, even on those estates which were owned by Junker families the sense of responsibility towards dependents was usually conditional on the same family occupying the estate for successive generations, and this grew more and more rare.

For those peasants who had owned holdings above a certain size and who possessed draught-animals, the land reform had one of two consequences: either they paid up part of their substance as the price of independence, and through care, skill and good fortune, rose to be middle-sized and even prosperous farmers, making money in the boom years for agriculture, between the 1830s and the 1870s, or they found themselves unable to meet the new demands and were forced to sell out and become either rural labourers or move into the city. Emigration in the first half and migration in the second half of the century made labour scarce on the land and improved wages for the rural labour-force, though not in line with the rise of industrial wages. In the last years of the century the east German landowners tended to bring in seasonal workers from Russia and the Austrian province of Galicia, who were prepared to work for low wages and in conditions not acceptable to the Germans. This again accelerated the flight from the land. For the peasantry in regions near growing towns the second half of the century could provide prosperity through improved markets for their produce; for example dairy farmers and market gardeners did well. Here innovation and improved productivity were impressive. The structural crises of German agriculture in the 1870s onwards had very adverse effects on the grain-producers and to a lesser extent, on the producers of root crops. In Bavaria, primogeniture ensured the survival of a sturdy peasantry, but in other states, as for example in Baden, division of land between all the sons brought impoverishment to the land as well as to the population. Socially, however, the rural community in Baden remained fairly cohesive, since here the continued survival of common land largely removed the difference of status between peasant-proprietor and rural wage-labourer in the same village. In the country as a whole the growth of credit organisations and rural savings banks, (the most famous of which was founded by the philanthropist Raiffeisen and which still exists), the creation of insurance and co-operatives helped the peasantry in the second half of the century. However, it was usually the medium and large farmers, not the small ones, who took advantage of these.

The political attitudes of the farming communities, however diverse in economic and social character these might be, tended, in common with many other social groups in the nineteenth century, to approximate to those of the Conservative ruling class. Most labourers, especially in the east, had little political awareness, but received their opinions from 'the master'. Moreover, as in the case of the domestic servants, the law governing the employment of rural labourers (*Gesindeordnungen*) was weighted in favour of the employer. The peasantry and the large landowners alike saw the growth of industry, and the increasing economic power of groups other than their own, in terms of conspiracy against themselves. They felt, as did the *Kleinbürger*, as though their contribution in terms of work and loyalty entitled them to special protection by the state. It was this which gave such conviction to the high-flown claims of the Agrarian League of the 1890s, which to other ears sounded so hypocritical. Although constituting only a tiny minority, some 1% of the membership, the large landowners from eastern Germany dominated this agrarian pressure group, and the 'Green Front', as it was called, won the support of such diverse groups as the Catholic farmers in Westphalia and Silesia and small-holders in south and west Germany.

The Jews

Although they no longer formed a physically separate and hence easily identifiable group within society as had been the case in previous centuries, the German Jews in the nineteenth century still retained a distinctive sense of identity in an age which wrought many changes in their external condition. The social origins of the German Jewish community, which averaged roughly one per cent of the total population over the century as a whole, were generally of three kinds. There were the old-established and wealthy families, settled in cities, such as Vienna, Frankfurt, Hamburg and Cologne, connected by marriage with similarly situated Jewish families in Amsterdam, Paris and Bordeaux. These represented a small minority of the community, and, in common with the vast majority, who were poor pedlars, purveyors of small luxuries in the sparsely populated regions of eastern Germany, or tailors, craftsmen and small traders, scattered across the country, they were Orthodox in the practice of their religion. The third group were usually, though by no means exclusively, traders or traders' sons and grandsons who came from Poland and Russia to settle in Germany in the eighteenth or early nineteenth century. Through their ability, hard work and family connections, they became well-to-do merchants in Königsberg, Berlin, Breslau, Nuremberg, Augsburg etc, and sent their sons into the professions. Most of the many Jews who made a name for themselves in business, the arts, politics or public life in the nineteenth century were sons and daughters of such men. Thus the lawyer Heinrich Simon, who played a prominent role in the 1848 revolution and his first cousin, Fanny Lewald, whose best selling novel, *Jenny* (1842) dealing with the relations of young German Jews with their Christian environment, won its author fame overnight, were children of merchants with business in Königsberg and Breslau. The somewhat younger Socialist leader, Ferdinand Lassalle, was a businessman's son from Breslau; the composers Meyerbeer and Mendelssohn came from similarly situated families living in Berlin, while the father of Bismarck's banker, Gerson Bleichröder, worked for the Rothschilds. Most Jews active in some area of public life were baptised in their youth or early manhood, Bleichröder being an impressive exception. They decided to submit to Christian baptism in order to enter certain professions or simply to get round the restrictive legislation operative, for example, in Frankfurt and Königsberg before 1848, which limited the number of marriages in the Jewish communities there to an arbitrary figure of fifteen. Few experienced a crisis of conscience over the decision, though Heinrich Heine for all the apparent flippancy of his famous *bon mot* on baptism for Jews as 'the entrance ticket to European culture', was one of those who did. For him, and those who felt as he, the decision to convert was less a religious problem than a crisis of identity, and one which the progressive integration of Jews into the rest of German society in the course of the century did not solve.

The history of the emancipation of the Jews in Germany is a complex one. Representatives of the Jewish communities in the city states of Hamburg, Frankfurt and Bremen, tried and failed at the Congress of Vienna in 1815, to win a general measure regulating the rights and obligations of German Jews in the new Confederation. States legislated piecemeal for their Jews, or ignored their existence altogether for decades to come. The different states were not in step with one another and the removal of disabilities was therefore not only gradual, but measures to alleviate the problems encountered by Jews were often withdrawn in subsequent years in response to a changed political climate. Thus Napoleon emancipated the Jews in German territories under his rule, but his measures were withdrawn after his defeat. Meanwhile the Jews in the old provinces of Prussia had benefitted from Wilhelm von Humboldt's Prussian Edict of Tolerance in 1812, but the provisions were not extended to the rest of the state, when Prussia recovered her lost territories in 1815 and advanced further into western Germany. A similar situation occurred in and after the 1848 revolution. The very fact that so many Jews had identified themselves with the liberal cause and played such an active role in revolutionary assemblies made reactionary ministers in the 1850s vindictive towards Jews in general. Both before 1848 and thereafter, German governments allowed themselves to be convinced by the specious argument that a gradual removal of disabilities on the Jews, so long pariahs in German society, was in the best interests of all concerned. This approach served to create a 'Jewish question' in people's minds, and delayed both emancipation and integration. The removal of outstanding civic and legal disabilities only came in 1874, as part of a body of liberal legislation which accompanied the process of German unification.

Jews of the two first types did not in general seek integration. Those of the third group, with their rational and optimistic approach to social and political problems, which was a product of the German Enlightenment, tended to take it for granted. Many were bitterly awakened to the reality of prejudice at some stage of their career. Anti-Semitism was a gut reaction, but flared up in times of economic distress. The bad years after the Napoleonic wars, especially between 1816 and 1822, which affected rural communities especially severely and forced indebted noblemen to sell up family estates, saw many sporadic outbreaks of violence against the Jews and their property. This was particularly the case in southern Germany. In the east, where the Jewish population was disproportionately high, especially in the towns of West Prussia, Pomerania and Posen, where it could be as much as 50% of the total, the influence of the pogroms in nearby Russia was a constant threat. The anonymity of the industrial cities, as well as the greater opportunities of personal advancement, proved attractive for Jews from the middle of the century onwards. The villages of Bavaria lost nearly all their Jews to the towns in these years, and the Jewish population in the eastern provinces fell sharply. By contrast the numbers living in the growth areas, such as Berlin and Breslau, increased rapidly every year; bankers, merchants and industrialists included a large percentage of Jews among their members, as did professions such as the law, medicine and journalism. Many poor Jews settled in the city to work for the clothing industry or in other traditional Jewish trades.

The opportunities offered by the German educational system for personal advancement and as a means to gain entry to positions of status in government service had a special appeal for liberal Jews. 'Heinrich (Simon) probably chose a post in the civil service, since it was easy to hide one's racial origins', wrote a close friend of his in later life, and such reasoning was fairly typical of the first generations of Jewish families to become Christians. Increasing numbers from well-to-do families took advantage of grammar school and university education, and, although most encountered the endemic prejudices of their Christian environment, they identified themselves more and more as the century progressed with the values of the society in which they lived. Middle class Jewish homes cultivated the German classics, art and music. In countless such homes, as the biographer of Franz Rosenzweig of Kassel, later a distinguished rabbi, put it, 'Goethe and Beethoven played a chief part and Judaism none at all.' In the later decades of the Empire, most liberal Jews identified with German nationalist values and many gave expression to a sense of euphoria about Germany's future and their own role in society. The highest legal offices were still closed to them, despite emancipation, and anti-Semitic prejudice in military circles was particularly hidebound, yet Jews preferred the legal career to almost any other and a sizeable number aspired to membership in the Reserve and the student fraternities. But many of the student organisations became closed to them from the 1880s onwards, and, as has already been said, a number of the pressure groups also. In the so-called 1892 Tivoli programme, the Conservative party adopted anti-Semitism as one of its official policies, some fifteen years after political anti-Semitism, based on race rather than religion, made its first appearance in Germany. In the last years of the century anti-Semitic utterances were increasingly heard and came to be frequent among members of the establishment, including the emperor himself and his court, and despite the fact of William II's friendship for individual Jews, such as the industrialist, Emil Rathenau and his son, Walter. What is more, anti-Semitism was widely regarded as intellectually respectable as well as socially acceptable.

However, the history of the German Jews in the nineteenth

century, as that of Germans generally, was too persuasive a story of success against many odds not to have inspired optimism and a certain complacency. The Jewish community, taken in its widest sense, could congratulate itself on the position in society of its members. Moreover, those liberal Jews who had long ceased to practise their faith remained conscious of their obligations to fellow-Jews less fortunately placed. The old-established families had augmented their wealth and connections, not alone in Europe, but throughout the world, especially in the United States. The traditional Jewish communities in eastern Germany still lived a ghetto-type existence, but they continued to produce clever children who won fame and fortune in the outside world. The liberal Jews occupied positions of trust and influence in the German community, as bank managers and doctors, scientists, artists, university teachers and journalists. They knew their race had made an outstanding contribution to the national life, and while they retained in general a pride in their racial origins, they felt and thought as Germans.

I I
The Family

Conditions of life for women in the family were modified
substantially in the course of the nineteenth century. At the same
time, the image the Germans had of women altered subtly. Our
image of the kind of life led by women in Germany, and of the
education and environment of children, is much more influenced
than we realise by conditions and attitudes which prevailed in
Germany from about 1867–1945. Yet when one studies literature,
music and painting in the years *c*. 1800–1860 in terms of those artists
who were popular at the time, it is clear that a great deal of care and
imaginative concern was lavished on children in German families
and that discipline was by no means regarded as the most important
element in family life. In particular one is made aware of the fact
that it is a characteristic of German literature and painting to be
especially sensitive in depicting the child's world from the child's
point of view, as well as that of the understanding adult.

What follows is an attempt to describe conditions of life on the
domestic scene. In the absence of sufficient area studies, it must be
impressionistic, but the attempt is surely justified in view of the
remarkable body of literature (both imaginative and periodical), of
painting, letters and memoirs dealing with family life which survive
from the nineteenth century.

The German household
i) Women

A major social change affecting women, especially in the middle
ranks of society, in the early 1800s was the gradual disappearance of
the traditional 'whole house' ('ganzes Haus') family structure. For
centuries the household had consisted of the extended family and
the indoor servants, and it included also those who worked for the

231

master, whether they were farm labourers, apprentices of a craftsman, counter clerks, scribes and carriers in a commercial enterprise. The gradual separation of home and place of work was a feature of the late eighteenth century and early nineteenth century. The passing of a centuries' old tradition was much commented upon at the time as heralding the end of a patriarchal social organisation, which went back, it was alleged, to Roman times and beyond. The wives of merchants or craftsmen in towns and villages, and the wives of large farmers in Schleswig-Holstein, in parts of Hessen and Hanover found themselves no longer responsible for the feeding and maintenance of their husbands' employees, when these began to live away from their place of work. This development was not general throughout Germany but varied according to region. In rural areas of Bavaria and Austria and in Switzerland, as the Swiss novelist, Gotthelf, attests in his novels '*Uli der Knecht*', '*Uli der Pächter*', '*Geld und Geist*' etc, the old patriarchal structure continued to pre-dominate well into the nineteenth century. The mother of the family presided over her maids and the herdsmen and labourers, among whom strict hierarchy prevailed, and cared for the material and spiritual well-being of the household. Where the 'whole house' economy ceased to exist, its passing had important implications for women's status and education, The reduction of their duties of supervising and providing for such large households gave women an interest in their own education, or encouraged them to devote themselves more to the care and education of their children. Contemporaries were very aware of the changes. There was no lack of critical voices to allege that women in the middle ranks of society from the late eighteenth century onwards wasted a considerable portion of their time on frivolous novels. It was certainly true that the female reading public increased rapidly from the middle of the eighteenth century onwards and that 'the reading rage' (*Lesewut*) was a feature of middle class life in the early nineteenth century.

It would seem however, that family life benefitted from the greater leisure of the mistress of the household and her helpers, though how far there was a direct co-relation between this development and the greater refinement of home life characteristic of the so-called Biedermeier period (*c.* 1815–50) is impossible to say. Certainly the cult of family life extended throughout the upper class and middle class circles in these decades. It is recorded in stylised painting of musical evenings, play readings, in birthday poems and the many customs of the German family, which became ritualised in these years. The special feature of this cult of family life is that it was not confined to particular areas or merely to the well-to-do. The craftsmen and small traders, who would rank as *Kleinbürger*, shared a common ideal of cultivated family life with those who were better educated and far more well equipped with the material goods of this world. Skilled workers, in common with their social and material superiors, tried to acquire books for their homes, and innkeepers and local traders – such as Robert Bosch's father and countless others – had themselves painted with their families 'for posterity'. Festivals and leisure activities had a very special place in people's lives, and hospitality within the family was an aspect of this, a welcome interruption of traditional thrift of everyday life in the German household. The German home was (and indeed is) much more accessible to the friend or the visitor than was the case in Britain, France, Italy or Spain. This derived in part from a tradition of hospitality stretching far back in Germany's history and partly from natural curiosity about the stranger in a country where communications were poor. Moreover, the extending of hospitality did not on the whole place undue strain on slender resources. The housewife did not feel called upon to provide more than some extra item for the family meal or perhaps just devote special care in presenting her table. This was also true of larger gatherings. Memoirs of life in Berlin of the 1840s and 1850s recall the literary salons, frequented by popular writers such Lewald, Auerbach and Spielhagen, where the hospitality consisted of little more than tea.

The German household remained a fairly self-sufficient unit in the sense of providing for the family needs in terms of goods and services, for far longer than was the case in western European countries. It was also still common for unmarried female relations to share a home with their married brothers or sisters, especially in the middle and upper ranks of society, and to help in the various household tasks. Household management books, which became popular in the nineteenth century as wedding presents, give some indication of the variety of tasks performed in the home – hair-cutting, dressmaking, making of soap, candles, beer, cultivation of indoor plants, and the massive task (still common in western Germany ten years ago and widely prevalent in the Democratic Republic still), of stocking the larder for the winter with preserves of all kinds. The volume and variety of household activities, and an imaginative concern for their children's physical and moral development, which goes back to the popular works of the Enlightenment, gave women in these social groups in the post-Napoleonic age a fuller life than their grandmothers had enjoyed.

Women in employment

But as the century advanced, it became clear that social conditions
in certain strata of society did not permit many women to enjoy the
benefits of a secure and protected, if restricted, family life.
Differences in the conditions of domestic life between the
bourgeoisie and the traditional German middle classes grew more
pronounced. In the late 1830s and the 1840s, *Kleinbürger* circles
began to be affected by a rapidly rising population and diminishing
chances of earning a living. Prussia in particular, where the
population increased by some 60% between 1815 and 1840,
provided an example of a state with very serious social problems.
Here many professional men, for whom a contemporary coined the
term 'academic proletariat', as well as other social groups within the
broad spectrum of the middle classes, lived on or below the breadline.
The consequence for women in these social groups was pressure on
them to contribute to the family income or in fact to support
themselves. But the attitude of society and of the authorities in the
nineteenth century Germany towards working women was a
thoroughly ambiguous one. Social change, rising population,
recurrent food shortages, rising prices, were driving women to seek
employment. This was a fact of life, a feature of the economy, but it
was a feature of life which was sedulously ignored both by the public
and governments. It was clear that the notion of 'bourgeois' (i.e.
respectable) women working was an abhorrent one to society.

Part of the reason for this attitude was the widespread lack of
employment opportunity for the educated classes in Germany and
in western Europe generally, in the first half of the nineteenth
century. But this fact was much less important in people's thinking
than the deep suspicion felt about any form of 'emancipation' in
itself, which working, especially working outside the home, was seen
to be. Even liberal thinkers throughout the century seemed to fear
anarchy more than tutelage, and the implications for society of
female emancipation were much more far-reaching, than, for
example, the removal of disabilities on the Jewish minority. The
churches, especially the Evangelical church in Prussia as spokesman
of the Crown, were bitterly resentful of suggestions that women
should become involved in interests outside the home. Leading
Prussian clerics castigated women for appearing at public meetings
in the 1830s and 1840s in support of a liberal religious movement
known as the Friends of Light; in fact it was against the law for
women to take part in public meetings throughout the nineteenth
century. The very fact that female emancipation had been taken up

'Picture of the future' Munich (1847). The German woman student of the future. (Note the Jewish star, implying the Jewish associations with women's emancipation.)

by the French Saint-Simonist movement, which gained support among the academic youth in Germany in the 1830s, confirmed people's prejudice that women's emancipation in any form was something both ungodly and subversive. The French war scare in 1840 aroused the nascent chauvinism of many middle class Germans; it was associated by such people with the strictures on French manners and French novels levelled by popular journalists

in the 1830s and 1840s – one of these being Wolfgang Menzel, editor
of the fashionable *Morgenblatt für gebildete Stände*. The lack of
political experience and social 'nous' among the angry young men
known as the Young Germans and the Young Hegelians and their
womenfolk in the 1830s and 1840s, provided their opponents with
effective arguments to attack their basic social criticisms. The
subsequent polarisation of social and political responses into
'radical, democratic, atheistic, prone to foreign influence' on the
one hand, and 'German, paternalist, pious, patriotic' on the other,
persuaded the general public in Germany to overlook the genuinely
progressive quality of these young mens' social thought.

During the revolutionary upheaval of 1848–49, some redoubtable ladies caught the attention of the public – among them Emma,
wife of the poet Herwegh, who helped finance and even lead the
German legion to fight in the Baden revolution. (Satirists on both
sides suggested that she was much more resolute than her somewhat
fainthearted husband.) Johanna, wife of the revolutionary
Gottfried Kinkel, whose home in their London exile was a meeting-
point for European radicals in the 1850s, Malwida von Meysenbug,
author of the widely read '*Memoirs of an Idealist*', and the highly
intelligent novelist, Fanny Lewald were other remarkable women of
their generation. The opponents of revolution made much of the
'unnatural' character of female participation in the revolution in
whatever capacity this might be; and they gained the ear of many a
paterfamilias who was disappointed and shocked by the revolution or
who felt betrayed by the events of 1848–49. The experience of
revolution greatly increased the polarisation in German society over
questions of social reform. The total failure of democratic radical
movements in these years, the failure to challenge the traditional
authorities or to win a measure of general popular approval for
social reform had serious consequences for all liberal and reformist
movements, of which women's emancipation was but an aspect.

But whatever members of governments and the representatives of
public opinion, as expressed in the literary and philosophic journals
of the early and mid-nineteenth century might deem proper for
women, the fact remained that more and more women were being
forced by circumstances to seek employment. For indeed the most
striking change affecting the family between 1800 and 1914 was the
rise in the number of women at work outside the home, though the
most spectacular change occurred only in the last decades of the
period. The following table gives some indication of a social
phenomenon which received too little publicity from a society,

which professed paternalist values and from a state which was alleged to care for the material welfare of its citizens.

Employment of women in the Second Empire (in 1,000s)

Economic sector	Year	Total no. of employed	Women absolute	in %
A. Agriculture	1882	8,236	2,535	30.8
	1895	8,293	2,753	33.2
	1907	9,883	4,599*	46.5
B. Industry	1882	6,396	1,127	17.6
	1895	8,281	1,521	18.4
	1907	11,256	2,104	18.7
C. Commerce and Transport	1882	1,570	298	19.0
	1895	2,339	580	24.8
	1907	3,478	931	26.8
D. Domestic service	1882	1,723	1,466	85.1
	1895	1,772	1,548	87.4
	1907	1,736	1,570	90.4
E. Administration, Military and the Professions	1882	1,031	115	11.2
	1895	1,426	177	12.4
	1907	1,739	288	16.6
F. Together	1882*	18,957	5,542	29.2
	1895	22,110	6,578	29.8
	1907	28,092	9,493	33.8

From: Hohorst, Kocka, Ritter, *Sozialgeschichtliches Arbeitsbuch*, Munich 1975, p. 66.

It was more difficult for middle-class women to find work than for manual workers' wives and daughters, but it was also less necessary for them to do so. Social studies and records from individual manufacturing concerns or branches of manufacture and industry suggest that, from the late eighteenth century onwards, considerable numbers of women and children were in fact seeking

---

* These figures, taken by the authors from the *Statistik des Deutschen Reichs* for the appropriate years, should, they point out, be revised upwards, giving the overall percentual share of women in employment as 35.9% for 1882, 34.9% for 1895 and 34.9% for 1907, while remembering the continued rapid rise in the population.

employment to support themselves or supplement the family income. This was particularly true of women in the textile industries, where the depressed wages and conditions of work bore all the marks of an industry where female labour was easily available and was therefore exploited. Domestic manufacture, most notoriously the weaving industry in central Germany and Silesia, as also the stocking manufactury of Franconia in northern Bavaria and other regions, whose spokesmen protested so plaintively to the Bavarian king in the 1840s, used female and child labour extensively in the first half of the century. The advent of the sewing machine in the 1850s extended womens' ability to support themselves by their own work. The ready-made clothing industry, centred mainly in Berlin, which expanded with tremendous rapidity from the 1850s onwards, offered employment to seam-stresses working at home or in the workshop of a foreman. In this way, the wives, sisters and daughters of those tens, later hundreds of thousands, who left rural areas for the cities in the 1850s and 1860s, but particularly from the seventies onwards, could hope to earn their living, to find lodgings and be respectable, or almost respectable – as Luise Eisold was (Gutzkow's '*Die Ritter vom Geiste*' 1850–52), or the incomparable Lene Nimptsch, heroine of Fontane's '*Irrungen, Wirrungen*' (1888).

Domestic service remained an important option for girls from rural or village backgrounds throughout the century, but it was no longer acceptable from about the mid-century onwards, for middle-class girls to go, as they had formerly done, to a neighbouring 'big house' to learn the domestic arts prior to marriage. Female domestics were widely sought, since it was part of the ethos of the European bourgeois to delegate every menial task to an employee. As in other countries, the status and the conditions of domestic service could vary enormously. German fiction, especially in the latter half of the century, has many vivid portraits of household servants, from the tyrants of the kitchen and the confidants of their mistresses, to the victims of the system, including even those who, like Hedwig (in Fontane's '*Der Stechlin*' of 1898), could find some considerable pleasure in the more obvious forms of exploitation of female dependence. If a servant girl was ill-treated, she was likely to find it very difficult to win redress. If the wrong was on her side however, if she stole or got pregnant, the police were likely to be called in and she to be dismissed 'without a character'. Very many girls who gave birth to illegitimate children had conceived these in their villages and sought the anonymity of the city. Such a girl often looked for domestic employment of some sort to support herself and her child if it survived. This created a pool of labour ready to be exploited both in terms of wages and conditions as well as hours of work. From a legal point of view, domestic servants were less well protected than almost any social class, being subject to a variety of anti-diluvian measures governing their employment which were not brought up to date until after the outbreak of the revolution of 1918 and the collapse of the monarchy. Yet, as a social group, domestic servants, like agricultural workers, were in general staunchly conservative or simply a-political. Neither group showed interest in party-political organisations, unlike women workers in industry. The Socialists in their turn tended to neglect or ignore them, whether as a social group or in their capacity as potentially interested parties in the women's movement.

The aspirations of middle class girls to prepare themselves for employment were not widely voiced until the second half of the century. But in the years preceding the 1848 revolution, individuals agitated to win support for their cause. Fanny Lewald, born in 1811 in Königsberg as one of ten children of a Jewish businessman of not very ample means, gives a vivid account in her

The German woman lecturer of the future (1848).

diaries (published 1858 to 1861) of the difficulties she had encountered from a tolerant and affectionate father and from society in seeking to support herself. She eventually did manage to earn a living as a novelist, writing initially under a pseudonym, and she won a surprising degree of social recognition as well as independence in later life.

Most women striving to be teachers or nurses (the latter thought highly indelicate, though this was by no means unique to Germany), were not very successful and had often to suffer social opprobium. Friederich Fröbel's ideas for training Kindergarten teachers (1839 onwards) had a certain limited success in the first decade of the movement's existence. The popular encyclopedias of the 1830s and 1840s expressed enlightened interest in this and similar projects. But here again the revolution of 1848 seems to have been a watershed. Not only were the Kindergartens suppressed in Prussia after 1848 (cf. section on schooling), but both official policy and public opinion as expressed in journals and encyclopedias showed a growing suspicion and resentment of anything that smacked of female initiative, or of institutions which enabled mothers of families to work.

The women's movement

The women's movement in Germany grew up as a direct response to the sense of a need for improved education for women as a prerequisite to employment. The *Allgemeiner Frauenverein* was founded in 1865 by a writer and teacher, Luise Otto-Peters. It was 1889, however, before girls had their own grammar schools and could take university entrance examinations and 1908 before the last German state to do so (Prussia) allowed them to be admitted to university. 'What we do not want and have never wanted is political emancipation for women', declared Wilhelm Lette, founder of the so-called *Lette Verein* set up to promote technical training for women. It was a sentiment which most German women, even the most politically aware, would have agreed with, at least until the Socialists Klara Zetkin, Rosa Luxemburg and others championed female emancipation as part of the liberation of the proletariat. In other words, in contrast with the women's emancipation movements in the United States and western Europe, the German equivalent lacked a political dimension.

As the result of public debate and its being a favourite theme of popular novels, especially those serialised in womens' magazines and family journals such as the *'Gartenlaube'*, women's education and professions enjoyed tremendous vogue in the last decade of the century. Lectures on the subject drew large audiences, especially in northern Germany, and provincial towns formed their own study groups; Theodor Fontane devoted one of his socially most acutely observed novels to the subject, *Mathilde Möhring* (1896). Women and girls read serialised novels, where quietly confident girls confronted their fathers with plans to study, only to be brought down to earth by the socially conformist views held by their mothers. A typical example of such serials was '*Trotzige Herzen*' (1897) from '*Die Gartenlaube*', where the heroine Anne pleads to be allowed study music in Dresden:

> Her mother cut her short: 'Don't talk such rubbish ... you are not a boy, and that's all there is to it. You be grateful', she added sharply, 'that you have your parents, and don't have to go out into the world.'
>
> 'I'm supposed to do nothing, learn nothing?'
>
> 'Do nothing! There's plenty to do, cooking, mending, dusting, caring for your mother ... you are in the world to be useful, to give joy to your parents and later to be the wife of a good man – that's enough of that. I don't want to hear another word on the subject.'

But the publicity in no way reflected the actual facts; the achievements of womens' movements in the nineteenth century were negligible. The new civil code of 1896 did little to improve the legal position of women. This was disadvantageous by comparison with most western European countries, especially with regard to married women's status and their rights over property. A more fundamental reason for the lack of progress was the tendency of society as a whole, and one which was sedulously fostered by the authorities from the emperor downwards, to see attempts to change women's status or even their economic situation as part of a nationwide assault on the achievements and values of the German Empire – as a mere appendage, in other words, to the programme of the bitterly opposed Social Democratic party.

The ideal woman

Just as the political and social mores of Germany grew less tolerant as the century progressed, so too did public attitudes towards women become increasingly restrictive, and expression of these ever more dogmatic. The revolutionary changes in the economy, in the size and distribution of the population and the effects these had on the position of a substantial proportion of the country's female population were simply left out of account. The accepted womanly ideal, projected by writers, painters and others, and viewed with complacency by society – including the majority of women – was that of female submissiveness. Even the language and content of articles in the popular encyclopedias reflect this trend. While, for example, the entry on *Frau* in the 1818 edition of the Brockhaus encyclopedia dwells almost exclusively on the beauty of the female form and the refinement of the feminine nature, and those in similar works published in mid-century show a pragmatic and often very open approach to questions of education of children, family life and the relationship of the sexes, the editions of the Brockhaus encyclopedia after 1871 concentrated on the notion of the female sex as by its very constitution an inferior one. The inability of women to understand conceptual thinking, women's finding fulfilment in the knowledge of their dependence on men, and a chauvinistic (both national and 'male') satisfaction at the greater chivalry with which Germans treat their womenfolk, characterise the later entries.

> Man's achievements lie in the fields of action, communication and creativity, woman's special qualities are patience, receptiveness, care for others ... Man's thinking is consistent and logical, woman does not think, she perceives, instinctively, intuitively.

So reads a typical article from 1876.

It is important to emphasise the contrast between the earlier decades and the period of the German Empire in this as in other areas of social life. It is also a necessary correction to a common tendency, when dealing with Germany, for people to read attitudes of mind back into Germany's past, which as a generally accepted view belong to one particular period of her history. Certainly the theme of woman's natural subordination to man had had a long history in the German states, as elsewhere, but the experience of the decades between the end of the Napoleonic wars and the revolution of 1848 had seemed to suggest that a more open-minded attitude was beginning to establish itself in the broad spectrum of the middle classes. And indeed in the earlier part of the century, practice was often more liberal than theory. A study of memoir literature and of private correspondence in the nineteenth century in this context provides evidence of a much greater degree of naturalness and openness in the relationship of the sexes than the existing institutions of society would lead one to suppose.

Such study provides the opportunity to modify current generalisations about the authoritarian character of German society in the century as a whole. An impressive body of correspondence exists, mainly, but not only, between husbands and wives, whose tone testifies to the intelligent interest which the male partner knew his wife, fiancée or friend to take in political affairs and in social relationships. This is especially well documented for the Democratic Left in the 1840s; examples are the letters of the Rhinelander Robert Blum to his wife Jenny, Emma Herwegh and her husband, the poet, or the philosopher Arnold Ruge to his wife. Very different in the political views of the partners, but equally unprejudiced in attitude are the letters which were exchanged for nearly half a century between the novelist Fanny Lewald, who married to a divorcé after many years as his mistress, and the grand duke of Weimar, son of Goethe's friend Karl August. The letters from the 1870s and the 1880s between Theodor Fontane and his daughter Mete are a particularly fine example of such exchanges. In this case, however, the changing atmosphere of the times is very apparent, and one sees from the correspondence how intense family bonds of affection and interest must compensate an intelligent woman for the lack of opportunity to employ her talents in a profession or public life.

Another instance where one can observe a change of public attitudes over the century, concerns prudery. In general, the decorum which governed the relationship of men and women in the Biedermeier period was free of the kind of prudishness on the one hand, and sultry eroticism on the other, which frequently characterised both society and the arts in the later decades, for, contrary to what critical literature on the history of women's emancipation in Germany sometimes appear to suggest, the nature of women's emotional and sexual needs did not go unexplored in the nineteenth century. The arts, especially painting, literature, and the popular sub-literary almanacs and commemorative verses, attest this freely. At the beginning of the century, in the years when the Romantic movement was at its height, the attention of society was focussed on a relatively small segment of society, where women from aristocratic and bourgeois backgrounds seemed to enjoy a degree of freedom in their personal morals and their expressed feelings, which was almost unparalleled until after the Second World War. Influenced as much by the presence of remarkably gifted women with strong personalities, Romantic writers had ascribed to women a powerful influence over men's mind and actions. A number of writers, most notably Fr. Schlegel in his provocative fragmentary novel 'Lucinde' (1799), and H. von Kleist in his (unperformed) drama 'Penthesilea' (1808), had treated the subject of female sexuality with an openness which was not matched for nearly a century. While the permissiveness of the Romantics and their associates during the Napoleonic wars provoked a sharp reaction from about 1810 onwards, especially among the pious aristocratic families of Prussia, a domesticated version of the Romantic feminine ideal survived the restoration of the monarchy in 1815. This ideal found a wide and receptive audience among the readers of almanacs and pocket books produced in subsequent decades. Erotic subjects were discreetly treated, as for example through the idiom of Oriental verse and painting. Persian love poetry, translated, or as later Iranian poets have attested, re-created by that immensely popular and now almost forgotten figure, Friederich Rückert, enjoyed a wide vogue in middle-class homes. Many other poets, such as Friedrich Bodenstedt and Emanuel Geibel used the imagery and verse forms derived from Oriental erotic poetry, and found a similar response. In painting, Carl Blechen of Berlin whose fame rests mainly on his landscape paintings, also enjoyed wide popularity among his contemporaries for his Oriental paintings on erotic themes. Rückert's poetry also included a vast amount of occasional verse on family life and friendship – he is the author of *Kindertotenlieder*, which Mahler later set to music. He appealed strongly to an age which did not share the taboos current in modern times on the expression of sentiment in love, grief or friendship. The sensual character of verse in anthologies, albums, and almanacs from the Biedermeier period strikes the modern reader. By contrast, the erotic poetry of Theodor Storm on the subject of married love in the 1850s and 1860s, when attitudes were already beginning to alter, earned him a censorious reception. Gottfried Keller was one of the few to voice his unqualified admiration but even Fontane, while expressing his appreciation, reminded Storm that he was held to be something of a sensualist by his contemporaries.

For German women from families who enjoyed at least a modest competence, life was fuller in the Biedermeier period and the homes more obviously reflected feminine sensibilities than had been the case in previous centuries. The relative poverty of the times meant that most people's homes were simple, and thrift was still regarded as a pre-eminent female virtue. However, the political stability encouraged the acquisition of treasured household possessions. The presence in the population of a high percentage of unemployed craftsmen meant that these goods were cheap and therefore within the capacity of even humble households. Household articles produced in those years are of simple design and material but delicate workmanship. This includes larger items of furniture and such things as porcelain, lamps, kitchen equipment and cotton prints. Social life was centred on the home and family, even for those who enjoyed a relative degree of wealth and status in the community, and colleagues often came to visit the family. Within the means at their disposal, women tried to make the setting a reflection of their own personalities.

In literature and painting the contemporary feminine ideal combines the virtues of the domesticated with a discreet acknowledgement of the pleasures of the senses. Women are pictured in a setting that is both orderly and beautiful. The rooms in which they live and care for their family, the gardens in which they sit and do their handiwork are neat, practical and pretty. The austerity of the domestic environment is relieved by the beauty of a few treasured objects or by nature's hand. In many paintings of the time, particularly those of painters' wives or fiancées, the objects surrounding women, both works of art or natural objects, are meant by the artist to be understood symbolically. They represent the harmony that is seen to exist between the two aspects of the woman's life, her role as orderly and diligent housewife and affectionate mother, and that of woman as a lover, the last-named always to be understood in terms of married love. Domesticity as an ideal, an idyll in a wicked world, is a familiar theme in the art of these years. Genre paintings show contented nursery scenes, little boys brawling – and they *do* brawl – while indulgent parents watch and young girls busy themselves with their needlework. When the man is portrayed as husband and father, the affectionate reliance of the woman on his strength and wisdom is generally evident. She leans on his arm, looks up into his face and is almost invariably considerably smaller and slighter (and younger) than he. Yet in the countless portraits of these wives and sweethearts, executed in the Biedermeier period, the notion of such dependence is not stressed. Portrait painters convey different aspects of women's nature in their rendering of the face and upper part of the body. Character and virtue are shown in the firm mouth and chin, the erotic element in expressive eyes, full, white bosoms and softly rounded arms and neck, and in the gently clinging draperies they wear. Queen Louise of Prussia, mother of seven, who died in 1810 at the age of 37, approximates most closely to this ideal which indeed she helped to inspire. And even the grandmothers of the Biedermeier age, in contrast with the embattled or sharp-nosed matrons of the Empire, are invariably depicted as kindly, and wise, if sometimes comfortably corpulent.

Frau Wilhelmine Begas. Painting by K.d.A. Begas.

Of course the tendency to idealise women and women's role in art is clearly apparent in the Biedermeier period, but evidence from biography, correspondence and diaries written in these years, show that there was also an attempt to realise the ideal in practice, that is, in those circles where the economic basis of life was reasonably secure. Moreover, the psychological realism with which a number of German writers depict women is of a far superior order in the early and middle decades of the century than is the case with the more famous* writers of later decades. Grillparzer portrays his heroines with an unusual degree of explicitness, yet never offends in actual expression against the decorum demanded by the literary and social conventions of his time. Examples of his art are the passionate Spanish Jewess ('*Die Jüdin von Toledo*'), the priestess Hero

---

(* famous, that is, in their time)

Queen Louise of Prussia. Painting by G. Grassi (1802).

in '*Des Meeres und der Liebe Wellen*', and Erny, married to her dead father's friend, in '*Ein treuer Diener seines Herrn*', the last two of whom are torn between shame and delight in the discovery of their own sexuality. Friedrich Hebbel, who wrote his dramas in the 1840s and 1850s, has a different emphasis. In contrast with Grillparzer or earlier German dramatists, he treats the theme of feminine sexuality in terms of the battle of the sexes. Surprisingly, perhaps, this aspect was not generally censored, though it was disregarded or underplayed in performance in Hebbel's lifetime. The realistic depiction of a very different social type from the heroines of German drama, namely the peasant women of Gotthelf's tales and novels, share with these the same freedom from stereotype.

By contrast, the literature of the later decades, or at least the works of writers regarded by the age as leading figures, are marred by utter lack of psychological realism of the women characters – the

novels and epics of the best-selling Gustav Freytag and Friedrich
Spielhagen, of the historical novelist Felix Dahn and Viktor von
Scheffel, and the early and more popular works of Wilhelm Raabe
illustrate this. Moreover, it is a feature of the literary scene in
nineteenth century Germany that the woman of strong character
and independent judgement virtually disappears from German
literature after about 1860. (The Swiss writers, Keller and Meyer,
and the Prussian novelist, Fontane, provide in their different ways
an exception to the rule.) Characters comparable to Stifter's
Brigitta, Gotthelf's forthright mothers, Hebbel's highly self-
conscious heroines, Judith, Marianne, Rhodope, are absent from
drama or fiction of the 1870s to 1890s. It is perhaps symptomatic
that the women figures in the novels of Fontane, which provide
plenty of evidence to question the above assertion, were not well
received in his time, and that he was frequently accused of
immorality. His tender and realistic novel, '*Irrungen, Wirrungen*', for
instance, was dismissed by one leading critic as that 'frightful story
of a whore'.

Women and society

Fontane belonged by birth (1819) to a generation earlier than that
in which his novels were written, namely the years 1878–98. Both as
a novelist and a critic, and as incomparably the finest letter writer of
the century in Germany, he is a full and most subtle commentator
on contemporary society. Towards the end of his life, it was clearly
apparent that the German establishment was putting a great deal of
effort into projecting a particular type of society as the only
acceptable one, and as part of this, into presenting the home and the
family as the only 'natural' place for women. It was clear too that
the majority of Germans outside the ranks of the Social Democratic
Party shared this opinion, and that the agonised protests of the
rebellious spirits or indeed the much publicised discussions on the
question of women (*die Frauenfrage*) in the 1890s were having little
effect. Even the leaders of the Social Democratic movement, notably
August Bebel*, were known for their ambivalent attitude to the
women's rights movement, while those who were committed to it,
such as Klara Zetkin and Rosa Luxemburg, (termed by malicious
contemporaries 'the only men' in the Socialist movement), refused
at any point to make common cause with the bourgeois feminists.

---

* This feature has been treated with considerable flair by Günter Grass in his recent novel,
'*Der Butt*' (1977).

Mᶫᶫᵉ Chauvin: — Und nun zum Schluß, meine Herren Geschworenen,
hier meine letzten und besten Beweise!

'The first woman advocate' as seen in 1897. The caption reads: 'And now,
gentlemen of the jury, I present you with my last and best evidence!'

Despite the lack of progress on this front, despite the slowness in
conceding greater educational facilities to women on the part of the
state or the institutions, such as the universities, the establishment
reacted violently against any notion of women changing the
conditions of their legal and social status. 'The establishment' is to
be understood here in the broadest sense. It included members of
the government and the ruling classes, the Conservative political
parties and fringe organisations, the pressure groups characteristic
of late nineteenth century politics and society, church leaders and
members of the teaching professions, civil servants; it also included
a considerable section of writers for the weekly and daily press. Even
royalty conformed to the accepted image of the 'German woman' in

the Empire between 1888 and 1918. In the preceding decades, Vicky, daughter of Queen Victoria, who married Crown Prince Frederick of Prussia in 1858, (Emperor Frederick III for 99 days in 1888), had been intelligent and dominant. She had been the object of hatred and even ridicule in upper class circles for this, while chauvinists lower down the social scale resented her as an Englishwoman. By contrast William II's empress, Princess of Schleswig-Holstein-Sonderhausen, affectionately known as Dohna, seemed to embody to perfection the acceptable 'Kinder-Küche-Kirche' feminine type*. She had given six sons (and one daughter) 'to the fatherland', and her ample but well-corsetted figure was constantly seen in public, when she opened bazaars and functions for charitable purposes, and was heard reiterating current clichés about the threat to religion (always to be understood as Protestantism), the danger of Social Democracy, or the British envy of Germany. In conclusion, one can say that both Dohna herself and the official and socially acceptable image of German womanhood she represented, is a particularly striking instance of what the American historian, Fritz Stern, in his brilliant study of the epoch, '*Gold and Iron*', has called 'the sentimentalised self-righteousness of Imperial Germany'.

ii) Childhood

The quality of family life in nineteenth century Germany is not easy to re-capture, but there is a great deal of evidence to support the notion that childhood, particularly in the early decades of the period, was the object of special and imaginative concern by the adult world. Although it is impossible to quantify existing evidence, the survival of certain traditions of family life dating from that time into the late twentieth century, suggest that childhood was full of pleasures more intense than in many of the western countries, at least where the economic basis of family life was secure. By this I do not mean 'bourgeois' and upper-class families, but rather those where children were not forced to work in factories or in domestic industries from a tender age, as was the case in the textile towns of the Rhine/Ruhr area, or in Saxony and in the decaying weaving villages of Silesia and Hessen, or to do more than their share of labour in the parental farm or small-holding.

---

* Literally 'children-kitchen-church': it implied that such women had no interest outside their family and home except for church-going.

Details from 'Panorama from the Werdersche Church' by Edward Gärtner. Note how realistically the children, especially the older one, are portrayed, and how ready the parents are to enter in the spirit of the thing, but at the same time pointing a moral.

'Sums',
a mid-century
painting by
Marie Wunsch.

The arts

The evidence of literature and the arts is eloquent here, nor is it
exclusive to those writers known for their sympathy with, and
closeness to children, such as Jean Paul (1763–1825) or the
Austrians Adalbert Stifter (1805–68) and Peter Rosegger
(1843–1918). In the years from about 1800 to 1860, the world of a
child is frequently the subject of sensitive studies in prose and
poetry, and also drawings and paintings. It is true that many of these
were trite and sentimental, seeking to prettify experience for the
unlettered and uncritical. However, it is a striking feature of
German art of this period, which had children as its subject, for the
child's world to be seen through the eyes of the child, and the
mysteries and apparently illogical character of the adult world to be
allowed to impinge gradually on his experience. Many minor
writers, such as the Jewish pedlar's son, Berthold Auerbach
(1812–82), Gustav Schwab, (1792–1850), the Austrian, Marie von
Ebner-Eschenbach (1830–1916), Friedrich Rückert, professor of

Oriental languages, and the Catholic priest Christoph von Schmid, wrote dearly loved stories and poems for almanacs, school primers and later for the immensely popular family journals, which show an intimate understanding of the child's mind and the child's world. The account by Theodor Storm (1817–88), for example, of the ten-year-old Nesi awaiting the arrival of her new stepmother, half hidden behind the banisters on the first floor, (in his novella '*Viola Tricolor*',) is an excellent instance of the originality of German literature in this area. The awkward positioning of Nesi's body, described so precisely by the writer, expressed the contradictory feelings she could not yet understand or articulate. Even more impressive for its insights into the childish world, because more sustained, is Gottfried Keller's account of his early boyhood in his semi-autobiographical novel '*Der Grüne Heinrich*' (1854–55). Many writers, popular in their time as contributors to the much read almanacs and anthologies, offered children a glimpse into the adult world in terms they could understand, although one must not exaggerate the availability of such literature to children. An example could be Berthold Auerbach's portrait of the teacher Eugen in his '*Anfang in der Schule*' (First Day at School). Eugen is depicted very realistically trying to conceal from the children on his first day at school, his fears and his total inexperience in controlling a class of ninety-two. The portrait is quite at odds with the accepted picture of the authoritarian school system and the high moral tale. From a slightly later date (1860), one could mention Peter Rosegger's account of a child's first train ride with his godfather, on the famous Semmering railway, a remarkable feat of railway engineering across the eastern Alps which was completed in Austria in 1854. The naive response of the boy when he first catches sight of the train, 'a whole village with lots of windows rolling by', is equalled by that of his companion, who calls out in amazement and horror as the train passes them and disappears into a tunnel: 'Look at those conceited souls, gone to their grave they are!' The godfather suddenly decides to impress the people back in the village, they pool their money and go for a ride. 'That's my funeral bell tolling', remarks the old man lugubriously as the train approaches, but no sooner are they in than he gets a taste for it and they stay on beyond their stop. Having no money to pay the excess, they are interned in the station for the evening and are eventually let out to find their way home in the dark. The events of the day bring home to the child the limits of grown-ups' authority and their ability to cope with situations, which hitherto he had taken for granted. These are no isolated examples but are representative of much writing for children and adults at this time.

At the same time it would be wrong to deny the fact that children's literary diet was more frequently moralistic, where the good triumphed and the bad were punished, often gruesomely. Examples of moralistic literature for children abound throughout the century, none more famous than the work of the brilliant graphic artist and versifier, Wilhelm Busch (1832–1908), and his older contemporary, Heinrich Hoffman, whose *'Struwwelpeter'*

'At the window'. Painting by F. Waldmüller (1840).

(1845) has delighted children and horrified their squeamish parents for generations. Wilhelm Busch's '*Max und Moritz*' (1865), his '*Pious Helene*' (1872), '*Balduin Baalamb, the would-be poet*' (1879) and many of his other works have long been household names in Germany. Frightful things happen to naughty children in Busch and Hoffmann, some of them guilty of only minor transgressions. Undoubtedly the evil pranks of Max and Moritz invite stern punishment but hardly the gruesome end of being ground to pieces by the miller, whose flour they had ruined, and finally fed to the chickens whose relations they had strung up on the widow's clothes-line. The superb illustrations and eminently quotable verse of Busch put him into a class of his own in nineteenth century children's literature. From a grown-up's point of view he was ideal for reading aloud. His tales are so very funny, both in the story and the neat formulation of his verse and his works are full of sage (and sometimes very nasty) observations on the human race and on middle-class German social mores in particular. One of the more harmless tales recounts the story of Balduin Baalamb, prevented from developing his poetic muse by his family commitments. He retires to a bucolic existence among farm animals and milkmaids; they prove less inspiring than he hoped, and considerably less naive, and so, plagued by a frightful toothache, he scurries home to the bosom of his loving family.

In general the popularity of literature about childhood and the child's relations with its natural environment, and the variety of registers in which such literature was written, suggest a concern for, and an understanding of children, which is one of the less widely appreciated aspects of life in Germany and Austria in this period.

Memoir literature

The quality of domestic life in nineteenth century Germany also finds expression in memoir literature, among which an abundance of vivid memoirs of childhood survives, with that gift of selective recording of individual moments of experience, which is the stuff of a child's world. One of the most vivid is Gutzkow's account of the reconciliation of neighbours through the death of a child in his '*Aus der Knabenzeit*' (Boyhood Memories). This is a remarkable evocation of living conditions in a densely populated area of Berlin in the 1820s. It provides impressive evidence too that a proletarian home environment need not stifle a child's fantasy. Gutzkow's family were forced to share a kitchen with the neighbours; 'Each (of the two mothers) did at least have a room for her family with three beds for the children or at least enough room for chairs to be made up into children's beds at night', but the two 'had to share one and the same kitchen. The two stood at the same stoneware basin, cleaning their vegetables, peeling their potatoes, picking over their peas and lentils; and they had to cook them on the same stove.' The two women got on each other's nerves and quarrelled irrevocably. Two lots of 'potatoes, beans and peas boiled side by side, emitting their steam into the common chimney ... Through the tiny kitchen a demarcation line had to be drawn, and this might only be crossed on entering. For the rest, buckets and washtubs, cupboards and firewood, chopping boards and market baskets were placed with mathematical exactitude in such a way that neither obtruded by even a centimetre into the territory of the rival.' Then one of the neighbour's children, Marianne, died. The mother 'hid her tears lest the enemy perceive her agony'. There was no room in the bedroom and therefore the coffin had to be placed in the shared kitchen. 'The narrow room could only serve to harbour a bier for the little corpse if each woman gave up some of her territory. And so it happened. The demarcation line was set aside. The body lay for two days in the shared kitchen and on the third day, the day of the funeral, the two mothers looked at each other and silently offered each other a hand in reconciliation ...'

Family festivals – Christmas
In almost all these memoirs, which were usually written in middle life or old age and hence usually, though not inevitably, tend to stress the more positive aspects of childhood, the family festivals played a special role. Celebrations of birthdays, with birthday tables arranged with presents from the immediate family but also from neighbours and quite distant relatives, helped to give a child a real sense of his own importance. Even in a household of modest means, and in contrast with the traditional thrift of everyday life, presents were included which were not merely utilitarian. Above all, Christmas was a festival associated with a host of much loved rituals – the lighting of Advent candles on the four Sundays preceding, baking the special Christmas biscuits, which were sent to one's friends and received from them, and the Christmas market, *Christkindlmarkt*, full of delights. There were marzipan figures and the wonderfully imaginative German toys, which, at least up to the last decades of the century, were cheap to buy. Nuremberg had the most famous Christmas market, but in other towns all over Germany one could buy decorations and toys for very small sums.

Father's birthday. Photo (1880).

The best known, and to small children the most delightful because of their scale, were the little painted wooden villages, farms, figures and animals, associated with the Erzgebirge region of central Germany. For boys, the famous Nuremberg *Holzschächtelchen*, wooden boxes filled with painted tin soldiers, allowed all but the poorest to amass collections to re-fight the campaigns of *der Alte Fritz* (Frederick II of Prussia), of the wars against Napoleon and the campaigns of the wars of unification. They included not only famous regiments of the German army but most foreign ones too, and could be had in all conceivable positions – attack, fire and drilling, wading through water, lying, kneeling down, falling, dying etc. – above all, they were cheap.

In the last decade of the century the increasing wealth of bourgeois circles was reflected in the massive expansion of the toy industry and the successful promotion of what were virtually luxury toys, from miniature prototypes of German industrial achievements such as locomotives, sewing machines, guns of various kinds, three-dimensional lead soldiers, magnificent dolls, prams, dolls houses etc. At Christmas time the shops in German towns began to be filled with goods thought appropriate to the nurseries and playrooms of the children of the solid citizenry. Both in the stress laid on material

Christmas day. Augsburg, early 19th century etching.

goods as a due reward for the industrious and patriotic little citizens,
and in the inevitable barriers raised between those who could afford
to indulge themselves and those who could not, the characteristic
tensions of Imperial society at large were reflected. It was
particularly because the authorities and their spokesmen actively
promoted a view of German society in which all righteous burghers
had a share and that the celebrations of family festivals was so
deeply rooted in nineteenth century German family life at all levels,
that disappointment of expectations seemed particularly cruel.
Proletarian childhood memoirs are full of reminiscences of parents'
efforts to defy circumstance and produce something special for the
occasion. Among such accounts there are few more bitter passages
than the Socialist Adelheid Popp's recalling Christmas preparations
in her home and their sequence:

> One Christmas when I was not quite five still remains vivid in my
> memory. On this own occasion I nearly got a Christmas tree. My
> mother wanted me, who was her youngest child, to see just for once what
> Christmas *could* be like. For weeks she had strived to save a few coppers to
> buy me a toy kitchen set. The Christmas tree was decorated with
> coloured paper chains, with gold-painted nuts and with the little toys.
> We waited for the lighting of the candles until Father came home. He

had gone to deliver some goods to the factory-owner. He was to bring money with him. Six o'clock came, then seven, then eight. Still Father hadn't come. We were all hungry and clamoured for our food. We had to eat the lovely poppy-seed noodles, the apples and the nuts on our own without Father, and then I had to go to bed without seeing the candles alight on the tree. Mother was too upset and too anxious to light them. I lay wide awake in my bed. I had so longed for the Christ-child to come and now he hadn't come. At last Father arrived. He got a poor reception and a quarrel started. He had got less money than Mother expected and he had gone to the pub. He had had to walk two hours and he wanted to warm up. But he'd stayed longer than he intended and came home a bit drunk. The noise made me peep out from where I slept to look at my parents, and then I saw – Father with an axe chopping the tree and everything on it into pieces. I didn't dare scream, I just wept.

The sentimentalisation of German Christmas and its exploitation by chauvinist writers as evidence of the superiority of 'German Culture' was a phenomenon of the late nineteenth century. Christmas was presented as a microcosm of German social life, with father as the omnipotent provider, mother as the busy executor of his wishes, and the children happy and grateful. Inevitably the trend in bourgeois circles to make the Christmas festivities the occasion of ostentatious present-giving and entertainment attracted the attention of satirists. Both publicists and literary writers mocked at the self-esteem and self-indulgence masquerading as *Kultur*. A lighthearted instance of this is Max Müller's satirical poem entitled '*Die Kolonien*'. The author shows father asking the family what they would like for Christmas – grandfather wants a cane with an ivory handle, mother a fur coat, daughter a sewing-machine and the son wants a bicycle. 'Our colonies will provide all', the father declares, and so they did. The satisfaction of their wishes is hailed by the family as a triumph of German foreign policy in the age of imperialism. Perhaps the most famous account of Christmas in German literature is to be found in Thomas Mann's '*Buddenbrooks*'. In its ironic account of bourgeois ritual it belongs to the body of literature associated with the names of Thomas and Heinrich Mann, Robert Musil and others, who began the process of critical evaluation of bourgeois society under the German Empire, more than half a century before historians began to submit the period to critical scrutiny.

School

For the German child, school intruded all too soon on his consciousness. It was the exception rather than the rule for children, even of the well-off, to be educated by private tutors and governesses. Compulsory schooling had existed longer in Germany than in any other European country. Particularly among the middle classes, the prosperous and the impecunious, education was held in particularly high esteem. Most of those who read at all were interested in education, which they saw both as a means of achieving upward social mobility and also as a moral institution for society and humanity.

Education and the German Enlightenment
For the last decades of the eighteenth century had seen a remarkable flowering of interest in the education of children in German-speaking countries, an interest which was directed both at the rearing of young children in the home and their schooling. This owed a very great deal to the seminal work of J. J. Rousseau, namely the novel '*Emile, ou l'éducation*' (1762) which appeared in a German translation, published at Berlin, in the same year. This interest in education found expression in a number of experimental schools and in an impressive volume of literature which was both systematic, as was Basedow's '*Elementarwerk*' (1786), and pragmatic, as were Sintenius' '*Vater Roderich unter seinen Kindern*' or the great educationalist Pestalozzi's novel, '*Lienhard und Gertrud*' (1781–83). Basedow, who was responsible for a famous boarding school, the *Philanthropinum* in Thuringia, engaged the prolific graphic artist, Daniel Chodowiecki, famous for his drawings of Frederick the Great, to illustrate his massive compendium. The *Elementarwerk* contained information and guidance on a bewildering variety of educational problems, from methods of teaching the three R's to sex education for children. It was too expensive for all but the wealthy to buy, but its fame was considerable and it served to stimulate public interest in educational matters which was sustained throughout the following century. Much interest was shown among middle-class circles during the German Enlightenment for the idea of the educational formation of the child as a future citizen. Not only the role of the parents and teachers, but also the child's reading matter were recognised as important elements in that process. In 1775 a certain Christian Felix Weisse started a periodical for children called '*Der Kinderfreund*' (twenty-four volumes – 1775 to 1782). He decided to start it as his child had nothing to read and, although its contributions were prosy and moralistic, the children of that age, as far as one can judge from tributes written in later life, loved it, for they had little access to books. It was J. H. Campe

(1746–1818), headmaster of the *Philanthropinum*, best known for his version of Robinson Crusoe, which was known as '*Robinson der Jüngere*' (1779), who exercised the most powerful influence on writings for and about children in the nineteenth century. His collected works for children and adolescents appeared between 1806 and 1832, in thirty-seven small volumes, and his name is very frequently cited in memoirs.

Education in imaginative literature

How far the influence of these and many other enlightened pedagogues actually modified educational institutions in the nineteenth century is open to question. Most of the progressive educational institutions such as the *Philanthropinum* were short-lived and did not even survive until the beginning of the new century. The function of school seemed in general to continue to be regarded as the place to instil obedience and authority, and this was reflected in the type of reading material to be found in school primers from Prussia and Mecklenburg in the north to Bavaria and Württemberg in the south. It is probable that the most important and lasting influence of enlightened pedagogues was rather on the minds and educational practices of individual teachers. Moreover, the writings of imaginative literature continued, at least for about the first sixty years or so of the nineteenth century, to be stimulated by their ideas, and literary works in their turn acted as a guide for open-minded parents and teachers in their treatment of the young. An example is the Romantic writer, essayist, novelist, and pedagogue, Jean Paul, whose work was widely read in bourgeois circles for most of the century. Writing about his childhood memories, which like those of another great nineteenth century pedagogue, Fr. Fröbel, were not happy ones, he warns parents to increase childish joys and to avoid being too stern, since, as he notes, childhood experiences are so intense and so formative of the future character. Similarly, Pestalozzi's writings and his rather simplistic but highly regarded novel, '*Lienhard und Gertrud*', pay tribute to the woman's role as educator, as did Stifter's great *Bildungsroman* three quarters of a century later, '*Der Nachsommer*' (1857). This was a fruitful theme, both in serious and in popular literature, for the first fifty years or more of the century. The portrayal of the teacher in early and mid-nineteenth century literature in Germany owed much to the influence of these pedagogues. Thus Zschokke, a German philanthropist who settled in Switzerland and whose novels enjoyed a wide vogue in the Restoration period, portrayed

the ideal type of village teacher who becomes the leader of the
community. In his '*Die Branntweinpest*' (1834) the schoolmaster
weans the peasants away from hereditary drunkenness and pioneers
new farming methods in line with the government's agrarian
reforms of the early nineteenth century. By contrast there was the
tyrannical bullying pedagogue familiar in German literature and
cartoons throughout this period. The disparity between ideal and
practice is made manifest in satirical novels such as '*Die
Schulmeisterwahlen*', which was published in Saxony in 1805 by K. Fr.
Döhnel; here the local landowner, who has the appointment to the
village school in his gift, derides the young graduate. He asks, 'Why
do you want to be a schoolmaster? Why have you studied – all you
need to be a schoolmaster is to be able to sing and to thrash – you
don't have to go to university for that!' Or there was Karl
Immermann, whose abominable schoolmaster Agäsel delighted
admirers of his satirical novel, '*Münchhausen*' (1838–39).

Educational reform and the state

The high reputation enjoyed by the German school system in other
European countries in the nineteenth century rested primarily on
the reforms introduced into the Prussian state in the early years of the
century, which were copied in a number of other German states
subsequently, among them Saxony and Bavaria. In 1807 Baron
Stein had placed education in Prussia, which hitherto had been
largely under church control, under the ministry of the interior. He
created a special department in the ministry entitled 'cults and
public instruction', which Wilhelm von Humboldt was appointed
in 1809 to direct. In the following year Humboldt introduced state
examinations for teachers, a measure which, however, proved
difficult to enforce. Humboldt's ultimate aim was to introduce
compulsory elementary education into Prussia of a kind which
would prepare his fellow countrymen for the role they would play as
citizens of a liberal state. In the event, neither the financial
resources nor the political attitudes of the authorities proved
adequate to implement his ideals. Humboldt went into the
diplomatic service after his brief but immensely stimulating time at
the ministry of the interior, but found himself obliged to resign along
with other liberal ministers and civil servants in 1819. In the
following years more authoritarian policies emanated from
bureaucrats in charge of education. The law on compulsory
schooling was strengthened in 1825; in 1834 the school-leaving
examination, the *Abitur*, which had been instituted in Prussia in

'The school yard'. Painting by Ludwig Knaus (1892).

1788, was made obligatory for entry into the professions, the civil service and the university. The Prussian Constitution of 1850 made elementary education free to all; this did not become a general feature of education in Germany as a whole until considerably later, namely 1888. (Even after the founding of the Empire in 1871, education remained under the control of the individual states, as is the case in the Federal Republic today.) In the year 1850 Prussian teachers at secondary schools were made civil servants, with all attending privileges, already enjoyed by university professors. In Saxony, which had long enjoyed a high reputation for educational standards, a matter in which her rulers had shown consistent and enlightened interest, vocational education received particular attention; in 1873 attendance at some form of further education, vocational or professional, was made compulsory for three years in the case of boys leaving school at fourteen. This measure was adopted in the following decade by Baden, Württemberg and Bavaria.

However the development of education in Prussia in particular and in Germany generally was much less liberal after 1819 than the policies of the previous decade had suggested. The leading official at the department of education, von Altenstein, declared in a decree of 1832 that the king

> wished to record his appreciation of the keen interest being currently shown in elementary schooling, but that he felt constrained to point out that this must be kept within bounds, so that the common people might not be transformed into 'over-educated and semi-literate' persons, in a manner quite unsuited to their status as working men.

It was for political reasons that experiments in teaching methods and course content, which had been a feature of mid-century, were firmly suppressed after the 1848 revolution. In 1854 the notorious 'Stiehlische Regulations' or guidelines for elementary education, introduced by the Prussia civil servant Stiehl, were applied to Prussian elementary schools. These limited the curriculum broadly speaking to the three R's and the catechism, and this was done at a time when the expansion of industry, particularly in the towns and cities of Prussia, was creating a growing demand for skilled labour. In a letter to his publisher, Wilhelm Hertz, Fontane, who knew Stiehl, observed sardonically that, apart from a single individual, none of the Prussian officials responsible for the administration of schools had any children of their own. Eighteen years after Stiehl's measures, the then Prussian minister, Falk, whose name is associated with the *Kulturkampf*, introduced a more modern curriculum into the elementary schools. Subjects such as geography, history and nature-study became part of the programme; the number of hours devoted to the teaching of religion was reduced. However, the new programme did little to modify the system traditional in Europe of teaching large classes by drumming facts into the children's heads. Falk also concerned himself with the type of school-building in which the children were taught, and indeed throughout the Second Empire considerable sums of money were spent on the provision of school-buildings at all educational levels. Popular encyclopedias devote much space to 'hygienic desks' where the child will learn to sit and write correctly and without strain. Popular lectures on the subject had an increasing vogue in the latter decades of the century. It was rather typical of that age that such mechanical and material matters pre-occupied the officials and the informed public, while the fundamental issues such as curriculum, teaching methods, course content, the aims of modern schooling, engaged their attention so little. In 1871, Prussia, which comprised some three-fifths of the German Empire had 33,120 elementary schools with 3.9 million pupils. By 1911, the number of schools had risen to 38,164 and the number of pupils to 6.5 million. However, a most striking reform was achieved in one area with the increase in the number of teachers – 30,805 in 1871 and forty years later, 117,462. In consequence the proportion of teacher to pupil dropped rapidly, despite the population increase, from about 1 to 80 at the beginning of the Empire, to 1 to 50 in the later period.

However, the percentage of state budget spent on education remained low, usually in the smaller states, but in Prussia especially so, by comparison with military expenditure. Within the education budget, the amount devoted to the elementary schools was extremely small in relation to what was spent on the grammar schools, to which only 3% of the population gained access. Nor did society and state in the nineteenth century make real provision for the change in the structure of the society consequent on the industrial revolution. The rudimentary education offered by elementary schools to the rural populace was no doubt intended to fit them for their future menial tasks. But for the many hundreds of thousands of children moving from the land and growing up in a poor urban environment after 1870, few technical skills were learnt at school which might have assisted them in their emancipation. Practical skills were available in a limited degree to the sons of the lower middle and middle classes, such as, for example, Fontane had received in the 1830s at the Berlin *Gewerbeschule* (vocational school).

The well-known Gymnasium (grammar school), Joachimsthal.

The problems of the poor

A far more serious indictment of the government was the failure to implement legislation to protect children against exploitation by employers and parents. In the early decades of the century, children could be forced to work as much as fifteen hours a day and the mortality rate among such children was estimated as high as 30% per annum of the labour recruited. Orphans in particular, as in the Dresden, Potsdam and Stuttgart orphanages, were especially susceptible to brutal forms of exploitation. The first legal measure in Germany prohibiting work for children under nine and restricting that of juveniles to ten hours per day, was passed after some considerable opposition from factory owners in Prussia in 1839. Seven years later, official statistics put the number of children under fourteen in the state who were working in factories, at 32,000 or 10% of the adult population so engaged.

Between 1850 and 1869 relatively effective inspection of children working in factories was introduced gradually. In fact it was not until 1860 that school became compulsory in fact as well as in theory for children up to the age of twelve. The inclusion in the school readers of idyllic accounts and illustrations of children at work in domestic industry (as well as in factories and coal-mines), suggest that the authorities were well aware of the problems of child labour but cloaked their reluctance or their inability to alleviate human distress by misrepresentation. A crass example of such attitudes is provided in the weaver-song ('*Weberlied*' – 1816) by one Johann Genersich, which tells of the happy life of a weaver lass at her loom from dawn to dusk:

> Wohl hört oft meine Lieder
> die stille Mitternacht
> und Arbeit ruft mich wieder
> so wie der Tag erwacht.
> Die Arbeit stärkt die Glieder
> und macht gesundes Blut,
> und sing ich fröhlich Lieder
> so geht es wieder gut.*

---

* 'Stilly midnight hears my songs
  Many a time and oft.
  And with the dawning of the day
  I'm called back to my work.
  For work adds strength to my limbs
  And gives my blood its health,
  And when I sing my joyous songs,
  I'm happy once again.'

Legislation existed in the German Empire to protect children from abuse, but a reading of contemporary views on the subject of child labour in the popular encyclopedias from the period of the Restoration up to the latter years of the nineteenth century, suggests that bourgeois attitudes became less, not more liberal in that period. Thus Spamhaus Encyclopedia, published in Berlin in 1876, declared sententiously that, once provision had been made for the education of children and a certain amount of time reserved for play, the employment of children was an excellent thing. It brought benefit to the character of the children concerned, and redounded to the good of the state.

Memoirs by members of the urban and rural proletariat of their early lives under such conditions, which began to appear in some numbers between about 1890 and 1914, encouraged by Socialist leaders, offer a very different interpretation. The one feature stressed by these writers is the lack of a real childhood among the proletariat. Although Germany was the first country to provide institutions to look after the children of working mothers as far back as the 1820s, and the popular encyclopedias of mid-century expressed keen interest in and offered encouragement to such work, as late as 1912 only some 8% of such children under three years were being looked after in crèches. The authorities showed very little understanding of the real problems of life for the poorer classes in this regard. Fröbel's Kindergarten, which was opened in Blankenburg in his native Thuringia in 1837 was aimed at awakening and developing the child's interest and skills by what we would call educational toys and games. He also provided for the training of Kindergarten teachers to look after the children. Fröbel's work was shortlived in mid-century Prussia, however, because the Prussian government closed down his schools in 1851 on the grounds that they were Socialist organisations. The ban, which originated in the case of mistaken identity – Friedrich Fröbel was thought to be the revolutionary, Julius Fröbel – remained in force until 1860, and the movement recovered only slowly from this intervention by the state. The general neglect by the state authorities of the care and education of young children, is perhaps surprising in a country with such a high reputation in matters educational as nineteenth century Germany enjoyed, but it is nonetheless true. Indeed, primary schools received far less attention than this reputation suggests, and the attitudes of the authorities in the era of the German Empire is aptly summarised in three Reich decrees, issued in 1889, 1901 and 1908. These dealt with general

principles of primary school education and suggested that the
teachers' most important duty was to counteract Socialist ideas, as
evident in the very choice of set textbooks and readers prescribed for
German primary schools from the 1870s onwards. In the years
1889–1914 many literary works appeared in Germany containing
portraits of young people who suffer at the hands of society, either
through active cruelty on the part of those in authority or through
culpable neglect by parents or teachers. Among some of the most
notable of literary works dealing with young people in crisis are
'*Frühlings Erwachen*' (1891) by Franz Wedekind, Gerhart
Hauptmann's '*Hanneles Himmelfahrt*' (1893) or his '*Rose Bernd*'
(1903), and Robert Musil's '*Die Verwirrungen des Zöglings Törless*'
(1906). Among the many critical portraits of teachers in German
literature in the same period, Arno Holz's Prussian bully in '*Papa
Hamlet*' (1889), Thomas Mann's Headmaster Wulicke and his
brother Heinrich's grotesque grammar schoolmaster Professor
Unrat from the novel of the same name (1905), are probably the
most notorious; in the literature of that time written by somewhat
younger writers, the teacher is almost invariably a negative figure.
Yet we know from a large variety of memoirs of adolescence relating
to these years that there were many kindly and dedicated teachers,
who played a willingly acknowledged role in their pupils'
formation. Indeed Thomas Mann's 'frightful' Direktor Wulicke,
Hanno Buddenbrooks' headmaster, was expressly described as the
successor of 'that jovial and humane old man' who taught his father
and his uncle. Gustav Wyneken, a Berlin headmaster was an
example of just such a dedicated individual, the object of his pupils'
deep devotion. He lent his support to the *Wandervogel* movement
and openly professed his belief in the reality and worth of such an
autonomous youth culture. But it must be said that such men
appear to have been the exception rather than the rule, and it seems
likely that the negative portrayal of school and its representatives by
those who were the most gifted writers of their age in Germany was
not a distortion. It was an attempt to stress the representative
character of teachers as agents of what was felt to be an intolerably
authoritarian state. The grotesque character of many of these young
writers' satire was a device to reveal the stultifying and socially
injurious nature of paternalist authority in its many manifestations.
The very names given by writers to their schoolmaster characters
express their outrage – Heinrich Mann's Professor *Unrat* (i.e. filth,
excrement), which is the nickname given Herr *Rat* (i.e. councillor),
or Arno Holz' three proponents of corporal punishment at the

elementary school in '*Papa Hamlet*' : Affenschmalz (monkey grease)
Knüppeldick (truncheon thick) and Knochenbruch (bone break).
Thomas Mann uses such devices much more sparingly, but he is at
least as aware of the exemplary character of the situation he is
describing. With characteristic clarity and judiciousness his account
of the new regime of Direktor Wulicke in '*Buddenbrooks*' (1901)
contains an indication of the changes which had taken place in
German education in the last decades of the nineteenth century. In
describing these changes he associated them with the more
fundamental process of the 'Prussification' of German society,
which had been gaining momentum since 1871.* A certain
idealisation of former days, which must have seemed a little precious
in one so young as Mann then was (he was born in 1875), informs his
account of the changes wrought in the school by the new
headmaster Wulicke:

> Wo ehemals die klassische Bildung als heiterer Selbstzweck gegolten
> hatte, den man mit Ruhe, Muße und fröhlichem Idealismus verfolgt, da
> waren nun die Begriffe Autoritat, Pflicht, Macht, Dienst, Karriere zur
> höchsten Würde gelangt, und der 'kategorische Imperativ unseres
> Philosophen Kant' war das Banner, das Direktor Wulicke in jeder
> Festrede bedrohlich entfaltete.†

But the system remained impervious to satirical onslaught from the
pens of impatient, bitter or merely critical young men. However,
there is evidence of widespread, if piecemeal, questioning of
inherited authoritarian traditions in late nineteenth century
Germany. This was expressed in a variety of ways, one of which was
dress. The cult of 'natural' clothes, inspired in part by a new interest
in folk-art, favoured loose garments and outdoor pursuits for a
generation whose mothers were confined in whalebone corsets and
who passed most of their lives indoors. Some few parents rebelled
against the endemic German habit of wrapping their children
remorselessly up in woollen garments, by going to the opposite
extreme and allowing them to wander naked (at least in summer).

---

* The Manns came from the old Hanseatic city of Lübeck, which, like the other Hanseatic
cities of Hamburg and Bremen, had a detached and critical attitude towards Prussia.

† Where once a classical education had been looked on as an end in itself, the source of serenity,
to be striven after calmly, in a fashion that was at once leisurely and filled with a joyous
idealism, now instead concepts such as authority, duty, power, service, career, were exalted
above all else, and the 'categorical imperative of our philosopher Kant' was the intimidating
banner, which Headmaster Wulicke unfurled at every school speech day address.

'The sun-children'.

This, it was held by a handful of progressive parents, would make relationships between the sexes less problematic when the children grew to adolescence. It was hardly surprising that such notions aroused a passionate response in a nation whose new colonial empire and expanding economy made it favour sailor-suits for boys and clothed its daughters in starched cotton, lace and flounces, which equated prudery with sexual morality, and sexual morality with morality. Any infringements of the accepted code in this sphere were regarded as little short of anarchistic. Indeed, 'modernism' in any guise was something to be feared and resisted as questioning the whole foundations of society and state policy. The youth movements of the pre-war years with their folk music and back-to-nature ideas, are a somewhat pedantic adjunct of the same spirit of modernism, though they had features which commended them to parents and to the establishment in general. The pressures of the establishment on most spheres of activity were strong and it was only the resolute who resisted them. The youth movement, especially the *Wandervögel*, became increasingly chauvinistic in the years leading up to the outbreak of war in 1914, reflecting the temper of bourgeois society. Even the Socialist youth organisations were affected by the conformist spirit of the age, as the young Marxist Ludwig Turek found in the 1900s, when to his horror he was required to wear a white shirt and black suit on joining a Social Democratic youth rambling club.

It was indeed a striking fact of German society in pre-war years how ineffective criticism of contemporary values was. It was surprising in view of the very real social tensions and the fact that a great deal of energy on the part of Germany's ruling classes went into stifling or denying them. In particular, German family life and the environment of childhood and youth remained unassailed either by the attack of novelists or the brilliant caricatures of some of contemporary Europe's greatest graphic satirists, such as Th. Th. Heine or the Norwegian Gulbransson, then working in Berlin. Despite their efforts and the many fringe organisations which offered a brief protest against some aspects of German life, society continued to accept a system in which paternal authority was writ large, since it was held by most people that the father represented in the family what the state represented in the community. Women's opportunities for self-fulfilment, while perhaps more considerable within the home than later generations have appreciated, were severely and consciously curtailed outside. Yet while witty attacks on emancipated women in satiric journals amused a wide audience, the traditional German *Hausfrau* escaped relatively unscathed. Even a radical writer such as Wedekind, as Roy Pascal has pointed out, makes the emancipated women of his works seem grotesque and ridiculous. It was not peculiar to Germany that sons and daughters remained dependent on their fathers long into adult life, but to a later generation it was surprising that the extreme opprobium with which German society regarded those who deviated from the norm, or what was held to be the norm, did not arouse a more vigorous reaction. And there is abundant evidence that the ruling classes and their agents, the churches, the military, police, civil servants at all levels and teachers, as well as the greater part of bourgeois and petty bourgeois society, linked a rigidly conservative social and sexual moral code with true patriotism.

For political reasons, the preservation of the status quo was made to seem the highest civic virtue. And the malice, rather than mere casual interest, in the tone of gossiping relations and neighbours about those who did deviate was a special German characteristic. From the state's point of view, the stabilising influence of the family at all social levels, from the Hohenzollerns and the Bismarcks to its most menial farm and factory hands, was undoubtedly its most important feature, and school was required to be an extension of that influence, a bridge between the disciplined joys of childhood and an adult life of service to the nation state.

12
The German Writer and his Public

The German poet and writer invariably sets his sights on Parnassus, and is inclined to overlook the Forum.

(Georg Gervinus)

Economic and social situation

The social status and economic position of the German writer in 1800 was largely determined by two factors, which continued to be influential throughout the following century. These were firstly the late emergence of a bourgeois class, and secondly the lack of a capital city in consequence of the internal divisions of the country. After the unification of Germany in 1871, when Berlin became the capital, the opportunity of earning one's living by one's pen improved radically. Unification coincided with the emergence of a well-to-do and self-conscious bourgeoisie who bought books – if not always the right ones. Consequently, even those poets who lamented the passing of the old Germany, who felt affronted by the lack of discrimination in the reading public, could not but agree that the economic situation of the writer was incomparably better than it had been thirty or fifty years previously. The social status of the writer was another matter. The idea that the writer fulfilled a public function in society was something which the authorities throughout the century, and in the last decades of the nineteenth century even the bourgeoisie also, were reluctant to concede. And German poets themselves had unusual, not to say conflicting views as to what that function might be.

In his short story entitled *Die Geschichte vom braven Kasperl und dem schönen Annerl* (1817), the Romantic poet Clemens Brentano observes through the figure of the narrator, 'How odd it is that a German is always a little bit ashamed to admit he is a writer.' The

273

DAS ENTSCHULDIGT. Kommst du heute nachmittag mit spazieren? – Nein, da habe ich keine
Zeit, da will ich eine neue Kultur entwerfen.   O. GULBRANSSON

Cartoon by O. Gulbransson. The caption reads:
A good excuse.
'Are you coming for a walk this afternoon?' 'No I'm too busy. I'm drafting a new
culture.'

Romantic idea of art as a divine gift, the fear – to use a then contemporary phrase – of 'prostituting one's art' by accepting payment for a work of art, as though it were a pair of shoes or a loaf of bread, died hard in the nineteenth century. A pseudo-religious character was attributed to the creation and to the enjoyment of art. When Germans went to the theatre or to a concert, even in provincial towns, they dressed up and behaved as if they were taking part in a ritual act. The novelist and short story writer, Adalbert Stifter, a fairly representative figure of the Poetic Realist school of writers, could refer in 1848 to the function of the poet as that of 'teacher, leader and friend of his fellow men, an interpreter, a priest.' A poet liked to speak of his *Berufung*, his calling, and there was widespread agreement that this calling was concerned with the task of improving and edifying his readers. It was not thought that he should make them critically aware, at least outside the ranks of the controversial 'political' writers, to whom the majority of artists would deny the title of poet. The use of the term *Honorarium*, as payment for published work, was in keeping with such ideas; its acceptance could enable a man to keep his self-respect and yet at the same time to earn a living. Goethe, who had a sound business sense and something of a reputation among publishers as a 'hard man', commented in his '*Dichtung und Wahrheit*' that 'the production of a poet was looked upon as something holy, and people regarded it almost as simony to accept a fee, much less to try and bargain for an increase in the payment of their work'.

In the early nineteenth century the profession of letters was not established in Germany as either profitable or respectable. The very term *freier Schriftsteller*, (free-lance writer), although in current use at that time, did not suggest a laudable or even enviable estate, but rather had and continued to have associations of rootlessness, lack of substance and general indiscipline. The political and social organisation of the German Confederation after 1815 discouraged mobility. Indeed the small-town mentality which characterised the sedentary population of most of the country, made people suspicious of those who were mobile, whether students, journeymen or Jews. After the revolution of 1830 a number of talented and ambitious young men, who were encouraged by what they regarded as the favourable social situation of the writer in France, attempted to make a living with their pens. In his '*Briefe aus Berlin*' (1822) Heine underlined the differences between the two nations in this respect:

> The French writer spends his life in society, indeed in high society ... the poor German writer, because he is badly paid and rarely has the chance

of travelling, since he is without private means ... locks himself into his attic room, creates a world of fantasy ... writes novels with characters and objects in them which are glorious, divine, highly poetic, but which have no substance in reality.

The writers of Heine's generation, reaching manhood in the 1820s and 1830s, found themselves the object of the strictest police surveillance; a number served prison sentences for alleged offences against society and morality. Their position was a difficult one in any case. The restricted employment prospects open to the educated in Germany between 1800 and 1850 (as in western Europe generally), made it difficult for intellectuals to find their place in society. In the Restoration period the majority solicited state appointments; those who failed to get a post, often joined the opposition. State appointments offered not only security, but status also. When he was a student, wrote Karl Gutzkow, a leading figure in the Young Germany movement and probably the first genuine professional writer of note, 97% of all students aspired to be state employees. Contemporary literature is full of references to their efforts, none more rumbustious than the comedy entitled '*Die politische Wochenstube*' or 'The Scene of Germania's Confinement' (1845) by the political journalist Robert Prutz. Heinrich Laube, also a member of Young Germany and afterwards director of the Vienna Burgtheater, where his bust adorns the façade, had a similar experience to that of Gutzkow. He studied in Breslau in Silesia and in the central German town of Halle, where he found that

everyone simply clung to the state. Any kind of job which had some state connection was what people were after, and only that. Any independent activity, in which one relied on one's own resources, was regarded as adventurous and dubious.

It was not just a matter of economics. Status was just as important. Thus the Romantic philosopher Fichte, grown somewhat pompous since he became rector of Berlin university, referred to 'the superior class of person, those with a higher education ... whoever has not had a higher education belongs to the common people, the *Volk*'. Not wealth or fame, but officially attested learning was the ladder to position and standing and general reliability for the middle-class German. Many provincial writers in the Restoration years simply arrogated the title of *Doktor* to themselves in the hopes of attracting attention to their work. It is striking how many of Germany's well-known writers in these years and later had a university training; very many of them also had what is known as a bourgeois profession. The Romantic poets, E. T. A. Hoffmann and Eichendorff, for example, were lawyers in the Prussian civil service; the novelist Immermann and his younger contemporary Theodor Storm were judges. The Austrians Stifter and Grillparzer were also civil servants, while Mörike and the Swiss novelist Gotthelf were parsons. Many poets, including Heine and Uhland, the dramatist Grabbe and the dialect novelist Fritz Reuter, studied law, as had also the Grimm brothers. Reuter and the Young German poet, Hoffmann von Fallersleben, had dearly wished to be artists, but their fathers, mayors of small towns and especially status conscious, forced them to enter the legal profession. Hebbel too went to university after working in domestic service for eight years; he studied at immense physical cost to himself, because he was too poor to feed himself properly, and had to make the journey between home in Hamburg and university in south Germany on foot. Karl Gutzkow and Heinrich Laube studied theology, though they did not take it professionally. The high proportion of writers who followed this course is less a reflection on the piety of middle-class homes than an indication of the availability of scholarships for poor students in the faculties of theology. Such a qualification stamped one as a reliable and pious soul, deserving of patronage, which was an important matter for the penurious in the pre-March period.

'Literature is only esteemed when its creator has another source of income and respect, apart from his writing', observed the schoolmaster poet, Christian Weise, in his 'Curious Thoughts on German Verses', published in 1691, and his views held good until late in the nineteenth century. It was widely held that the pursuit of a respectable calling by a writer was a pledge of the general 'morality' of what he wrote. On the other hand, those who attempted to create a career in writing, as did the gifted journalist and democrat from the Frankfurt ghetto, Ludwig Börne, or Heine, or the group of radical writers known as the Young Hegelians, encountered criticism, persecution and in some cases exile, even before the revolution of 1848 in which so many took part. Besides the hostility of the authorities, there were other major obstacles to be overcome in the first half of the century, if they were to succeed. These included the lack of a mass market for books and journals, the political divisions in the country, the lack of cities, and poor transport and communications. A national press did not exist in Germany, the local press was scarcely developed, and, not least, there was the problem of the censorship.

Censorship

The role of the censorship in Restoration Germany owed much to the example given by Napoleon. '*L'imprimerie*', he had declared before the French Council of State, '*est un arsenal qu'il importe de ne pas mettre entre les mains de tout le monde.*' There were in fact relatively few printing presses in Germany in 1815, certainly by comparison with France, and they were generally regarded as potentially disruptive in character as regards society. The Prussian authorities appointed a censor in every town where a printing press existed. On Metternich's instructions the Federal Diet had overall responsibility for controlling the activities of writers within the federal borders. However the situation was complicated by the fact of state autonomy, and censorship operated with varying degrees of severity in the different states. Thus Prussia was less severe in this regard than Austria, but more efficient; Hamburg, Hesse-Darmstadt and the central German states were more liberal. The Karlsbad Decrees of 1819 included much sterner measures of control over the printed word, and up to the revolution of 1848 writers were considerably harassed. Not only writers, but publishers also, and they had to pay the censor for his pains ('pencil turned into a man' as Nestroy called him). Yet even when a manuscript had been passed by the censor for publication, the work could still be seized without compensation. Censorship was more or less limited to publications of twenty sheets or less, that is, it was aimed mainly at controlling periodicals and pamphlets.

Repeated bouts with the censor could lead to a total ban on a man's work, which happened to Gutzkow, who was also imprisoned in 1835 on the appearance of his novel, '*Wally, die Zweiflerin*'. At the same time the federal diet banned the works of his fellow Young Germans, Laube, Mundt and Wienbarg, and also those of Heine, on the grounds that they were 'unchristian and blasphemous', that they 'trample underfoot all morality, modesty and decency'. In 1841 the whole list of one of Germany's leading publishing houses was forbidden, Julius Campe of Hamburg. Authors and publishers became adept at dealing with the censor, and in doing so they created a bond with their readers, who learned the rules of the game, as it were. Authors made use of fictitious settings, allusion and parody; they encouraged reading between the lines, and became expert at attacking contemporary political abuses or personalities in the form of reviews of literary works. Many moved their domicile after publication or brought out censored work in another, more liberal, state. In 1840 censorship on illustrations was lifted in Prussia, as a concession to the liberals, and this measure gave immense stimulus to the vogue for illustrated satirical journals. The following years saw the publication of '*Kladderadatsch*' in Berlin, the '*Fliegende Blätter*' in Munich; the most famous of such journals, '*Simplicissimus*', was not founded until 1896. The viciousness of satire and caricature in the 1840s, and particularly in the revolutionary year, when censorship was lifted, the widespread use of personal invective and the general bad manners of writers in mid-century Germany were a natural response to the attitude of the authorities in treating writers and journalists as immature and irresponsible elements in the community. After the revolution, censorship was re-imposed in a less stringent form, but its more absurd features were only gradually abolished.

Copyright

Yet the system had none of the advantages normally to be expected from a paternalist system. No protection was offered by the state to authors from those seeking to exploit their talents. No federal copyright law existed in the early decades of the century, and the generally low levels of payment were in part dictated by the risks to the publishers of literary works from piracy. A work published in one German state under privilege could be pirated in another state three miles away. Goethe was the first German writer to submit a successful application to the Federal Diet for protection from piracy in the Confederation. He submitted it in 1825 for the forthcoming edition of his collected works. (This was the famous '*Vollständige Ausgabeletzter Hand*', published by Cotta in Stuttgart 1827–30.) He supported his submission on the grounds that an author had the right 'to some advantages and reward for his work, which however is generally denied to the German writer'.

But Goethe was no average German author, either in terms of the quality of his work or his commercial success, and the benefits of his enterprise did not become available to others for a number of years. In 1835 a law was introduced to impose penalties on literary pirates, but it was easy to evade, and no such measure existed for Germany as a whole until 1871. In 1837 Prussia showed some initiative in the matter: the works of all writers who had died before 9 November 1837 were declared copyright for a period of thirty years. Thus the profits of Goethe's and Schiller's works, and those of other 'classical' writers, were reserved for their dependents and heirs, and the price of such works remained extremely high in consequence until 'the year of the classics', 1867. Piracy by foreign publishers continued to be something of a problem until 1886, the year of the Berne Copyright Convention. Several German states made bi-lateral agreements with England, France, Switzerland and Italy, but two states, Holland and the USA, pirated works from German authors, the latter for its growing German community. Holland proved a more serious threat, as the works could be smuggled over the border and sold at low prices, particularly the popular political poets of the 1840s, Freiligrath, Herwegh and others.

The book trade

The image of Germany in the Goethean age as the land of poets and scholars, the enormous growth in demand for reading material and in the number of books published, gave a false impression of the state of the book trade in that country in 1800. Its organisation was thoroughly haphazard. There were relatively few bookshops, and booksellers came to the annual fairs at Leipzig and Frankfurt, taking books back home for their customers, who perhaps would not buy them; in this case the booksellers returned them to the publisher the following year. Publishers were widely regarded as the writer's enemy in the eighteenth century, and undoubtedly some made a good deal of money and continued to pay minimal sums to authors. But the element of risk was considerable, and it was not until the advent of an enterprising young publisher named F. C. Perthes, who joined the Hamburg firm of Hoffmann and Campe in the late eighteenth century, that the book trade in northern Germany was gradually rationalised. Perthes travelled widely in Germany in the early years of the nineteenth century and encouraged booksellers by organising a steady supply of titles. He was helped by the spread of the lending libraries and reading societies, which could be counted upon to take a regular number of new books. As he observed in his memoirs, Perthes found the situation in southerm Germany, apart from Württemberg, much more backward than in the north, and for most of the century the cultural divide between north and south was amply attested by its reading habits. The number of bookshops continued to grow in subsequent years. Including the shops selling musical scores there were in Germany and Austria the following number of bookshops.

Year	Number of bookshops
1800 (an estimated)	500
1834	859
1843	887
1867	1,325
1880	3,378

Book sales were boosted in the 1830s and 1840s by the novel fashion of window dressing; sales were extended to include paper and fancy goods, as well as writing materials, which brought the present-loving Germans into the shops. Both bookshops and publishing firms tended to be sited along trade routes and university towns in the first half of the century, rather than in state capitals. Thus Leipzig and not Dresden was the leading centre of the book trade in Saxony, and in the Confederation. Its primacy remained unchallenged until the later nineteenth century, when Berlin and Vienna became prominent in this respect. Leipzig's reputation, dating from the time of Lessing and the young Goethe as 'Little Paris', made it a favourite place for writers to live throughout the nineteenth century.

German publishers

The growth in the number of books published in the first half of the century struck contemporaries forcibly. 'If authorship goes on in a similarly progressive ratio to that which it has lately done', wrote an English visitor whimsically in the 1830s, 'it may safely be argued that the number of living German authors will exceed the number of living German readers.' Johann Georg von Cotta wrote wryly to a Munich professor in 1834, 'Tell me, dear friend, why is it that we have become a sedentary nation, a nation of scribblers, readers and printers?' The expansion of the book trade is reflected in the figures compiled by contemporaries as shown in the graph overleaf.

The fashionable 'reading craze' (*Lesewut*) in the pre-March era owed much to the entrepreneurial talents of individual publishers, among them Cotta's father. The philosopher Kant had likened the publishers of his time to factory directors. The great names in the early nineteenth century publishing world, Perthes, Cotta and Göschen, were men of a different order, men of vision, cultivated and urbane. Of these Cotta was the most distinguished. He came

The number of books published in 19th century Germany

from a Tübingen publishing family and was responsible for publishing many of the most famous works of German literature. An immensely hard worker, he had studied law and mathematics in Tübingen before spending time at Paris, where he made contacts which proved useful under the Napoleonic administration. He settled down in Tübingen to restore the family fortunes, made a lifelong friend of Schiller, and through him met Goethe, who had been publishing hitherto mainly with Göschen. Cotta was both generous and shrewd. Schiller's family was cared for after his early death in 1805 as a result of the contracts made with Cotta, but the firm made a great deal of money on the transactions, as they did through Goethe's later works, and the collected editions of the 1820s and subsequent years. Cotta used some of the profits to finance little known authors, as well as publishing in fields other than literature. It was he who launched Alexander von Humboldt's '*Cosmos*', a compendium of contemporary knowledge in the field of science. His descendant, Bernard von Cotta, could observe in 1869, the year of Humboldt's centenary and of the launching of the jubilee edition of '*Cosmos*', that it was 'the most widely sold book after the Bible' (in Germany). Cotta, made a baron by the Austrian emperor in 1824, had represented Württemberg at the Congress of Vienna in 1815. He was in a position to protect his authors from the full rigour of the censorship, and did so for Heine, among others. Heine wrote for his newspaper, the '*Allgemeine Zeitung*', published at Augsburg, and the leading newspaper of the Confederation. When Cotta died, fittingly perhaps, in the same year as Goethe, his son continued the firm's policy. Until his own death in 1864 Johann Georg von Cotta continued to give a special place in his list to lyric poetry, even though there were few profits to be made from it after mid-century. In time the firm merged with the Leipzig firm of Göschen (whose descendants became prominent in British business and politics). In the late nineteenth century the house was bought by Kröner, whose popular cheap editions of the classics had few rivals in Germany, at least before the advent of paperbacks in our own times.

A younger man, Julius Campe, was a more modern figure, with much less capital behind him, but he became a leading publisher in the 1830s. He specialised in the work of controversial writers, such as Heine and the Young Germans. He was adept at avoiding conflict with the authorities, and though he paid low fees, he managed to finance his main authors through profits from the sort of thing that the public wanted, such as the patriotic Prussian '*Hohenstaufen*' dramas by Ernst Raupach.

The popular encyclopedias (Konversationslexikon)

While Cotta and Campe are of particular interest to the student of literature, for the history of public taste in the nineteenth century two other publishers are important: F. A. Brockhaus and the much criticised C. J. Meyer, Under the genial slogan *Bildung macht frei!* (education liberates!), Meyer set up the so-called 'Groschen Library', on the lines of the English Penny Magazine. He engaged a veritable army of colporteurs, a species of commercial traveller, who delivered advertisements for his cheap classics to people's houses and solicited subscriptions. At a time when books were still expensive, Meyer's organisation succeeded in selling several hundreds of thousands of copies at two groschen (or about 1p) each.

The Brockhaus organisation was much more respectable, indeed the Brockhaus Universal Encyclopedia represents one of the great cultural achievements of the century. The success of both ventures–and Meyer's own encyclopaedias, modelled on Brockhaus– marked the emergence of publishing as a capitalistic enterprise, catering for a new mass market. In 1809 Brockhaus produced his first encyclopedia in five volumes in an edition of 2,000. The fifth ten-volume edition appeared in 1819–20 in 32,000 copies. By the time the eleventh edition appeared in the 1860s, some 300,000 copies had been sold. 'No work of reference has been more useful and successful, or more frequently copied, imitated and translated than that known as the Conversational Lexikon of Brockhaus', reported the Encyclopedia Britannica in 1948. Not only was it a great commercial success, but, with its imitators, the 'Brockhaus' helped to form contemporary thinking on social and political issues among its predominantly middle-class readers. For the student of Germany in the nineteenth century the encyclopedias are a fund of information and a truly fascinating record of how opinions and manners changed in the course of the century.

The flair and commercial skill responsible for the success of Brockhaus and his imitators were also responsible for the unusual success of a number of other ventures, notably the 'World History' by the Freiburg professor Rotteck, a prominent liberal, and also his joint venture with his colleague, Welcker, the '*Staatslexikon*', which became a popular and influential work of reference on political and social questions in the constitutional states of southern Germany in the decades before the 1848 revolution.

Later in the century, success on a similar scale was achieved through the small and under-capitalised firm Reclam. In 1867, when the copyright on the German classics was lifted, Reclam, in common with many other publishing firms, launched cheap editions of the major works of German literature. However, whereas others concentrated on collected works, Reclam produced single copies priced at only two groschen each. Thus Schiller's '*Don Carlos*' which had cost two taler in October (about 30p) could be had for the equivalent of one penny a month later. In the winter of 1867–68 20,000 copies of the first volume of Reclam's famous series were printed; it was Goethe's '*Faust*'. To this day low cost Reclam texts continue to be printed in Leipzig in the German Democratic Republic and Stuttgart in the Federal Republic, with the signal advantage that they do not go out of print.

Lending libraries

The publication of narrative prose, of drama and verse epics, and the autobiographies and travellers' tales so popular in the first half of the century was made possible by the institution known as the lending libraries and, to a lesser extent, to the so-called *Lesezirkel* or magazine rental service. This was intended for the local notables, the *Honoratioren* of the small towns across the country, who began to use the 'reading cabinet' (*Lesekabinett*) as a kind of club or a venue for the holding of lectures, meetings and borrowing books and magazines. Booksellers were encouraged to open a room next to their shops, where the latest books and periodicals were laid out for their perusal. Membership fees were high and the societies were elitist in character. Lending libraries, on the other hand, which, like the magazine service, started in the eighteenth century, were probably the most democratic institution in Germany. Aristocratic ladies might dislike the idea of handling books read by domestic servants, but they wanted to read the same kind of books, namely popular novels, tales of fantasy and devotional works. By 1800, when many such libraries already existed throughout Germany, it was becoming more profitable to lend books than to sell them. A Munich library owner had 2,500 books in 1801, 4,000 five years later; a Bremen bookseller, who had started his venture in 1800, had some 20,000 in 1824. From Würzburg in 1800 Kleist remarked in a letter to his fiancée, 'Nowhere can one gauge the degree of culture of a town or the spirit of its taste more rapidly and yet accurately than in its lending libraries.' Like other northern visitors, he was not impressed by what he saw in this south German town, but authors of popular works, including devotional writers, benefitted hugely from the system. Christoph von Schmid, a Catholic priest from Dinkelsbühl in Württemberg, and a fellow priest called Ludwig Donin in Vienna, each sold several million copies of their works in the course of the century.

The lending libraries actually determined the size of editions of books, for this began to be calculated on the basis of how many copies the libraries would buy, plus a couple of hundred more. Vieweg of Brunswick, publisher of Keller's '*Der grüne Heinrich*' (1854–55), reckoned that 800 libraries would take it and printed a thousand copies, but he was proved wrong and twenty years later the edition was still not yet sold out. As late as the 1860s and early 1870s, books remained difficult to sell to private individuals, though the lending libraries continued to play a useful role in their distribution. In these years the larger libraries 'serviced' the small provincial ones, by selling surplus copies at low prices. It was not until the late 1870s onwards that Campe's observation to Heine in 1833 ceased to hold good, namely that the Germans were 'a nation of readers but not of book buyers'.

The press

Germany's political backwardness was reflected in the state of her press in the first half of the century. Political news, if one could call it thus, had long been the monopoly of the authorities, who published the doings of the court and some foreign news items in the so-called '*Intelligenzblätter*'. In 1844 the Foreign Quarterly Review observed pertinently that the newspaper

> in England but ancillary, and in France the parent of a political party, may be regarded in Germany as one of the regalia of the Crown. The preparation, manufacture and sale of political intelligence, are as much a royal monopoly in Germany as those of tobacco in France.

Other newspapers existed on a limited scale, the most famous being the '*Vossische Zeitung*'. Founded in 1725, it still preserved a justly earned reputation in cultural matters when Fontane joined the staff as drama critic in 1870. Cotta founded the paper which was undoubtedly the best German newspaper in the first half of the century, the '*Allgemeine Zeitung*', in 1798. It moved to Augsburg after being previously published in Württemberg, and in the 1830s enjoyed a circulation of about 10,000, compared with about 8,000 for the '*Vossische*'. The period of French rule in Germany gave considerable stimulus to press ventures. It was the Romantic essayist and critic, Joseph Görres, considered one of the most talented of German journalists, whose paper, '*Der Rheinische Merkur*' (1814–16) earned from Napoleon the title so often applied to the press since, that it was the 'fifth power in Europe'. However few newspapers survived the stringent censorship regulations imposed as part of the Karlsbad Decrees in 1819, and even Cotta, despite his power and connections, encountered many problems with the authorities over his '*Allgemeine Zeitung*' and associated publications.

The periodical press
From the point of view of Germany's writers, the periodical press played a much more important role in their lives as a purveyor of information and as a source of livelihood than either the newspaper

or book publishing. Periodicals were generally published by the leading book publishers, and in the pre-March era, and more particularly between the years 1830 and 1848 leading writers were employed as editors and journalists. Hermann Marggraff, radical social philosopher and journalist, summed up the situation in the early 1850s:

> The journals were the vehicle of public expression, and in a sense the leaders of public opinion. They put into words what people felt and were concerned about, and they could only exist so long as they could continue to perform this function.

Their number and variety was considerable, reflecting the variety of political, philosophical and religous opinion in the Confederation as a whole. But they were directed at a national rather than a local readership, for, in line with national and liberal thinking characteristic of the majority of writers on contemporary affairs, they aimed to foster a sense of cultural nationhood in a politically divided country. Cotta's '*Morgenblatt für gebildete Stände*' (Morning Gazette for the cultivated classes – 1807–65) had an influential literary supplement, under its editor Wolfgang Menzel, who acquired considerable authority in intellectual circles in the 1820s and early 1830s. He employed Karl Gutzkow after the latter graduated from Berlin university. The '*Morgenblatt*' was aimed at the educated upper class, as was Campe's avowedly liberal *Telegraph für Deutschland* (1838–48), also edited by Gutzkow, who had fallen foul of Menzel in 1835. The '*Rheinische Zeitung*', which Karl Marx edited for a short time in 1842, catered for the new commercial bourgeoisie of the Rhineland. Friedrich List, the economist, edited a number of journals designed to awaken interest in the Customs Union and the railways as a preliminary to national unity on an economic basis, while Brockhaus' '*Deutsche Allgemeine Zeitung*' in northern Germany advocated free trade and political liberal policies. Conservative traditional views were also represented in the journals, the most notorious of which was the '*Evangelische Kirchenzeitung*', edited by the Lutheran churchman Hengstenberg, who had much of the demagogue in him. A short-lived but highly influential journal was edited by the Young Hegelian, Arnold Ruge, the '*Hallischen Jahrbücher*' (1838–42). First published in Prussia, then, on account of the censor, in Saxony, the '*Jahrbücher*' exercised immense influence on young intellectuals from Königsberg in East Prussia to Hamburg in the north-west and Heidelberg and Stuttgart in the south. Most of the leading radicals wrote for it, including Friedrich Engels. The majority of journals included a section on imaginative literature, with a preference for verse tales, lyric poetry and short narrative prose pieces, which enabled poets to 'place' their work on a more or less regular basis. A further means of publication, which disappeared largely after about 1850, were the so-called pocket-books or almanacs, favoured especially by women, which were generally published by the same firms which sponsored the journals.

The family journals and periodicals press after 1848

The revolutionary year 1848–49 proved to be a watershed in the history of the press, as in so much else besides. The editors of the pre-March journals had catered for a relatively small but socially homogeneous readership. The readership had grown politically ever more aware since 1830, and was, with some notable exceptions, predominantly liberal in sentiment. After 1848 this changed. Sections of the middle class, such as large or medium farmers, innkeepers, teachers, minor civil servants, became progressively disillusioned with political liberalism and indeed with political issues generally. In the aftermath of the failed revolution, reform and change lacked the topicality it had possessed a decade earlier. At the same time more money came into circulation, improved techniques led to a reduction in costs, and publishers began to aim at a mass readership. The so-called family journals made their appearance, starting with the famous '*Gartenlaube*' ('Garden Bower') in 1853, which had a readership of some 5,000 at the end of its first year. The *Lesewut* of the Restoration era was transferred from novels and biographies to magazines. Book production figures continued to drop from the high point reached in 1843, and this trend was not reversed until the late 1870s. Circulation figures for the most popular magazines give an indication of the extraordinary success of this new phenomenon, which had important long-term effects for writers and imaginative literature in Germany. The '*Gartenlaube*', which accommodated its liberal views to the conservative climate of Prussia in the late 1860s and Germany in the 1870s, sold 135,000 copies in 1863, 382,000 in 1875 and 234,000 in 1883; the Stuttgart based *Illustrierte Welt*, reached a figure of some 100,000 copies in 1867; *Über Land und Meer* which had a more literary flavour, enjoyed a circulation of 55,000 in 1867 and 150,000 in the late 1870s. The more prestigious journals published a number of major prose works of German literature in the 1870s and subsequent decades. These included Julius Rodenberg's *Deutsche Rundschau*, founded in 1873, and Paul Lindau's *Die Gegenwart* (1872). If they never reached more than a fraction of the circulation figures of the popular magazines, at best something around 10,000 copies per annum, they represented a vital force in the literary life of the nation.

Commercial considerations dictated editorial policy to an ever increasing extent, and authors were forced to take heed of this in their choice of literary forms. Drama and lyric poetry declined in popular appeal after 1848, as reading matter and for performance on social occasions. Novels were initially hard hit by the vogue for the journals, since a subscription to a family magazine, which could be expected to include matters of interest for everyone in the household, cost no more than a book. The *Novelle* on the other hand, a literary genre in which German writers excelled, began to sell well. While Keller experienced difficulty in getting a reasonable price for '*Der Grüne Heinrich*' (666 talers for a very long novel), he was well paid for his '*Seldwyla Tales*' (290 talers), published a year later, in 1856. Stifter earned 2,000 talers for his cycle of *Novellen*, '*Bunte Steine*', in 1853, and only twice that amount for his two long novels '*Der Nachsommer*' (1857) and '*Witiko*' (1865–67). Raabe, admittedly an unknown author in the 1850s, did much less well. The publisher Vieweg required a payment of fifty talers from him for the publication of his first novel, '*Die Chronik der Sperlingsgasse*' (1857), which afterwards became such a favourite of the public, and gave him only 150 talers for his second novel.

However in the course of the 1850s an innovation improved the situation of the writer of prose fiction generally and the novelist in particular. This was the policy of serialising novels in magazines prior to publication.* Throughout the following decades, and in the large national newspapers at the end of the century, novels were serialised and increasingly well paid. Now writers found themselves less and less dependent on a 'bourgeois' profession, although many, including Keller and Storm, still held to the view that such a profession provided the artist with needful discipline. Successful novelists now began to make a lot of money. Fritz Reuter, who once eked out a living giving private lessons at a few pence an hour, was able to move into the villa he had built himself on the

---

* This helps to account for apparent disagreement about dates of first publication of prose works in this period; the first date refers to the serialisation, the second, usually the following year, to book publication.

slopes of the Wartburg twenty years later, in the late 1860s, on the profits of his three novels in *Plattdeutsch*: '*Ut de Franzosentid*' (1859), '*Ut min Festungstid*' and '*Ut min Stromtid*' (1862–64). Gustav Freytag, author of the greatest financial success of the century, '*Soll und Haben*' (1855), and Friedrich Spielhagen, who adapted his novel-writing technique to the demands of the serial and Paul Heyse, a writer of much admired Novellen which were serialised in the press, became wealthy men. By 1880 Keller could command fifty talers per sheet for the serialisation of the second edition of '*Der Grüne Heinrich*', and 20% of that sum for the book edition. Even the less successful writers, such as Fontane and Raabe, doubled their earnings from royalties between 1870 and 1880.

Many writers voiced the opinion that the commercialisation of publishing had a demeaning effect on art, but Fontane, always a realist, recognised the advantages of the new situation. In a letter to the editor of the '*Gartenlaube*', who had asked him to make some alterations in a manuscript, he observed:

> There can be no question of my feeling aggrieved afterwards, not even in my own mind. For there must be something in it, if the actual material permits it, to please three hundred thousand subscribers, or whatever the number is. And the dish which feeds three hundred thousand Germans, shall feed me too.

In private he expressed similar views. In 1884 he wrote to his wife:

> The days of a penny (*groschen*) or a penny ha'penny a line are over ... Thank God I've lived to witness the change. For the pure poet, who won the patronage of princes, the former age may have been better, but as far as humanity in general and the average writer are concerned, the progress of our own day is colossal.

At the end of the 1870s book publishing picked up sharply. The growing wealth of the middle classes encouraged the purchase of books, which came to be seen as part of the life-style of the educated man. *Prachtexemplare*, beautifully bound editions of the classics, the equivalent of the modern coffee table books, became fashionable, the more so since they were seen as a monument to German craftsmanship. Moreover the reading public felt a need for roots in the new national state and responded avidly to writers and publishers who supplied them with historical works, both of scholarship and of fantasy, about the origins and development of the new Germany. Examples of such works of very different genres but which enjoyed immense success, are Franz Kugler's 'Life of Frederick the Great' (first published 1855), Viktor von Scheffel's medieval romance '*Ekkehard*' or his vastly popular verse epic '*Der Trompeter von Säckingen*' (1852), which went through 299 editions in fifty-nine years, and Heinrich von Treitschke's 'History of Germany in the nineteenth century' (1878–94). Freytag's '*Die Ahnen*' ('The Ancestors'), a well-informed and easily digested account of Germany's cultural origins, which appeared in six volumes between 1872 and 1880, earned him nearly half a million marks, and Felix Dahn's historical novel about the Germanic conquest of Rome, '*Der Kampf um Rom*' (1876), had a similar appeal. The negative picture of the German Empire now current in history books has drawn works such as these into the general condemnation of popular culture in late nineteenth century Germany. There is much justification for this, especially with regard to the stereotype presentation of Germany's rivals and enemies, notably France, and at a somewhat later date, England. However a comparison with popular reading material in Britain or France – of novelists such as Merriman, for example, suggest that such prejudices were a European rather than an exclusively German phenomenon. Modern critics overlook the narrative talents displayed in many such works, which help to account for their popular success, as much as did their political prejudices. That these latter undoubtedly operated is clear from the lack of success accorded to Fontane's major historical novel, '*Vor dem Sturm*' (1878). Set in the emotive period of the wars of liberation in Prussia, 1810–13, Fontane here challenged the accepted notion of German patriotism and upset the sensibility of many of his readers by presenting the French as brave and chivalrous, the Poles as kind and dignified.

Professional organisations

A number of attempts were made at different times during the century to create associations to protect writers and their interests. They were not particularly successful. The first attempt was undertaken by a number of politically progressive writers and editors, including Hermann Marggraff and other Young Hegelians, at Leipzig in 1842. They called their organisation the *Literatenverein*, and were joined by the publisher Brockhaus and his colleagues, Wigand and Hirzel. In 1845 they held a successful writers' conference, but soon fell foul of the authorities. However, few prominent writers associated themselves with the undertaking, and the liberal journal, '*Die Grenzboten*', damned the enterprise by observing that the conference had been dominated by writers 'of the materialistic and political persuasion', while the 'artistic and idealistic writers were scarcely represented'. One of the leading members of the *Literatenverein*, Karl Biedermann, who had published his fine history of Germany in the eighteenth century, '*Deutschland im 18, Jahrhundert*', in 1858, defended his associates vigorously:

> There is no shame in earning a living by means of our intellectual capital and mental effort in the way others do with dead money or with the mechanical work of their hands.

The incident showed that the old conflict of conscience was not yet laid to rest, that professionalism in letters was still held to mean the end of literature as art.

Several decades later, in 1878, a national writers' organisation was set up, again in Leipzig. This was the General German Writers Association, and it proved itself to be an apt representative of what the public regarded as the 'literary world'. Of some 194 members of the organisation in 1880, the year in which they held their first conference at the Wartburg, Luther's erstwhile residence, where he translated the Greek New Testament into German, 150 were writers of note. Only two of them, however, styled themselves thus, a fact reminiscent of Brentano's observation quoted at the beginning of this chapter. Thirty-two were editors, several were civil servants, and eighty had the title of *Doktor*. 'An excellent buffet, splendidly presented, lackeys with wine, champagne and beer, served in old-fashioned drinking goblets' graced the final assembly of 'literary folk'. But those whom posterity regards as Germany's major writers were absent. 'In my opinion,' observed the novelist Raabe, 'there simply isn't any such thing as a social class of writers, and there never will be.' In their views on the function of the arts in society, in their rigid notions of what constituted good taste and aesthetic principles, the official representatives of literature in the German Empire were the living embodiment of what Nietzsche described in the opening chapter of his '*Unzeitgemässe Betrachtungen*' (1873–75) as the German philistine.

The writer and society

The response of Germany's writers to efforts made to organise them throws light on the uneasy relationship between them and the society in which they lived in the second half of the century. In an anonymous article entitled 'The social status of the writer', published in 1891, Theodor Fontane referred to the *aufgeklebter Zettel* (official label) which the authorities and the public liked to attach to the artist, so that they knew where they were with him. 'Examinations, certificates, official approval, public office, titles, decorations, in short everything which derives from state patronage' was what persuaded people of a writer's artistic worth. People did not trust themselves to respond intuitively to art. They did not wish to be disturbed by what they read (or saw or heard), but rather looked to art for confirmation of their principles and their way of life. The success of men such as Freytag and Spielhagen, and of the authors enjoying a wide following in the family magazines, owed much to the fact that they interpreted 'the eternal verities' to mean the conservative social values of Imperial Germany. Among writers themselves, disagreement separated those who, like the Young Germans in the 1830s and 1840s, and the Naturalists in the 1890s, believed that literature should be critical and radical, concerned to change and improve society, and those who, like Stifter and, in a very different manner, Hebbel, considered art to be concerned with the quest for 'eternal truth', and that topical issues had no place in it. Those who, like Grillparzer and Annette von Droste-Hülschoff, Storm and Fontane, Raabe and Meyer, could identify themselves with neither position, complained of a growing sense of isolation in the community of German-speaking peoples. This feeling was exacerbated in the last years of the century by the alienation of German popular culture from that of the rest of western Europe, a process which preceded her political isolation at the beginning of the twentieth century.

When Prussia set up the North German Confederation in 1867, a preliminary to unification four years later, a writer called upon her to 'place German poetry under the wings of the Prussian eagle'. In a sense this is just what happened. 'National' values were at a premium in literature as in the arts generally. Virtues which were frequently held up as ideals to emulate, such as loyalty, honour, comradeship, integrity, rarely appeared without being preceded by the epithet 'deutsch', and it was implied, and often openly stated, that these qualities were not shared by other European nations. The decline in the appeal of liberalism as a political creed or a code of conduct for the individual after 1848, was accompanied by a growing dislike of those of a different background, nation or race. Associations for co-operation in the field of international understanding were viewed with suspicion, and among the various nationalist pressure groups, with open derision. The provincialism of German intellectuals struck even well intentioned foreign visitors forcibly. Provincial chauvinism was a common characteristic of German academics too, and of upper class circles apart from the high nobility, and it found expression in the resentment shown to qualities such as sophistication of taste and urbanity of manner. If political and economic rivalry bred dislike and envy of Britain in German society at the end of the century, a special hostility was reserved for French intellectual traditions. The known influence of French writers and of Ibsen on the generation of the 1890s, the Naturalists, notably Gerhart Hauptmann, Heinrich Sudermann and their younger contemporaries such as Heinrich Mann, made them the object of open vilification. The Naturalists' concern to draw attention to the oppressed, especially in rural and urban working-class circles, associated them at once in the mind of society at large with the reviled Social Democrats, with European anarchists and those whom contemporary invective liked to term *vaterlandslose Gesellen*. It was an intrinsic part of the young Heinrich Mann's protest against the values of contemporary German culture that he chose to model his early novels on the work of leading French writers, and to publicise Germany's long cultural debt to France in the work of his maturity.

What to German poets who were growing old as the century grew to a close was a bitter heritage, the alienation of German artists from their society, proved to be an inspiration to the generation of the 1890s and 1900s. Thomas and Heinrich Mann, Franz Kafka, Robert Musil and Carl Sternheim, each in their different ways, made this the central theme of their works, as did many minor poets in their wake. They and their successors submitted the epoch in which they had grown up, and which was to be destroyed in the Great War, to a critical reappraisal which, as has already been said, anticipated the work of historians by almost half a century. Yet curiously enough, despite their merciless exposure of the culture of the German Empire, in satire, irony and parody, they all seemed to accept the prejudice of the bourgeois world that the artist was somehow 'unfit' to be a full member of the community.

Main historical dates

1803		Abolition of territorial sovereignty of ecclesiastic princes (= Mediatisation)
1806	July	Napoleon forms the Confederation of the Rhine
	August	Abolition of the Holy Roman Empire (founded AD 800)
	October	Battle of Jena
1807		Treaty of Tilsit
		Baron Stein initiates the Prussian reform programme
1809		Count (later Prince) Metternich becomes Austrian foreign minister
1813–15		The wars of liberation against Napoleon
1813		The Volunteers are formed
	October	Battle of Leipzig ('Battle of the Nations')
1814–15		Congress of Vienna
1815	June	German Confederation formed (till 1867)
	June	Battle of Waterloo
1816–17		Cattle plague and crop failure
1819		Karlsbad Decrees
1830		Revolution in the German Confederation
1832		Death of Goethe
		Hambach festival
1834		Customs Union
1835		First German railway (Nuremberg–Fürth)
		Federal Diet bans the works of Heine and the Young Germans
1837		Protest of the 'Göttingen Seven'
1840		Frederick William IV succeeds to the Prussian throne

1844		Hunger typhus in Germany – the Weavers' Revolt in Silesia
1846–47		Crop failure and potato blight
1848	February	Communist Manifesto
	13 March	Revolution in Vienna
	18 March	Revolution in Berlin
	31 March	'Pre-Parliament' in Heidelberg
	18 May	Frankfurt Parliament opens
	August	Artisans congresses in Frankfurt and Berlin
	September	Uprisings in Frankfurt and elsewhere
	October	Counter-Revolution begins
	December	Franz Joseph I becomes Austrian Emperor
1849	April	Promulgation of the German Constitution
	May, June	Revolutionary disturbances in Saxony and Baden
	May	Three class franchise in Prussia
1850	January	Prussian Constitution
1850–73		Take-off into sustained economic growth
1858		William becomes Regent in Prussia
1861		William I succeeds to the Prussian throne
1862		Trade agreement between the states of the Customs Union and France
		Bismarck becomes Prussian prime minister
1862–67		Constitutional conflict in Prussia
1863		First German Workers Party (Lassalle)
1864		War with Denmark
1866		Austro-Prussian War
1867		North German Confederation formed (till 1871)
1868		Military alliance with south German states
		Customs Parliament meets at Berlin
1869		Social Democratic Workers Party founded (Bebel and Liebknecht)
1870–71		Franco-Prussian War
1871	18 January	Proclamation of the Second Empire at Versailles
	May	Peace of Frankfurt
1873		'Gründerkrise': the great crash
1874–95		'The Great Depression'

1875		Socialist Workers Party of Germany founded at Gotha (later Social Democratic Party)
1878–90		Anti-Socialist Law
1878–79		'Second founding of the Empire': conservative re-orientation in domestic policy
1879		Dual Alliance with Austria
1883–89		Bismarck's state Socialism programme
1887		Re-insurance Treaty with Russia (till 1890)
1888	March	Death of William I
	June	Death of Frederick III
1890	March	Bismarck's resignation
	June	Accession of William II (Kaiser Bill)
1893		Pan German League and Farmers League founded
1904		Entente Cordiale
1907		Russia joins Entente
1914	4 August	Germany invades Belgium

Museums

Selection of museums in the Federal Republic of Germany which contain material of special interest from the nineteenth century.

BERLIN Neue Nationalgalerie, Schinkelpavillon/Schloss Charlottenburg, Verkehrsmuseum (Transport museum)

BREMEN Kunsthalle

COLOGNE Wallraf-Richartz Museum

DÜSSELDORF Kunstmuseum

ESSEN Museum Folkwang

FRANKFURT Historisches Museum, Städelsches Kunstinstitut, Bundespostmuseum

HAMBURG Kunsthalle

KARLSRUHE Staatliche Kunsthalle

KASSEL Städtische Kunstsammlungen

KIEL Gemäldegalerie und Graphik Sammlung

MUNICH Neue Pinakothek, Schackgalerie, Städtische Galerie im Lenbachhaus

NUREMBERG Germanisches Nationalmuseum, Spielzeugmuseum (Toy museum), Verkehrsmuseum

SCHWEINFURT Georg Schäfer Sammlung

STUTTGART Staatsgalerie

WUPPERTAL Von der Heydt Museum

Some suggestions for further reading

Chapter 1

G. Mann, *A History of Germany in the 19th and 20th Centuries*, London 1961
F. Meinecke, *The Age of German Liberalism 1795–1815*, Calif. 1978
A. Ramm, *Germany 1789–1919. A Political History*, London 1967
F. Schnabel, *Deutsche Geschichte im 19. Jahrhundert*, 4 vols., 3.ed., Frankfurt 1954 (still a standard work)
ed. H. O. Sieburg, *Napoleon und Europa*, Cologne 1971
D. Thompson, *Europe since Napoleon*, Harmondsworth 1966

Chapter 2
R. M. Bigler, *The Politics of German Protestantism*, Calif. 1972.
K. Demeter, *The German Officer Corps in Society and State 1650–1945*, London 1965
A. Dru, *The Catholic Church in the 19th Century: Germany 1800–1918*, London 1963
M. Kitchen, *A Military History of Germany from the 18th Century to the Present Day*, London 1975
L. Krieger, *The German Idea of Freedom. History of a Political Tradition*, 1957
R. Koselleck, *Preußen zwischen Reform und Revolution*, 2.ed., Stuttgart 1975
E. Sagarra, *A Social History of Germany 1648–1914*, London 1977
C., L. and R. Tilley, *The Rebellious Century 1830–1930*, Harvard 1975
M. Walker, *German Home Towns*, Cornell 1971

Chapter 3
I. Barea, *Vienna*, London 1966
H. Benedikt, *Das Zeitalter der Emanzipation*, Munich 1977

W. Conze, *Staat und Gesellschaft im deutschen Vormärz*, Stuttgart 1962
J. Droz, *Europe between Revolutions 1815–48*, London 1967
Th. Hamerow, *Restoration, Revolution, Reaction. Economics and Politics in Germany 1815–71*, 2.ed. Princeton 1972
E. J. Hobsbawm, *The Age of Revolution. Europe 1789–1848*, London 1962
P. E. Schramm, *Neun Generationen*, vol. 2, Göttingen 1964. (A most imaginatively presented portrait of the Biedermeier age, based on family papers)
F. Sengle, *Biedermeierzeit*, vols. 1 and 2, Stuttgart 1971–72. (Vol. 3 of this magisterial work on the literary, intellectual and cultural life of this period has yet to appear)
M. Walker, *Germany and the Emigration, 1816–85*, Cambridge/Mass. 1964

Chapter 4
K. Borchardt, *The German Economy 1870 to the Present*, London 1967
C. Cipolla ed., *The Emergence of Industrial Societies*, I and II. (Fontana Economic History of Europe Vol. IV), London 1973
J. H. Clapham, *The Economic Development of France and Germany 1815–1914*, Cambridge, 3.ed. 1936
A. V. Desai, *Real Wages in Germany*, Oxford 1968
W. Emmerich, *Proletarische Lebensläufe*, vol. 1, 1848–1914. Hamburg 1975
W. Fischer, *Wirtschaft und Gesellschaft im Zeitalter der Industrialisierung*, Göttingen 1972
W. O. Henderson, *The Rise of German Industrial Power 1834–1914*, London 1975
J. Kuczynski, *Die Geschichte der Lage der Arbeiter unter dem Kapitalismus in Deutschland von 1789 bis 1917/8*, 1961–7 Berlin
D. Landes, *The Unbound Prometheus*, London 1969

Chapter 5
ed. H. Denkler, *Der deutsche Michel. Revolutionskömödien der 48er*, Stuttgart 1971
J. Droz, *Les révolutions allemandes de 1848*, Paris 1957
F. Eyck, *The Frankfurt Parliament 1848–9*, London 1968
R. A. Kann, *The Multi-national Empire. Nationalism and National Reform in the Habsburg Monarchy 1848–1918*, 2.vols., New York 1964

P. H. Noyes, *Organisation and Revolution. Working Class Associations in the German Revolutions of 1848-9*, Princeton 1966

V. Valentin, *Geschichte der deutschen Revolution von 1848-49*, Berlin 1930-31 (A magnificent work of German prose, quite apart from being still the standard work)

Chapter 6

Th. Hamerow, *The Social Foundations of German Unification*, 2 vols., Princeton 1969-73

W. M. Johnston, *The Austrian Mind. An Intellectual and Social History 1848-1938*, Calif., 1972

H. Kohn, *The Age of Nationalism*, New York 1968

ibid., *Prelude to National States: the French and German Experience 1789-1815*, Princeton 1967

Th. Schieder, *Das deutsche Kaiserreich von 1871 als Nationalstaat*, Cologne 1961

ibid., *Sozialstruktur und Organisation europäischer Nationalbewegungen*, Munich 1971

F. Stern, *The Failure of Illiberalism*, London 1972

H.-U. Wehler, *Das Deutsche Kaiserreich 1871-1918*, Göttingen 1973

Chapter 7

H. Böhme ed., *Probleme der Reichsgründungszeit 1848-79*, 2.ed., Cologne 1972 (Neue Wissenschaftliche Bibliothek, essays by leading German, American and other scholars)

E. J. Hobsbawm, *The Age of Capital 1848-75*, London 1975

M. Howard, *The Franco-Prussian War*, London 1961

I. Lamb, *Free Trade and Protectionism in Germany*, Wiesbaden 1963

O. Pflanze, *Bismarck and the Development of Germany. The Period of Unification 1815 to 1971*, Princeton 1963 (for all its learning, like the books of Th. Hamerow and Mack Walker, very easy for students to read and enjoy)

The novels of Spielhagen are most informative 'background' reading – such as:

In Reih und Glied (early Socialism) 1866

Hammer und Amboß (industrialisation) 1869

Sturmflut (speculation by the Prussian aristocracy before the 1873 crash etc.) 1874

Chapter *8*

H. Böhme, *The Foundation of the German Empire*, Oxford 1971
A. Gerschenkron, *Bread and Democracy in Germany*, 2nd ed., New York 1966
W. N. Medlicott, *Bismarck and Modern Germany*, London 1965
G. A. Ritter ed., *Die deutschen Parteien vor 1918*, Cologne 1973 (Neue Wiss. Bibl.)
F. Stern, *Gold and Iron. Bismarck and Bleichroeder*, London 1977
H.-U. Wehler, *Das deutsche Kaiserreich*, op.cit.

Chapter *9*

V. Berghahn, *Germany and the Approach of War in 1914*, London 1973
G. A. Craig, *Germany 1866–1945*, Oxford 1978
R. Dahrendorf, *Society and Democracy in Germany*, London 1968
W. Mommsen, *Das Zeitalter des Imperialismus*, 6.ed., Frankfurt 1976
K. v. Riezler, *Diary* ed. K. Erdmann, 1972
G. A. Ritter, *Arbeiterbewegung, Parteien und Parlamentarismus*, Göttingen 1976
J. Steinberg, *Yesterday's Deterrent. Tirpitz and the Birth of the German Battle Fleet*, London 1965
H. J. Varain ed., *Interessenverbände*, Cologne 1973, (Neue Wiss. Bibl.)
H.-U. Wehler, *Bismarck und der Imperialismus*, 2.ed., Göttingen 1972

Chapter *10*

R. Engelsing, *Zur Sozialgeschichte deutscher Mittel- und Unterschichten*, Göttingen 1972
H. Henning, *Sozialgeschichtliche Entwicklungen in Deutschland 1815–60*, 2 vols., Paderborn 1977
W. Köllmann u. Peter Marschalck, *Bevölkerungsgeschichte*, Cologne (*Neue Wiss. Bibl.*) 1970
Fr. Lütge, *Deutsche Sozial- und Wirtschaftsgeschichte*, Berlin 1960
W. Pöls, *Deutsche Sozialgeschichte I 1815–70*, Munich 1973
G. A. Ritter u. J. Kocka, *Deutsche Sozialgeschichte II 1870–1918*, Munich 1976 (These volumes contain extracts from contemporary writings on a variety of social themes)
E. Sagarra, *A Social History* etc. op.cit.

Chapter 11

P. Aries, *Geschichte der Kindheit*, Munich 1976
J. Braun-Vogelstein, *Ein Menschenleben*, Tübingen 1932*
R. J. Evans, *A History of Feminism 1894–1933*, London 1976
H. Lange, *Lebenserinnerungen*, Berlin 1925*
F. Lewald, *Meine Lebensgeschichte*, Frankfurt 1979*
D. v. Schlözer, *Ein deutsches Frauenleben um die Jahrhundertwende 1770–1825*, Stuttgart 1923*
E. Shorter, *The Making of the Modern Family*, London 1976
M. Twellmann, *Die deutsche Frauenbewegung. Ihre Anfänge u. erste Entwicklung 1843–89*, 2 vols. text and documents, Meisenheim am Glan 1972
R. Varnhagen, *Ein Frauenleben in Briefen*, Weimar 1912*
R. Weber ed., *Briefe der Revolutionszeit 1848–9*, Leipzig (Reclam) 1973
I. Weber-Kellermann, *Sozialgeschichte der deutschen Familie*, Frankfurt 1974
ibid., *Die deutsche Familie*, Frankfurt 1976 (with copious illustrations)

A sample of German memoirs quoted in or relevant to this chapter and easily available in paperback.

Author collective, *Der rote Großvater erzählt*, (Fischer) Frankfurt 1975
A. Bebel, *Aus meinem Leben*, Berlin (East) 1975
M. T. Bromme, *Lebensgesch. eines modernen Fabrikarbeiters*, Berlin (1905–re-print 1971)
W. Emmerich ed., *Proletarische Lebensläufe*, I (rowohlt) Hamburg 1975
Th. Fontane, *Meine Kinderjahre*, Munich 1969. *Von Zwanzig bis Dreissig*, Munich 1973. *Von Dreissig bis Achtzig*, Munich 1975 (dtv)
M.-L. Könneker, *Die Kinderschaukel*, 2 vols. (Suhrkamp) Frankfurt 1976
L. Andreas-Salomé, *Lebensrückblick*, Frankfurt 1968
L. Turek, *Ein Prolet erzählt*, (Fischer) Frankfurt 1975

---

* It may seem tiresome to include material not readily available to the modern reader, but the effort to obtain these memoirs is really very well worthwhile in terms of insight into nineteenth century life as seen at the time.

Chapter 12

Th. Fontane, *Von Dreissig bis Achtzig*, Munich dtv 1975

H. G. Gerth, *Bürgerliche Intelligenz um 1800*, Göttingen 1976

K. Gutzkow, *Werke*, ed. H.H.Houben, vol. 3, Leipzig 1912

G. Keller, *Gesammelte Briefe*, Bern 1952

H. Laube, *Erinnerungen*, vol. 8 of *Werke*, Leipzig n.d.

H. Mann, *Ein Zeitalter wird besichtigt*, Berlin 1947

Th. Mann, *Autobiographisches*, ed. Erika Mann, 1968

F. C. Perthes, *Memoirs*, ed. by his son, C.T.Perthes, Edinburgh 1856

R. Schenda, *Volk ohne Buch. Zur Geschichte der populären Lesestoffe 1770–1910*, Frankfurt 1970

F. Sengle, *Biedermeierzeit* op.cit., vol. 2

A. Stifter, *Werke*, vol. 18, 1 Prague 1918

ed. R. Wittram, *Realismus*, vol. 1, Stuttgart 1976

Index

Abitur, 161, 262
Agrarian League, (see Farmers League)
agriculture, 27, 55, 81, 198, 225
Allgemeiner dt. Arbeiterverein (General German Workers Party) 150, 155, 296
Allgemeiner Frauenverein (General Women's Organisation), 240
Allgemeine Zeitung, 283, 286
Alsace-Lorraine, 28, 121, 138, 141, 144, 168, 184
Anhalt, 144
Anti-Socialist Law, 35, 146, 157, 165, 183, 296
Antisemitism, 86, 171, 228f.
Antisemite Party, 148
aristocracy, (see nobility)
army (see military)
Arndt, E. M. 3, 110, 115
artisans, 25, 55, 66ff., 75ff., 87, 113, 156, 170, 198f., 213ff., 296
Auerbach, Berthold, 232, 252f.
Augsburg, 5, 227, 283, 286

Baader, Franz v., 25f., 77
Baden, 2, 5, 20, 22, 43f., 49, 61, 94f., 97, 101, 104f., 116, 126, 138, 140, 144, 162, 184, 204, 225, 236, 263, 296
Bamberger, Ludwig, 116, 123
banks, banking, 81, 84, 129, 210
Bavaria, 5, 19ff., 28, 41, 43f., 49f., 67, 96, 132, 137f., 140, 144, 184, 202, 204f., 207, 225, 228, 232, 238, 263
Bebel, August, 22, 148, 153, 156, 158, 184f., 194, 221, 296
beggary, 67 (see also pauperism)
Belgium, 57, 64, 112, 175, 185, 297
Bennigsen, Rudolf v., 133
Berlin, 47, 53, 55ff., 62f., 65, 68, 73, 75, 84, 89, 96, 129, 138, 145, 150, 157, 198ff., 210, 213, 227f., 238, 244, 281, 296
Berlin National Assembly (1848), 94, 99, 104
Berlin, university of, 8, 109, 276

Berliner Bewegung (Berlin Movement), 181
Bethmann-Hollweg, Theobald v., 161, 196
Bernstein, Eduard, 184f.
Biedermeier, 62, 232, 243f.
Bildungsbürgertum, 208f.
Bismarck, Otto v., 12, 15, 26, 29, 35, 51, 65, 81, 85, 97, 116, 127ff., 157ff., 165ff., 177, 180, 191, 193f., 201, 205f., 227, 272f., 296f.
Blechen, Carl, 244
Bleichröder, Gerson, 84, 210, 227
Blücher, G.L.v., 110
Blum, Robert, 99, 243
Börne, Ludwig, 50, 52, 112, 277
Bohemia, 68, 96
Bonaparte, (see Napoleon)
book trade, 280–3
Born, Stephan, 214
Borsig, August, 209, 214
Bosch, Robert, 70, 191, 210, 238
bourgeoisie, 15, 30, 102, 128ff., 156, 199, 202ff., 259
Brandenburg, 2, 99, 198
Bremen, 41, 58, 62, 143f., 191f., 199, 227, 285
Breslau, 47, 65, 156, 199, 227f., 276
Brockhaus, F.A., 283f., 287, 291
Brockhaus encyclopedia, 242, 284
Brunswick, 45, 62, 76, 111, 144, 285
Büchner, Georg, 46, 52, 74
Bülow, Bernard, v., 186f., 174f., 188
Bund der Industriellen (employers organisation) 170
Bund der Landwirte (see Farmers League)
Bundesrat (Federal Council of the German Empire 1871–1918), 145
Bundestag (Federal Diet of the Confederation), 38, 43, 59, 62, 155, 278
Burckhardt, Jakob, 12, 112
bureaucracy (see civil servants)
Burgtheater, 92, 276
Burschenschaften, 45
Busch, Wilhelm, 254f.

Calvinism, Calvinists, 25, 69, 210
Camarilla, 105
Campe, J.H., 66, 260
Campe, Julius, 278, 280, 283, 286f.
capitalism, 3, 29, 69ff., 204f., 207, 225
Caprivi, G.L.v., 167f., 188, 206
Carlsbad Decrees (1819), 42, 44f., 278, 286
cartels, 84, 212
Catholic Church, Catholics, 24ff., 33, 35, 77, 120, 149, 153f., 169, 180f.
censorship, 15, 54, 278–9
Centralverband der Industriellen, 170, 186ff.
Centre Party, 148, 151, 153f., 157f., 181–2, 221
chemical industry, 82, 84
Chemnitz (Karl-Marx-Stadt), 67, 119
Chodowiecki, Daniel, 260
Christian Social Party, see Antisemites
Christian trade unions (see trade unions)
childhood, 233, 250–5
child labour, 72, 79, 217f., 236, 266f.
Christmas, 256ff.
churches, 22ff.
Civil Code (Prussia 1794), 27 (Germany 1896), 240
civil servants, 42, 48f., 87, 89, 92, 104, 146, 198f., 206ff., 249, 262, 288
coal mining, 68, 71, 76, 80, 82
Code Napoléon, 3f., 206
Cologne, 57, 64, 101, 111, 210, 226
colonialism, 166
Colonial League, 195
Commune (Paris), 162
Communist League, 101
Confederation, German (1815–1867), 19, 21f., 38ff., 59, 89, 99, 111, 124, 132, 138, 201, 224, 275, 281, 295
Confederation, North German (1867–71), 132f., 135, 138, 146, 160, 296
Confederation, of the Rhine (1806–13), 5f., 38, 295
Congress of Vienna, 11, 38, 40f., 47, 67, 227, 283, 295
Conservative Parties, 145, 148, 152f., 157f., 181, 192, 201, 203, 206, 229
Constitutional Conflict, 29, 127f., 133–6, 150, 161, 296

copyright, 179–80
'Corn and Iron', 170, 174, 206, 211
Cotta (publishers), 279, 281f., 286
craftsmen, see artisans
Craftsmen's Congress, 101
Customs Parliament, (*Zollparlament*), 138, 296
Customs Union (*Zollunion*), 138f., 296

D-banks (see banking)
Dahn, Felix, 248, 291
Dahlmann, Friedrich, 16, 46, 60, 92
Danzig, 58, 125
Defence League, 123f., 195
Delbrück, Rudolf, 125
Democratic Workers Associations, 101
Denmark 18, 40, 58, 97f., 131, 148, *Deutsche Handlungsgehilfenverband*, (German Shop Assistants Association), 216
Deutsche Allg. Zeitung, 287
Deutsche Rundschau, 289
Deutschland, Deutschland über alles, 114
Diet, Federal Diet, (*see Bundestag*)
'Dohna' (German Empress), 250
domestic servants, 81, 198, 223, 231, 238f.
Dortmund, 57
Dresden, 55, 64, 101, 156, 266, 281
Dronke, Ernst, 73
Droste-Hülshoff, Annette v., 293
Droysen, Gustav, 92, 97, 116
Duisburg, 57
Düsseldorf, 14, 101, 103, 156, 199

East Elbia, 27, 115, 167f., 181
East Prussia, 1, 53, 128, 193, 198, 204, 287
Ebner-Eschenbach, Marie v., 252
ecclesiastical princes, 1, 5, 295
education, 19, 33, 66, 77, 80, 202, 209, 218, 229, 260–5
Edict of Tolerance (1812), 228
Eichendorff, Josef v., 45, 277
electrical industry, 82, 84
emancipation, 3, 8, 19, 29, 49, 171, 227f.
emigration, 104, 197, 201, 224
Engels, Friedrich, 15, 35, 55, 61, 101, 116, 287
England, 9, 30, 33, 40, 57, 174f., 232, 250, 280, 291

Entente Cordiale, 175, 297
Enlightenment, 2, 228, 233, 260
Ernst August of Hanover, 47
Ernst II of Saxe-Coburg-Gotha, 149
Erzgebirge, 257
Essen, 57, 155, 199
Eulenburg, Philipp v., 169
Evangelical church, 234 (see also
    under Protestantism etc.)
Evangelische Kirchenzeitung, 287

Falk, Heinrich, 263
family, 31, 231–72
Farmers League ('Green Front') 28,
    158, 167, 181f., 188, 203, 226, 297
Federal Act (*Bundesakte*), 41, 43
Federal Diet (of German
    Confederation) see *Bundestag*
Ferdinand I of Austria, 99
Fichte, Johann G., 3, 109f., 276
Fliegende Blätter, 279
Fontane, Theodor, 66, 89f., 99, 104,
    137f., 162, 209, 238, 241, 243f., 248,
    263, 265, 286, 290f., 293
France, 1, 31, 33, 40, 65, 126, 136ff.,
    173, 175, 185, 232, 235, 275, 278,
    280, 291, 294, 296
Franconia, 43, 238
Frankfurt, 5, 38, 40, 46f., 50, 53, 62,
    84, 89, 102f., 132, 150, 156, 199,
    226f., 277, 281, 291
Frankfurt Parliament, 89, 91–5, 96ff.,
    105f., 115, 149, 296
Franz I (II) of Austria, 19, 38
Franz Joseph I, 99
French Revolution of 1789 (see
    Revolution)
Frederick II of Prussia, 17f., 23, 257,
    260
Frederick III, German Emperor, 149,
    250
Frederick William III of Prussia, 6f.,
    19, 23f., 44, 54, 110f.
Frederick William IV, 19, 22f., 89f.,
    97f., 105, 111, 295
Freiligrath, Ferdinand, 53, 74, 112, 280
Freisinnige Vereinigung (see also
    Progressives), 159
Freytag, Gustav, 248, 289f., 293
Friends of Light, 24, 53, 234
Froebel, Friedrich, 240, 261, 267

Fürth, 62, 295

Gagern, Friedrich v., 91
    Heinrich v., 91, 94, 97
Gartenlaube, Die, 240f., 288, 290
Gegenwart, Die, 289
Geibel, Emanuel, 244
Geiger, Theodor, 208
German National Assembly, (see
    Frankfurt Parliament)
Gervinus, Georg, 46f., 60, 92, 273
Gewerbeschule (Berlin Technical
    School), 65f., 265
Gneisenau, August Neithardt v., 7, 110
Goethe, Joh. Wolfgang v., 1, 3, 43, 52,
    107, 207, 229, 275, 279f., 282ff., 295
Görres, Josef, 112, 286
Göschen (publishers), 281ff.
Göttingen, 7, 19, 47, 295
Gotha, 102, 156, 296
Gotthelf, (Albert Bitzius), 232, 247f.,
    277
Grabbe, Christian Dietrich, 14, 52,
    277
'Great Depression', 80, 189, 218, 296
Green Front (see Farmers League)
Grenzboten, Die, 291
Grillparzer, Franz, 14, 73, 246f., 277,
    293
Grimm brothers, 20, 46, 92, 221, 277
Gründerzeit (see Promoters' Boom)
guilds, 2, 71, 198, 213
Gulbransson, O., 219, 271, 274
Gutzkow, Karl, 60, 73f., 238, 255, 276,
    287

Hallische Jahrbücher, 287
Hambach, 112f., 295
Hamburg, 2, 5, 12, 19, 41, 47, 59, 62,
    68, 72, 84, 102f., 120, 125, 143f.,
    150, 191f., 210, 226, 277f., 281, 287
Hanover, 7, 19, 28, 40f., 47, 49f., 62,
    76, 96, 126, 132f., 156, 158, 191,
    232, 250
Hansabund, 186, 192
Hansemann, David, 84
Hanseatic Cities (see also Bremen,
    Hamburg, Lübeck) (or Free Cities)
    62
Hardenberg, K.A.v., 44
Harkort, Friedrich, 77

Hauptmann, Gerhart, 69, 268, 294
Hebbel, Friedrich, 247f., 277, 293
Hecker, Friedrich, v., 91
Heckscher, J.G.M., 98
Hegel, G.W.Fr.v., 5
Heidelberg, 89, 287, 296
Heine, Heinrich, 14, 21, 24, 50, 52, 60, 74f., 84, 111, 227, 275ff., 283, 286, 295
Heine, Th. Th., 271
Hengstenberg, E.W., 287
Herder, Johann G., 23, 107
Hertz, Wm., 263
Herwegh, Emma, 91, 236, 243, 280
Herwegh, Georg, 53, 74, 91, 93, 112, 236, 243
Hess, Moses, 55, 101
Hesse-Darmstadt, 5, 20, 43, 46, 74, 97, 116, 138, 140, 144, 158, 204, 232, 250, 278
Hesse-Homburg, 39
Hesse-Kassel, 20, 45f., 132f.
Heyse, Paul, 289f.
Hirsch-Dunkersche trade unions, (see trade unions)
Hintze, Otto, 204
HKT, 193
Hoffmann, E.T. A., 42, 45, 277
Hoffmann, Heinrich (author of *Struwwelpeter*, 254, 277
Hoffmann von Fallersleben, Heinrich, 53, 114ff., 277
Hohenlohe, Chlodwig v., 28, 168, 174, 188, 205
Hohenzollern candidature, 136
Holstein (see also Schleswig-Holstein), 19, 40
Holstein, Friedrich v., 174f.
Holy Roman Empire, 1f., 20, 28, 38, 41, 46, 108, 132, 153, 201, 295
Holz, Arno, 268f.
Honoratioren, 48, 158
Hoverbeck, Leopold v., 129
Humboldt, Alexander v., 282f.
Humboldt, Wilhelm v., 7f., 44, 49, 107, 109, 207, 228, 262

Illustrirte Welt, 288
Immermann, Karl v., 45, 52, 262, 277
imperialism, 173f., 208f.
Indemnity Bill, 134

industrial revolution, 48, 55, 56ff., 198, 201, 214
infant mortality, 69, 197
Ireland, Irish, 52, 112, 177, 224
Italy, 173, 232, 280

Jacobin republic, Jacobins, 1, 4f., 101, 110
Jahn, 'Turnvater', 3, 115
Jean Paul (Richter), 252, 261
Jena, battle of, 6, 25, 111, 206, 295
Jena, university of, 45
Jérome, king of Westphalia, 6, 108, 206
Jews, 4, 14, 26, 35, 47, 52, 120, 151, 163, 169, 210, 216, 226–30, 234, 275
Jewish emancipation, 4, 226ff.
Johann, Archduke of Austria, 94
Jordan, Wm., 116
journeymen (see artisans)
journeymens congresses, 101
Junkers, 27, 128f., 205, 225

Kant, Immanuel, 3, 107, 281
Karl August of Weimar, 243
Kardorff, Wm. v., 152
Karlsbad, 92
Karlsruhe, 2, 102f., 150
Katholikentag, 153f., 182
Kautsky, Karl, 184
Keller, Gottfried, 244, 248, 253, 285, 289f.
Ketteler, Bishop, 25, 77
Kiel, 199
Kindergarten, 240, 267
Kinder-Küche-Kirche, 250
Kinkel, Gottfried, 236
Kinkel, Johanna, 236
Kiderlen-Wächter, Alfred v., 175
Kladderadatsch, 279
Kleinbürgertum, 48, 102, 201, 206, 212–216, 226, 233f.
kleindeutsch 97, 116f., 120, 126, 132, 141
Kleist, Heinrich v., 4, 9, 14, 100, 108f., 243, 285
Kolping, Adolf, 25
Königgrätz, 133, 136
Königsberg, 47, 53, 227, 239, 287
Kotzebue, August v., 44
Kreisordnung (1872) 29
Krupp, Alfred v., 57, 67, 71, 168, 192, 211, 217

Kugler, Franz, 290
Kulturkampf, 26, 120, 152f., 181, 264

Landrat, 28, 193, 202
Landtag (Prussian Diet), 29, 36, 127, 133f., 148, 152, 168, 180, 188
Landschaften (provincial assemblies), 205
Lasker, Eduard, 151
Lassalle, Ferdinand, 150, 155f., 227, 296
Laube, Heinrich, 92, 112, 277f.
Legien, Carl, 189, 192
Leipzig, 2, 10, 48, 64, 92, 102f., 155, 280f., 283f., 291f.
Lenau, Nikolaus, 51
lending libraries, 285f.
Lenbach, Franz, 158
Leo XIII, Pope, 158
Lessing, G. E., 107, 281
Lewald, Fanny, 46, 53, 93, 227, 233, 236, 239
liberalism, 9, 13, 26, 50, 100, 103, 125, 127, 132, 148, 174, 208, 228, 262, 288, 293
Liberals (see also Progressives, National Liberals), 35, 112, 127ff., 132, 152, 169, 179f., 182–3, 201, 230, 262, 288, 293
Lichnowsky, Felix v., 98
Liebknecht, Wm., 156, 184, 296
Lindau, Paul, 289
Lippe, 143f.
List, Friedrich, 59f., 287
literacy, 32
Louis Ferdinand, 110
Louis Napoleon, see Napoleon III
Louis Philippe, 88
Louise of Prussia, 7, 111, 245
Lübeck, 5, 41, 57, 143, 192, 210, 269
Ludwig I of Bavaria, 20, 22, 111
Ludwig II of Bavaria, 138, 143
Luther, Lutheranism, see also under Protestantism, 23f.
Luxemburg, 40
Luxemburg, Rosa, 240, 248

Maaßen, Karl Georg v., 59
Mainz, 1, 5, 25, 98
Mann, Heinrich, 34, 268, 294
Mann, Thomas, 57, 259, 268f., 294
Mannheim, 48

manorial estates, 27, 204, 224f.
Marggraff, Hermann, 287, 291
marriage, 24, 49, 197, 199, 224, 244f.
Marx, Karl, 12, 15, 35, 48, 55, 73, 75, 101, 106, 184, 213, 287
Mathy, Karl, 95
Mecklenburg, 28, 62, 95, 110, 144f., 204f., 261
Mecklen-Schwerin, 10, 143f.
Mecklenburg-Strelitz, 7, 143f.
mediatisation, 295
Mehring, Franz, 3, 189
Mendelsohn, Abraham, 84, 210, 227
Mendelssohn, Felix, 210
Menzel, Wolfgang, 115, 287
metal working, metal workers, 77, 214, 217f.
Metternich, Clemens v., 10ff., 15, 40, 44, 51f., 89, 95f., 278, 295
Mevissen, Gustav, 84
Meyer, C.F.M., 248, 293
Meyerbeer, Giacomo, 210, 227
Meysenbug, Malwida, v., 236
Michel, der deutsche, 109
middle classes, see bourgeoisie, *Kleinbürgertum, Mittelstand*
military, 8, 29, 33ff., 106, 127f., 134ff., 146, 160–64
Miquel, Johann v., 29, 168f., 174, 188
Mitteleuropa, 173
Mittelstand, 88, 169, 183, 214, 216
'new' *Mittelstand* (see also white collar workers), 216
Mörike, Eduard, 277
Moltke, Helmut v., 121, 131, 160
Mommsen, Theodor, 19, 149
monarchy, 17ff., 40, 44, 46f., 53
Morgenblatt für gebildete Stände, 236, 287
Mottek, Julius, 157
Mundt, Theodor, 278
Munich, 55, 67, 77, 111, 184, 199, 281, 285
Musil, Robert, 259, 268, 294

Napoleon, 2ff., 21, 28, 43, 45, 108ff., 113, 206, 228, 257, 278, 295
Napoleon III, 126, 137f., 204
Nassau, 7, 43, 61, 132f.
nationalism, 3, 107–123, 201, 208
National Liberal party, 133, 150f., 157, 182f.

Nationalverein, 125, 149f.
National Zeitung, 133
Naturalism, Naturalists, 293f.
Naumann, Friedrich, 166, 183, 195
navy, 160, 163, 168, 170–1, 174, 179
Navy League, 123, 186, 192, 209, 216
Netherlands, 40, 280
Neue Rheinishe Zeitung, 73, 75
Nietzsche, Friedrich, 124, 292
nobility, 23, 26–30, 163, 199, 201–6, 211
Nuremberg, 62, 199, 256f., 295

Oppenheim, Abraham, 84
orphans, orphanages, 266
Otto-Peters, Luise, 240

Palacky, Franz, 96
Palatinate, 43, 101
Pan Germans, 121ff., 193, 209, 216, 297
Panslavism, 96, 173
Paulsen, Friedrich, 18, 24, 57
Paulskirche, 93ff.
pauperism, 77f., 88, 199, 213
Peace Movement, 122
peasantry, 2, 8f., 29, 204, 224ff., 262
Perthes, Friedrich, 280f.
Pestalozzi, J.H., 260f.
Pfizer, Paul, 22
Philanthropinum, 260f.
Pietism, 110
piracy, 279f.
Platen-Hallermünde, August v., 51
Poland, Poles, 29, 106, 112ff., 116, 120, 148, 193, 227, 291
political parties, 148–57, 163, 180–6
Pomerania, 198, 204, 228
Popp, Adelheid, 31, 258
population, 48, 55, 62, 68f., 73, 81, 144, 173, 197–9, 234
Posen, 65, 193, 198, 228
Potsdam, 62, 266
pre-March (see *Vormärz*)
press, 278, 286ff.
pressure groups, 122f., 158, 163, 166, 169–70, 186–9, 203
Pretβische-Fahrbücher, 128
Progressive party (*Fortschrittspartei*), 129, 150f., 156, 159, 161, 182
proletariat, 25, 87f., 201, 214, 217, 258

Promoters' Boom (*Gründerzeit*), 64, 210
protective tariffs (see tariffs)
Protestantism, also under Evangelical, Calvinism, Church, Lutheranism, 22ff., 26, 43, 250
Prutz, Robert, 74, 276

Raabe, Wm., 248, 289f., 292f.
railways, 59, 61ff., 68, 75, 84, 215, 287, 295
Ranke, Leopold v., 86
Rathenau, Walter, 229
Raupach, Ernst v., 284
Reclam (publishers), 284
Reform Act of 1832, 202
Reform era, 7f., 48f.
Reich League against Social Democracy, 193, 216
Reichspartei, 152 see also Conservatives
Reichstag, 36, 145, 148, 152, 154f., 157, 163, 166, 180, 188
Reichsverweser (Regent of Germany 1848), 94
Reinsurance Treaty, 173, 297
reserve officer, 34
Restoration, 18, 38ff., 77, 87, 112f., 207f., 213f., 217, 224, 261, 276, 288
Reuß-Greiz, 144
Reuß-Schleiz, 144
Reuter, Fritz, 277, 289f.
Revisionism, 184
revolution, 3, 12f., 203
Revolution, French, 1789, 4, 12, 15, 201
Revolution, French, 1848, 103
Revolution of 1830, German, 14, 21, 42, 45, 52, 60, 87, 202, 275
Revolution of 1848, German, 5, 14, 29, 48, 55, 86–106, 116f., 124, 128f., 149, 155f., 202, 208, 216, 227f., 236, 239, 242, 263, 279, 288, 296
Rheimische Zeitung, 287
Rhine, Rhineland, 1, 5, 11, 22, 24, 62, 64, 66ff., 100, 108, 112, 124, 150, 152f., 155, 157, 187f., 191, 198, 207, 209f., 221, 250
Richter, Eugen, 148, 151, 161
Riehl, Wilh., 22, 218
Rodenberg, Julius, 289
Romantics, 3, 10, 42, 243, 273, 275
Roon, Albrecht v., 127f., 131
Rosegger, Peter, 250, 253

Rothschilds, 227
Rotteck, Karl, 43, 284
Rückert, Friedrich, 244, 252
Ruge, Arnold, 92, 243, 287
Ruhr, 62, 64, 66ff., 124, 210, 250
Russia, 29, 40f., 173ff., 177, 205, 224, 227, 297

Saar, 58, 62, 80, 124
Saint-Simonism, 235f.
Sammlungspolitik, 169
Savigny, Karl, 110
Saxe-Altenburg, 144
Saxe-Coburg-Gotha, 89, 144
Saxe-Meiningen, 144
Saxe-Weimar, 144
Saxony, 19, 24, 31, 36, 41, 50, 53, 58, 67, 92, 96, 105, 116, 124, 126, 132, 140, 143ff., 150, 157, 162, 183, 191f., 205, 208, 262f., 282, 296
Scharnhorst, Gerhard v., 7, 110
Schaumburg-Lippe, 144
Scheffel, Viktor v., 248, 290f.
Schiller, Friedrich, 3, 77, 280, 282, 284
Schlegel brothers, 108
Schlegel, Friedrich, 243
Schleiermacher, Friedrich, 45, 109f.
Schleswig-Holstein, see also Holstein, 18, 97, 105f., 115, 131ff., 150, 191, 198, 232
Schmid, Christoph v., 253, 285
schools – see also education 253, 285
Schwarzenberg, Felix v., 99, 104, 125
Karl v., 10
Schwarzburg-Rudolfstadt, 144
Schwarzburg-Sonderhausen, 58, 144
seasonal workers, 29
Sedan, battle of, 121, 138
Septennat, 134
serfs, 29, 68
Siebenpfeiffer, Philipp Jakob, 113
Siemens, Werner, 149, 210f.
Silesia, 57f., 62, 64f., 67ff., 73, 75, 80, 124, 152, 193, 198, 218, 226f., 238, 250, 276, 296
Simplicissimus, 34, 278
Social Darwinism, 173
Social Democratic Party, 35, 102, 148, 154–7, 162, 179ff., 183ff., 211, 241, 248f., 294, 296
socialism, socialists, 26, 35f., 72, 120,

152, 183–5, 191, 221f.
social imperialism, 121–3
social welfare, 71, 81, 83, 157f.
Spielhagen, Fr. 119f., 211, 233, 248, 290, 293
Stahl, Friedrich Julius, 28
Ständestaat, 2, 55
Standesherrn (mediatised princes), 28, 204f.
state, 30f., 37, 55f., 83, 143ff., 205ff., 215
steel industry, 82, 170
Steffens, Henrik, 10, 18, 45, 110
Stein, Baron, 7f., 43, 109f., 262, 295
Sternheim, Carl, 294
Stettin, 125
Stifter, Adalbert, 252, 261, 275, 277, 289, 293
Stöcker, Adolf, 181
Storm, Theodor, 18, 224, 253, 277, 289, 293
Stosch, Albrecht v., 171
strikes, strike-breaking, 162, 189f., 214
Struve, Gustav v., 90f.
Stumm-Halberg, Karl v., 168, 211
Stuttgart, 210, 266, 279, 284, 287f.
Sudermann, Hermann, 294
Switzerland, 157, 232, 261, 280
Syllabus of Errors, 25

tariffs, 65, 85, 146, 167, 170, 174, 192
Telegraph für Deutschland, 287
textile industry, 67ff., 82, 217, 238
three-class franchise, 35ff., 103, 127f., 145, 180, 183, 192, 296
Thuringia, 31, 53, 191, 260, 267
Tieck, Ludwig, 108
Tilsit, treaty of, 6, 295
Tirpitz, Admiral, 168, 170f., 193
Tivoli Programme, 229
Tocqueville, Alexis de, 22, 88
Tönnies, Ferdinand, 28
Trade Agreement (1862), 126, 296
Trade Ordinance (1845), 79
trade unions, 183, 185, 188–92, 222
Christian, 153, 188f., 191, 221
Free, 185ff., 215
Hirsch-Dunkersche, 154, 189, 191
transport (see also railways), 60, 68, 83, 198, 215, 278
Treitschke, Heinrich v., 45, 52, 116, 291

Tübingen, 43, 204, 282
Twesten, Karl, 128f., 132

Ueber Land und Meer, 288
Uhland, Ludwig, 92, 277
Uhlig, Pastor, 53
unification, 126, 131ff., 135ff., 228, 257, 273
universal suffrage, 35, 102, 145f.
universities, 33, 35, 249
Unruh, Hans Viktor v., 104, 129
urbanisation, 56f., 83, 198–9

Valhalla, 111
Versailles, 138, 296
Victoria, Queen, 19
Victoria, Empress (Vicky), 250
Vieweg (publishers), 285, 289
Vienna, 53, 55f., 66, 72f., 89, 96, 99, 105, 198, 226f., 276, 281, 285, 296
Vienna, parliament of, 1848–9, 94
Villa Hügel, 57, (see also Krupp)
Vischer, F. Th., 92, 94
Volksverein, (Prussian Conservative organisation), 149
Volksverein für das katholische Deutschland, 169, 181, 187
Vollmar, Georg v., 185
Vormärz ('pre-March') 43, 46f., 277, 287f.
Vorparlament, 89f.
Voßische Zeitung, 286

wage labourers, 67, 69ff., 130, 169 198, 201, 215, 217–226
wages, 67, 71f., 80, 179, 207, 217f.
Waldeck, principality of, 144
Waldeck, Benedikt, 129
Wandervögel, 268, 271
War, Austro-Prussian, 131ff., 150, 296
Danish, 131f., 296
Franco-Prussian, 131, 136–8, 156, 195, 296
war veterans, 195, 216
Wars of Liberation (*Befreiungskriege*), 9f., 45, 110f.

Waterloo, battle of, 11, 295
Weavers Revolt of 1844, 69, 75, 296
Weber, Max, 205
Wedekind, Franz, 268, 272
Weerth, George, 75
Weimar, 43, 45, 208, 243
Weisse, C.F., 260
Weitling, Wm., 55
Welcker, Karl, 284
Werner, Anton v., 120
Westphalia, 6, 9, 21, 40, 75, 100, 108, 155, 187f., 191, 198, 206, 224, 226f.
West Prussia, 193, 198, 204, 228
white collar workers, 81, 170, 198
Wienbarg, Ludolf, 278
Wigand (publishers), 291
Willkomm, Ernst, 74
William I of Prussia, German Emperor, 17, 106, 123, 125, 127ff., 135, 137f., 143, 147, 160, 296f.
William II, German Emperor, 35, 123, 164, 167f., 178, 183, 229, 250, 297
Windthorst, Ludwig, 148
Windischgrätz, Alfred, 96, 99, 115
Wolfenbüttel, 62f.
women, 10, 71, 216, 231–72, 288
women's education, 24f.,
emancipation, 234f.
employment, 71ff., 81f., 234–40
Wrangel, Friedrich v., 97, 100
Württemberg, 2, 5, 16, 19, 33, 43f., 49f., 126, 132, 138, 140, 143f., 204, 210, 215, 263, 285f.
Wuppertal, 68f., 210
Wyneken, Gustav, 268

Young Germans, 5, 22, 50, 52, 60, 74, 112, 115, 236, 276, 278, 283
Young Hegelians, 5, 22, 50, 236, 277, 291
youth organisations, 271

Zabern Affair, 164
Zentrum, see Centre Party
Zetkin, Klara, 240, 248
Zollunion, see Customs Union